Combating Corruption in India

As corruption continues to be a persistent problem in India, concerned citizens, academia and courts believe that empowered police agencies independent of political control are the solution to the ills of corruption in the country. Can a crime-and-punishment approach suffice to deal with such a colossal and complex problem? Besides, there has not been enough focus on related questions: What is corruption and how is it facilitated? What are the appropriate agencies to combat corruption professionally in India? Why are these not effective in deterring corrupt practices? Are the alternative solutions to tackle corruption successful? This book seeks to engage with these questions, discuss and analyze them and based upon enforcement experience, conduct a thorough analysis of law, bureaucratic organizations, official data, case studies and comparative international institutions.

With extensive policing experience, the authors argue that a corrupt state only maintains the façade of rule of law but will not permit any inquiry and any solution beyond that of individual deviance. The book, using criminological and enforcement perspectives, presents a novel mechanism of the 'doctrine of good housekeeping' for public officials to combat and, more importantly, prevent corruption within their own institutions.

Arvind Verma, formerly an Indian Police Service (IPS) officer, is Associate Professor in the Department of Criminal Justice at Indiana University, Bloomington.

Ramesh Sharma is Executive Director at Legasis Services Pvt. Ltd., India. He has served as the Director General of Police of the Economic Offences Wing of Madhya Pradesh during 35 years of service as an IPS officer with the Government of India.

Combating Corruption in India

Arvind Verma
Ramesh Sharma

CAMBRIDGE
UNIVERSITY PRESS

CAMBRIDGE
UNIVERSITY PRESS

University Printing House, Cambridge CB2 8BS, United Kingdom

One Liberty Plaza, 20th Floor, New York, NY 10006, USA

477 Williamstown Road, Port Melbourne, vic 3207, Australia

314 to 321, 3rd Floor, Plot No.3, Splendor Forum, Jasola District Centre, New Delhi 110025, India

79 Anson Road, #06–04/06, Singapore 079906

Cambridge University Press is part of the University of Cambridge.

It furthers the University's mission by disseminating knowledge in the pursuit of education, learning and research at the highest international levels of excellence.

www.cambridge.org
Information on this title: www.cambridge.org/9781108427463

© Arvind Verma and Ramesh Sharma 2018

First published 2018

Printed in India by Rajkamal Electric Press

A catalogue record for this publication is available from the British Library

Library of Congress Cataloging-in-Publication Data

ISBN 978-1-108-42746-3 Hardback

Contents

Tables and Figures

Acknowledgements

Arvind—for me this book would not have been possible without the stress on honesty, integrity and righteousness that was imparted by my father, Surya Kant Verma. Sad and almost disillusioned with the growing corruption in society, he nevertheless continued to believe that the promise of future can only be realized by the steadfastness of the present. He always cited the example of my grandfather who was a lawyer and refused to accept a case where the petitioner had committed the crime. He would say that one cannot drink milk knowing there is a fly floating in it. My mother, Shashi Lata Verma, was the perfect companion to my father and gladly accepted the hardships emanating from the strict and straight path that my father followed in his life. She continues to be the moral beacon for the family and has inspired everyone in our extended family to follow the dharma of probity. It was this upbringing and their personal conduct that taught me the values and strength to stand up to corruption in my own police career and thereafter.

But I could not have lived the clean life without the care, patience and encouragement of my life-partner, Chapla. Our household was uprooted every few months as a consequence of abrupt transfers from one post to another which is the fate of public officials standing up to the corrupt. Single-handedly she had to take care of our children and their education as I was barely home. Nevertheless, Chapla ensured that we pursue a life that we can be proud of and based upon honor and righteousness. Our children, Juhi and Rishi, have not only been the joy of our lives but strong-willed good citizens fighting every wrong that they see around them. Both have devoted their life to public service and concern for the downtrodden. My wife and children have been the shelter and pillar that gave me the time to brood, spend long hours and keep shaping and re-shaping this manuscript. This book would not have been possible without their unqualified support and inspiration.

Ramesh—I dedicate this book to my late father, Mr. Satya Narayan Sharma, a self-made lawyer par excellence, a passionate philanthropist, who was kind and compassionate and above all a man of impeccable integrity. I also wish to fondly remember my late mother, Mrs. Sharda Sharma, who steadfastly stood by the side of my father, facing all adversities arising out of his non-compromising attitude towards corruption.

Prior to my joining the Indian Police Service, my father cautioned me that the slightest corrupt act would be enough to cast an evil shadow upon the morals and values of my children. It is his honesty and upright values, in both his personal and professional life, that shaped my career and life and inspired me to write this book.

Acknowledgements

I wish to express my deep gratitude to my wife, Neeta, who was always by my side, in all my good and rough times, braving the difficulties that honesty brings in its wake and constantly inspiring me to share my experiences through this book. I am also grateful to my children, Rika and Dravya, and their spouses, Gaurav and Ashima, for their constant encouragement and support.

Finally, I must acknowledge the motivation and strength that I received from the well-known corporate lawyer Mr. Suhas Tuljapurkar, Founder Director, Legasis Services Pvt. Ltd. (Legasis), to complete this book. My special thanks to Mr. Arun Kulkarni, Director, Legasis, also for his unstinted support.

Foreword

No society or state will ever eliminate corruption but that is no argument against confronting or combating this practice. The dream of corruption-free society is always important as articulating discontent with systemic governance corruption (SGC, as I call it)[1] and reinforcing moral crusades against it. However, the nightmare of corruption haunts millions of Indians. Obviously, for each generation, the important task is to devise strategies for controlling corrupt conduct.

The threshold difficulty, however, dwells in the very word 'corruption'. Its social and juristic meanings do not always coincide. There are other allied words such as 'bribery', 'nepotism' and 'ethnoclientism'. Difference among them is not just an affair of idiosyncrasy in style; it often reflects conceptual confusion as well as a matter of elegant toleration. The authors of this work do well to mediate on many of these differences and they remain entirely right in the view that systemic corruption is the tendency and conduct to use public office for private gain.[2]

The learned authors of this thought-provoking work supplement their scholarship with the vigor of experience and imagination shaped by considerable amount of intense policing work. This is an infrequent occurrence, as work on corruption remains generally the preserve of social scientists and legal academics. It is puzzling that while corruption in public life is monumental, work on its amelioration is scattered and sporadic. In this respect as well, the learned authors make a substantial contribution to the sparse literature.

They are clear that mega institutional frameworks will not work; what are needed are organizational and institutional settings in which daily corruption may be confronted by and on behalf of citizens in meso- and micro-level settings. Despite their unconcealed enthusiasm for the India Against Corruption movement led by Anna Hazare, the authors maintain that such arrangements may lead to a possible diminishing of democracy. They unequivocally write: 'We also raise a red flag over

---

1 Upendra Baxi, 'Human Rights in "Controlling and Combating Corruption": The "Uselessness of Good Ideas?"– Synoptic Remarks', *Journal of Law & Social Research (JLSR)* 2 no. 1: 4–15. (Research Journal Anchored by Gillani Law College, Bahauddin Zakariya University, Multan.)

2 My favorite remains the work of Susan Rose Ackerman: see her magisterial work, *Corruption and Government: Causes, Consequence, and Reform* (New York, Cambridge University Prress,1999). See also Upendra Baxi, *Liberty and Corruption: The Antulay Case and Beyond* (Lucknow, Eastern Book Company, 1990).

the creation of an all-powerful enforcement agency in the country. An empowered, resource rich and independent police agency, though effective in combating corruption can also be a threat to democracy and open society.' A principal merit of this work lies precisely in the difficult reconciliation of democracy with the first principles of combatting corruption. A crime-and-punishment approach to corruption does not go far enough; it is to be realized, as the learned authors say, that it strikes at the very roots of confidence that gives public decisions their authority in democratic governance. At the same time expansion of power to govern corruption, bestowing incremental accretion of arbitrary power to cleanse and purify the society of corruption, remains dangerous for dissent and democracy. Put another way, as the authors rightly insist, ways must be found to draw a firm distinction between 'democracy' and 'kleptocracy' (and I add 'electocracy').

The learned authors aver, based 'on our experience and knowledge of criminal justice issues that the Lokpal will not be effective in handling corruption in the country because the roots of corrupt practices run deep'. Besides, the 'machinations of political and bureaucratic axis, the administrative processes of handling enormous number of complaints without matching resources in terms of investigating officers and finances pose impossible challenges to any anti-corruption institution, howsoever powerful'.

What then is to be done? Arvind Verma and Ramesh Sharma propose a middle level solution: a system of decentralized 'good housekeeping' which will energize constitutionally sincere citizens to seek 'accountability' via 'organizational culture'—a 'significant factor in shaping the behavior and inclination of officials through social interactional perspective'—which can be effective in 'developing preventive measures against corruption'. Methods of 'enhanced supervision, decentralization and e-governance' can assist micromanagement as well. The role of 'mangers' of public institutions in combatting corruption within their own institutions cannot be underestimated. Of distinctive nature is the extension of the doctrine of good housekeeping to semi-public and social institutions.

Eugene Malinowski famously named modern law as comprising 'courts, codes, and constables'. Confronting corruption, our authors suggest, in many ways requires changes in all the three domains of law. But equally crucial as the law are religion and education as agencies of social control and social change. Perhaps the time has come, without denying law its importance, of taking these forces also equally seriously.

The book in your hands is thought provoking and is aimed at generating a new kind of debate concerning systemic governance corruption. I am confident that its various messages will generate requisite thought before it gets too late for social action.

26 September 2017

Upendra Baxi
Emeritus Professor of Law
University of Warwick
University of Delhi

1

Introduction

April 2011 was the time when emotions were running high and the anti-corruption movement was in full swing in India. Hundreds of thousands of people from all age groups and backgrounds—young, old, male, female, educated and school dropouts—were out on the streets determined to end the scourge of corruption in the country. Led by Anna Hazare, who according to many, exhibited the same qualities of integrity, simplicity and steadfastness as Gandhiji, the movement for Lokpal had reached its zenith. Police raids, threats of arrests, questions about motives, foreign money and media manipulation all failed to stop the juggernaut from rolling on. The government was finally brought to its knees after months of obstinate refusal to accede to the demand of a Lokpal (an ombudsperson) to deal effectively with corruption.

Cabinet ministers came down from their high pedestal to negotiate with the leaders of the movement. The then Prime Minister Manmohan Singh, even offered to meet Anna Hazare and his compatriots. Assurances were given to establish the Lokpal though it would still take years to take shape. The movement finally did lead to the Lokpal and Lokayuktas Act, 2013 that provides for the establishment of a body of Lokpal for the Government of India and Lokayuktas for the states. These institutions can inquire into allegations of corruption against public functionaries, however high and mighty, including the Prime Minister under certain dispensation.

Like every citizen of the country and every person interested in ending corruption in India, we, the authors of this book, too were following the evolving protest movement keenly and with passion. While we appreciated the mass mobilization and the determination with which Anna Hazare pursued the demand for Lokpal, we were debating amongst ourselves if such an institution could really combat corruption effectively in the country. Both of us have served many years in the Indian Police Service (IPS) and have considerable experience in criminal investigation. One of us even commanded the premier anti-corruption agency of a major Indian state and handled a large number and variety of high profile corruption-related cases. Based on our experience and knowledge of criminal justice system of India, we were certain that the mass protest movement might, alas, be in vain. The Lokpal will not be effective in handling corruption in the country because the roots of corrupt practices run deep. The machinations of political and bureaucratic axis, the administrative processes of handling enormous number of complaints without matching resources in terms of investigating officers and finances pose impossible challenges to any anti-corruption institution, howsoever powerful.

The Lokpal will only add another layer to the existing enforcement agencies and institutions engaged in anti-corruption functions. As seen over the years, even multiple units with committed leadership have remained ineffective in combating corruption in India. The political economy and governance model of the country is such that the criminal justice system and institutions by themselves cannot dent the extensive corruption prevailing everywhere. We are already witnessing impediments in the establishment of Lokpal even before it has been operationalized and tested in practice. The new BJP government, elected to office in May 2014, with public expectation of combating corruption has already displayed dilatory practices to impede an independent Lokpal.

The Lokpal and Lokayuktas (Amendment) Bill, 2016 has also strayed into certain areas which can be construed as dilution of its earlier intent. Some of these purportedly include weakening of the accountability provision by not requiring the disclosure of assets and liabilities of public servants and politicians. The Parliamentary Standing Committee on Personnel, Public Grievances, Law and Justice, tasked with the establishment of the new Lokpal, has even recommended review of existing rules requiring disclosure of assets by public officials. The Committee has observed that these demands reflect 'colonial mindset of doubt and mistrust' and can be used to harass government servants rather than serve to safeguard against corruption. The original demand by the protesters and citizen groups to keep checks on the assets of public officials is being surreptitiously watered down.

Similarly, the rank of Lokpal Secretary has been downgraded to the status of Additional Secretary. Under this dispensation, the Lokpal Secretary will be junior to all officers holding the rank of Secretary to the Government of India. This will create a situation requiring the Lokpal Secretary to keep all senior bureaucrats in good humor in order to be promoted. The Lokpal Secretary would thus continue to be beholden to the elite bureaucracy. In the same vein, the Act has laid down that the Director of Inquiry and Director of Prosecution of Lokpal will be of the rank of Additional Secretary. The Committee has now recommended downgrading of this rank to the level of Joint Secretary, a move obviously aimed at diluting the strength of these powerful positions.

All political parties have been indifferent to the Act and charges of corruption are found in every corner of the country. No political party is untainted and, except for levelling charges against one another, no politician is sincerely committed to enforcing the Lokpal Act. The current Prime Minister, Narendra Modi does project an impression of desiring to curb corruption in India. The Prime Minister's abrupt demonetization process whereby 500 and 1,000 rupee notes were replaced with newly minted 500 and 2,000 rupee notes has been hailed as an example of his intentions to curb black money. Yet combating corruption in India is not going to be as simple. Our scepticism is well-grounded as we are well aware of the shenanigans of political class who, we believe, even after the creation of Lokpal, will strive to make it ineffective. Corruption is now part and parcel of every political party and no politician is going to axe the tree that supports his or her access to wealth and power.

It is with these realizations that we seriously began to discuss other options and methods of combating corruption in the country. We began by examining the efficacy of an enforcement agency to combat corruption effectively. We wanted to understand—to what extent a truly empowered and resourceful investigation agency can successfully combat the corruption occurring within its domain. We were aware that the proposed Lokpal would be bounded and limited, given the political discourse and mischief of the elite ruling class. So rather than focusing on the likely impact of Lokpal, we conducted a case study of an existing enforcement agency—Economics Offenses Wing (EOW), Madhya Pradesh (henceforth EOW MP)—to understand its effectiveness. One of the authors was the then chief of this agency and exercised complete freedom in its administration. Garnering substantial political, administrative and even financial support of the government in power, he empowered the agency and handled corruption cases effectively and without external influences. Under his charge, this agency was efficiently turned around to probe, inquire, investigate and prosecute corrupt practices going on in the state bureaucracy. Several prominent bureaucrats and political leaders were successfully charged and/or prosecuted during his tenure. Yet an empirical study of the statistics of thirteen years only revealed the limitations of EOW MP in combating/ curbing corruption. The agency barely made any impact upon the corpus of corruption in the state.[1] This experience was revealing in so far as it suggested that even the most powerful enforcement agency, however efficiently and effectively led, was unable to successfully combat corruption entrenched in every section of government. Given the deep roots and obstacles imposed by the system and existing procedures as well as processes of the criminal justice system, an enforcement agency can only play a limited and peripheral role in combating corruption.

In a democracy, there are multiple institutions that act independently and maintain checks and balances in the system. This is rightly so and we fully support and appreciate the prevailing system. However, this affects efficiency as different institutions function in accordance with their own priorities and organizational practices. While the enforcement agencies prioritize quick action against the suspected offenders, the judiciary necessarily keeps in mind their rights and emphasizes due process. The anti-corruption police agencies would like to see the corrupt individuals put behind bars and punished for their wrongdoings; the courts prefer to proceed cautiously. The judge demands evidence beyond reasonable doubt and through a process that ensures that the rights of the offender are duly upheld and protected. Trying to balance crime-control efforts with the due process of law causes natural delays and difficulties in prosecuting the offenders. Many corrupt individuals

---

1   The so-called Vyapam scam broke out *after* this co-author superannuated from police service.

are able to evade punishment due to the inability of overworked investigators and/or the prosecutors to process all cases properly without delay. Additionally, the overburdened courts process evidence carefully to ensure that not a single innocent person is wrongly punished. It is a time-tested principle and one that we all adhere to and accept even when many offenders walk away freely.

We realized this dichotomy in examining the functions and cases handled by various enforcement agencies. Professional and determined management, hard work, adequate resources and full political support could not become an effective deterrent to corrupt practices, as we found out, much to our dismay, in the case study of EOW MP. The sheer number of cases that needed professional investigation, the time-consuming task of collecting sound evidence mostly from a reluctant bureaucracy and challenge of filtering frivolous complaints from those that deserved attention was a Herculean task for any enforcement agency. In a democratic mode of functioning no agency holds supremacy and must necessarily seek cooperation from other organs of the state. These different departments of the government operate at their own pace and have their own priorities. The Chief Minister (CM) generally sets the tone to ensure smooth progress and collaboration amongst different functionaries of the state government. However, the CM (and the PM) must tred carefully through the mine-field of coalition politics and occasionally capitulate to the demands of their party-members and coalition partners. Reining in the police agencies from persecuting their political allies is a common phenomenon in Indian politics. Furthermore, criminal investigation is also a laborious process and more often than not circulars to various departments to cooperate with the enforcement agency remain unattended. Collection of evidence and examination of witnesses is a legal requirement governed by lengthy procedures. This cannot be short-circuited and curtailed. The Code of Criminal Procedure, 1973 (CrPC) and the Evidence Act, 1872 lays down the process that must be followed diligently to ensure that evidence against the offender stands the demanding scrutiny of the judiciary. There is thus a natural limit to the extent to which an agency can be made efficient and the procedure can be expedited.

Nevertheless, we also examined the data in various ways and developed models to judge if greater efficiency and resource mobilization could still make a difference. Our examination clearly suggested that even the best and most resourceful enforcement institution will not be able to combat corruption effectively. The malaise has spread deeply into the social fabric of society and the enforcement agencies can at best play a limited role of professional investigation and prosecution. Besides, with the Right to Information Act, 2005 (RTI) coming into existence, the number of complaints have increased. Determined citizens are procuring official documents and filing charges where they perceive irregularities or abuse of power. Under such circumstances, alternate and new methods are required to dent the monolithic corruption structure. This detailed case study of EOW MP led us to research other options of dealing with deep-rooted corruption in the country.

This book is based upon extensive research and our personal experience of administering criminal justice in the country. We argue for alternate methods and propound the 'doctrine of housekeeping' that we believe will be more effective than adding another supra layer to the existing anti-corruption institutions. We, however, do not argue that our suggestions, if implemented, will put an end to corruption in the country. Nowhere, and at no time in history, can corrupt practices be totally eliminated. As the proverbial 'lehron ka daroga'[2] story suggests, the corrupt will find some means or the other to indulge in corrupt practices. But what we offer are options that can empower the citizens, force public accountability of officials and make the disburser of funds responsible for the payment. We believe this is a novel idea and practical proposition that can help control and bring corruption down to a level that does not threaten the fabric of Indian society as is the case now.

Analytical and Methodological Framework

Our framework in analyzing methods to combat corruption are largely guided by criminological perspectives. As former police officers, we have designed, experimented and implemented a variety of organizational reforms to battle crime in the country. Criminology suggests that criminal behavior emanates from various sociological, psychological, political, economic and situational factors. While it is still unknown why a particular person decides to engage

---

2   This is a famous Indian fable in which the government sentences a corrupt official to live on an island and count waves believing that this will put an end to his shenanigans. However, he begins extorting from ships passing the island on the ruse that the natural number of waves reaching the island is being affected by their movement!

in criminality, criminology does help us understand that such behavior must take place in a specific context. Hence, studying the situational factors and the 'backcloth' (Brantingham and Brantingham, 1993) that facilitate criminal action is helpful in developing effective preventive measures. We have considerable experience in successfully handling theft, robbery, crimes against women and children, riots and homicides. In our long police career, we have also handled thousands of white-collar crimes like cheating, fraud, forgery, embezzlement and also those falling under the Prevention of Corruption Act of 1988. As leaders of the force, we have successfully subdued professional criminals, dreaded gangs and dangerous offenders enjoying political patronage, with determination and creative investigative methods involving other agencies, citizens, non-governmental organizations (NGO) and the media. Accordingly, we are fully aware that to deal with a serious, deeply entrenched and wide-spread crime like corruption, an empowered police unit cannot be effective by itself. We need a comprehensive approach that takes into account the nature and political economy of the state, its institutions, social processes and even historical experiences of the people.

We conceptualize a theoretical model based upon the notion of 'structures of irresolution'[3] that suggests corruption is a result of constructing an idealized abstract image of the state. By such a formalization, the deviance is blamed upon individual aberrations rather than the deviant nature of state itself. Failures to prevent, investigate and prosecute corrupt personnel are explained as emanating from the shenanigans of a few rotten apples and not systemic limitations of the institutions. The state assumes a dominant role by providing for extensive discretion exercised by bureaucrats and politicians. When such discretion is routinely misused for benefit of oneself and a few selected personnel, the blame is thrust upon the 'black sheep' and not the system that provides for options without accountability. This helps maintain the façade of a state based on due process while enabling the ruling elites to subvert the law in their own favor. We argue that to control corruption not only is there a need to strengthen investigative agencies but also to evolve decentralized accountability mechanisms that redefine the relations between the individual, the institutions and the state. We therefore propose ways of

---

3   We thank Dr Madhukar Shetty, IPS, for suggesting this term.

empowering the citizens to hold officials accountable as also a decentralized doctrine of housekeeping that holds managers responsible for corrupt practices occurring under their supervision. These broad-based and multiple mechanisms, we believe, will facilitate speedy investigation and prosecution of the offenders and be more effective in preventing corruption at the nascent stage.

This framework forms the basis of thorough examination of the literature on the nature of corruption, facilitators of corrupt practices, anti-corruption policies/institutions/regulatory frameworks, and the strengths and limitations of existing policies and mechanisms in the country. As we describe below, we will extensively assess various theories that explain the genesis of corruption. We also examine the history of 'baksheesh', 'mamool', 'hafta', 'najrana', bribery, kickbacks and other practices in the Indian context to help the reader understand comprehensively the roots of corruption. We describe corrupt practices in different institutions of the country and examine the factors and organizational culture that facilitate them. We conduct an empirical analysis using real data from a major anti-corruption agency of MP. This helps us provide evidence about the limitations of various investigative agencies in combating corruption effectively. Based upon mixed quantitative and qualitative methods, we develop promising approaches to understand and combat corruption in the country. Our solutions incorporate the empowerment of the citizens to question the state and its functionaries and make them answerable.

We do maintain a cautious approach since corruption, like criminal behavior, cannot be eliminated and can only be controlled to a certain extent. We take cognizance of the 'social interactionist' perspective that suggests corruption can also result from self-reinforcing social processes. People are influenced by what they see around them and learn corrupt practices from their fellow co-workers. Such learning takes place in close intimate personal settings where the offenders not only learn about taking bribes and extorting from hapless victims but also to justify and rationalize their corrupt actions. The social norms prevailing in any public institution influences the personnel to be corrupt and be part of the group. Peer pressure and threats of ostracism compel new employees to adopt the prevailing norms and act in accordance with them. Since organizational culture is a significant factor in shaping the behavior and inclination of officials, such a socially interactive perspective becomes important in developing preventive measures against corruption. Methods of enhanced supervision, decentralization and e-governance can have only a limited impact in combating corruption. We argue for effective methods to transform the organizational culture of public bureaucracies and bring changes in the attitudes of public officials as well as citizens.

We also raise a red flag over the creation of an all-powerful enforcement agency in the country. An empowered, resource-rich and independent police agency, though effective in combating corruption can also be a threat to democracy and open society. The tools of surveillance, covert operations and invasion of privacy that form part of police functions can also have unforeseen and undesirable consequences. The need to police the police agency has to be kept in mind when designing an effective enforcement mechanism. We refer to the history of the Federal Bureau of Investigation (FBI) under J. Edgar Hoover and the recent example of the Independent Commission against Corruption (ICAC) in Hong Kong to caution those demanding for the creation of a powerful Lokpal in India.

Structure of the Book

We begin by examining the concept and nature of corruption in Chapter 2. Not surprisingly, the term has varied connotations and implies different meanings to diverse people. Commonly, extorting bribes or siphoning public funds are unambiguous examples of corrupt practices but illegitimate exercise of discretion could also fall under this genre as well. In many instances, irresponsible conduct of a public functionary could be interpreted as a form of corruption. An official misusing his position need not personally benefit in distinctly material terms, however, his gain could be measured in various forms. He could use his act to garner favors from the beneficiary for future material benefits; for some friend or family member or even to satisfy his superiors who may have a soft corner for the suspect under inquiry. A traffic officer overlooking speeding violation to favor some friend or one who enjoys food at a restaurant without paying for it could, in certain circumstances, be instances of corruption. Many such innocuous acts could develop into serious instances of corruption as the Bofor's case illustrates. Quattrocchi used his friendship with Rajiv Gandhi to move unfettered within the corridors of power and manipulate favorable decisions from government officials. In India, where familial bonds are strong and people are well-connected with several administrative officials, enforcement agencies often need to tread carefully lest such kinship ties and friendships influence their decisions or intimidate them from taking appropriate course of action.

Corruption has largely been explained through theories spawned by political scientists and economists, and hence criminological perspectives have relatively been absent. The crime of corruption has generally been explained in the context of violation of a criminal law, whereby if an official conducts himself in a manner that is prohibited by law, then it is considered corrupt. But limiting the discourse on corruption only to the legal issues is unsatisfactory, as corrupt acts are perceived immoral by the society and undermine the legitimacy of government. On the other hand, economists base their theories on the concept of rational choice and explain criminal behavior, like corruption, in terms of reward and punishment. They explain corruption as a form of economic *rent* whereby a person, having something within his power, charges more than normal price for its use to earn a profit. Economic theories also point to the system where some people exert monopoly over goods and services and are unaccountable for their actions. This perspective suggests that corruption can be dealt by forcing officials to act in the interest of the citizens, something that is not so easy to do. Furthermore, economic theories of corruption are invariably colored by ideological biases and tend to promote specific forms of economic activities that favor some people.

We argue that criminological theories provide new insights and help question how, where and why corrupt practices take place and focus upon a wider definition of corruption. This is useful since it helps develop effective preventive mechanisms. Corrupt practices are generally not a rationally chosen individual decision as social-interaction perspective suggests that individual choices are influenced by group adoptions. Many people begin to indulge in corruption by observing the actions of their peers and following suit for not wanting to be excluded from the group. Criminological theories offer a range of explanations for criminal behavior that cover not only actions involving violations of specific laws but also deviant acts that are perceived to be corrupt.

We examine several criminological theories and argue that corruption should not be restricted to the acts of public officials but need to cover those from the private sector also. In modern economy where public–private-partnership models are becoming common, focusing upon only public officials will not be effective in combating corruption. Indeed, the supply side is as important as the demand side of bribery.

Furthermore, in this chapter we also examine various ways of measuring corruption. We discuss the efforts of Transparency International and its Corruption Perception Index, and also the work by the World Bank to assess the nature and extent of corruption around the world. We examine extensively the data on corruption published as *Crime in India* by the National Crime Records Bureau and analyze its reliability in measuring corruption in the country.

In Chapter 3, we next examine the nature and form of corruption in India. Officials misusing their power for personal gain have been around us for a very long period of time. *Arthashastra* by Kautilya (3rd–4th century BCE) describes vividly the nature of this problem in ancient India and cautions monarchs to guard against its insidious effects. While corruption is an old phenomenon, the etiology of corrupt practices in India has not been studied extensively. We turn to criminological research that explains the genesis of crime and ways in which offenders operate. In particular, applying the theories of situational crime prevention, environmental criminology and opportunity we seek to understand the facilitators that enable corruption to take place in the Indian society. Not surprisingly, an indifferent bureaucratic structure, lack of public accountability and functioning in secrecy are significant factors in promoting corruption. Moreover, the law is stated in general terms that leave a wide discretionary option to the public officials. Police officers in particular, exercise extraordinary discretion in the enforcement of laws. Such untrammeled discretion and absence of system of local accountability has been a major reason for corruption in the Indian police organization. Modern technology has further strengthened the corrupt to quickly transfer the ill-gotten wealth or camouflage it under multiple layers through money laundering. Understanding the facilitators of corruption provide insight into ways to deal with the scourge and develop effective measures to combat it. In particular, we examine some specific organizations, such as the police, civil administration, financial bodies and the political system to understand the ways and means through which corrupt practices have become prevalent within them. Specifically, we examine political shenanigans and criminality that has become the bedrock of corruption in the country.

In the fourth chapter, we examine the structure and organization of anti-corruption machinery in India. We examine the configuration and functions of various agencies such as the Central Vigilance Commission (CVC), the Central Bureau of Investigation (CBI) and some agencies functioning under the various state governments. We have also carried out detailed case studies of the CVC and the CBI that form the bulwark of anti-corruption functions in the country. Again, our inquiry is directed towards understanding their strengths and weaknesses so that the ability of these major investigation units in combating corruption can be judged. Our analysis clearly brings out the politicization surrounding these agencies. Almost all are seriously hampered by lack of personnel and resources. Their functioning is shrouded in secrecy and which in turn enables the politicians and bureaucrats to interfere in their operations. Even though the Supreme Court has intervened a number of times to ensure proper investigation into the charges of corruption against powerful leaders, these institutions have remained ineffective in preventing corrupt practices. With the help of several cases handled by the CBI, we point out that even if the Lokpal is able to ensure independence for such agencies and shield the officers from political pressure, the capability of India's anti-corruption units would continue to be limited.

In the fifth chapter, we conduct a detailed case study of the Economic Offences Wing (EOW) of Madhya Pradesh and where one of the co-authors served as the head of organization. We illustrate ways in which this agency received support from several Chief Ministers and built its resources with greater number of personnel, technology and funds. We also describe several legislations to empower the anti-corruption efforts in the state. Significantly, we examine and analyze a fair number of case studies to describe the work of this agency. In an unprecedented effort, we analyze the data for thirteen years of this agency, assiduously compiled by one of the authors, who headed this agency for around three years. No public official or researcher has, we daresay, examined the complex statistics of as many as thirteen years relating to the complaints received, preliminary enquiries held, FIRs registered, investigated, filed or charge sheeted, and the ratio of cases to be investigated vis-à-vis the number of investigating officers. It must be noted that this data was not presented in one record system and had to be procured and compiled from various sub-units.

The disappointing inference of our analysis is that, despite professional and competent handling of the agency, no significant dent was made against corruption in the state. Notwithstanding appreciably larger number of disposal of cases, the number of pending cases increased rather than decreased. The better performance and more sensitivity to people's complaints led to an influx of further complaints being filed with the agency. The sum total of it all was that the EOW was unable to address the cases brought to its notice and which marred its performance. The significance of this case study is the empirical evidence about the limitations of enforcement and police agencies in combating crime effectively.

We devote Chapter 6 to analyze the structure of Lokpal and Lokayuktas of various states. The Lokpal is based upon the concept of ombudsperson and therefore we proceed by examining the ombudsperson institutions from various countries. We argue that the importance of this institution lies in its capability to act on behalf of the citizens to keep public officials accountable to the people. The ombudsperson represents an empowered institution that enables a citizen to lodge his or her complaint against a public functionary and have it investigated independently. Furthermore, the ombudsperson exercises the powers to recommend changes in law, regulations and even bureaucratic organizations to force them to serve the people in a transparent manner. We highlight the forms and functions of various ombudspersons in different countries, including the Scandinavian nations, where this institution first evolved. We also describe the various provisions of the Lokpal and Lokayuktas Act and point to the possibilities that some of the rules can be misused or misinterpreted so as to weaken its effectiveness. Based upon detailed examination and evaluation, we argue that the ombudsperson has been effective in those countries where bureaucracies have, by and large, been functioning to the satisfaction of the citizens. In these nations, the public officials maintain a high degree of integrity, probity and accountability. The citizens expect and receive professional services and their grievances are quickly addressed. In such societies, the ombudsperson are not overburdened and set impossible challenges. All the institutions seek to maintain high standards and provide the best possible services to the citizens. When all the levers function smoothly and without obstruction, the instrument functions like a well-oiled clock keeping good time.

On the other hand, in those nations where public services are of poor quality, where officials are generally perceived to be corrupt and have no direct accountability to the citizens, the functioning of even well-structured ombudsperson leaves much to be desired. We cite the example of the ombudsperson in Caribbean nations that are perceived to be ineffective in the discharge of their responsibilities. We draw parallels and argue that the Lokpal in India, as conceived of at present, will similarly not be able to function effectively against corruption. The long tussle between the government in the appointment of judges and the delay in the appointment of Lokpal, is presented to draw the distinction from the ombudsperson of Scandinavian nations. We also present evidence that even comparatively well-functioning Lokayuktas tend to reinforce the notion of an idealized state where individual 'bad apples' are blamed for corruption. They focus on junior functionaries and do not take steps to prevent malpractices through institutional reforms. Based on our analysis of the effective ombudsperson, we also propose some steps that could strengthen the Lokpal and Lokayuktas in the country to play a more effective role in building the trust of the public officials. Our discussion includes examination of the problems faced by a number of Lokayuktas in the country.

Yet, in spite of the above-mentioned limitations of enforcement agencies, we make an honest attempt to examine methods that could still empower and strengthen the anti-corruption agencies in Chapter 7. We describe not only a large number of mechanisms that could enable the CBI to act effectively against white-collar crimes but we also look into new legal provisions that could assist the agencies to combat corruption in better ways. We describe the Whistle Blower Protection Law that was enacted in 2011 and which has now been finally brought into force. However, we also note with concern that even before it was operationalized, efforts to dilute it were afoot with the introduction of and passage of The Whistle Blowers Protection (Amendment) Bill in the Lok Sabha in May 2015, now pending in the Rajya Sabha. We also critically evaluate the Right to Information Act of 2005 that has opened the process for citizens to obtain information from the officials and thus hold them accountable. Furthermore, the work of the Standing Committee of the

Parliament, that examined the functioning of the CBI, is also evaluated. We point to the number of useful recommendations made by this Committee which unfortunately have not been implemented.

We also examine the recent demonetization action of the current government and analyze its impact upon curbing corruption. At this stage, we do not have adequate information to assess its short and long-term impact upon corruption but do believe that this has been an honest and determined attempt. We include some recent studies that have critically evaluated the impact of this anti-corruption drive by the current NDA government.

In circling the prevailing negativity about anti-corruption efforts in India, we have researched and developed lessons from successful efforts to combat corruption in many parts of the world. We focus, in particular, upon the strategies adopted in Singapore and Hong Kong where corruption in public institutions was admirably controlled out through determined political and administrative measures. However, our analysis suggests that anti-corruption agencies cannot cleanse public institutions where the political establishment itself is perverted and indifferent to corruption. We also turn to the European Union (EU) that has faced corruption in massive scale in newly emerging democracies of Eastern Europe. EU provides several practical methods such as financing of elections, acceptance of effective policies and making the political system accountable that could be adopted in India. Finally, we examine the path adopted in the US where RICCO was enacted to deal with organized crime and which became an effective tool in combating political corruption. Based on our study of some of the powerful independent bodies in different countries, we also strike a cautionary note. We raise the question—who will police the police itself? While a powerful independent agency can be effective in dealing with corruption, it can become a threat to the rights of the citizens as we see in the case of FBI in the US and ICAC in Hong Kong.

In the last chapter, we bring together our experience, research and lessons from various systems and nations to outline alternate solutions to combat corruption. We believe that empowering the anti-corruption agencies, making them independent of political control and accountable to the judiciary cannot be done unless the politicians act solely in public interest. This is untenable and unlikely to happen soon in our country. Politics is the path to power, wealth and status, and people are attracted to it for selfish reasons though they may proclaim otherwise. Accordingly, our solution is to empower the citizens directly and develop mechanisms using modern technology and social media to force officials to be held accountable. We argue that large-scale involvement of the private sector and non-governmental organizations provide new players who have a stake in honest governance. Accordingly, their involvement helps combat corruption. We provide several examples of this successful partnership and develop solutions that could work in India. Finally, we also emphasize the need for 'the doctrine of housekeeping' and role of managers of public institutions in combating corruption within their units. We propose that these managers be held responsible for organized corruption going on under their authority. They need to act first and ensure clean administration as well as accountability to the citizens. If they need greater power, then they need to present proposals and options to the government. However, they should not simply pass the buck to anti-corruption agencies and report incidents when they happen. They need to examine the processes and facilitators that lead to corrupt practices within their charge. They need to be the first responders and act decisively to provide honest services to the people. The anti-corruption agencies can only act as investigators to bring the culprits and offenders to justice. By its very nature these agencies can only deter by their effective investigation and quick prosecution. Prevention of corruption needs another mechanism and deterrence alone is not going to work. This is the major result and lesson that we wish to convey in our book.

In conclusion, the rationale for this book is that any independent institution howsoever powerful such as the proposed Lokpal will not be able to handle corruption effectively. The reason is the sheer enormity of the cases and the delays in the investigative process as well as at the trial stage. Furthermore, as we argue, any government agency cannot reform the government itself. If the political system is corrupt, then institutions functioning under the government are not going to be empowered enough to act against the politicians. Based on this realization we have embarked on a discourse where we outline innovative methods to handle corruption through alternate means. This book aims to set forth a public debate among policymakers as well as the citizens at large on the methods of combating corruption both from the point of view of its prevention and managing the aftermath of corruption, when the damage has already been done.

Part I
Corruption in India

2

Corruption
Criminological Perspectives

While corruption has become a common word it still carries different meanings for diverse people. It has been described in various ways and this poses problems for combating it effectively. We examine the various definitions and interpretations from the perspectives of law, political science and economics and argue that criminological viewpoints provide the best means to understand and deal with the crimes of corruption. The 'rational choice' perspective explains corruption as an economic rent but is limited, as it suggests prevention by enabling officials to function in desirable manner. Moreover, such conceptualizations also are ideologically biased towards free market economy and liberalism. These perspectives also limit the notion of corruption to public officials whereas, in the global integrated system corruption is also embedded in the private sector. This chapter argues that criminology presents a more nuanced explanation for the existence, nature and control of corruption. We reiterate the social-interaction perspective and suggest that people tend to emulate the prevailing norms and be part of the group rather than stand out alone. We argue that corruption as evil is perhaps the best manner to capture the damaging influence of this phenomenon. We also examine methods of measuring corruption and illustrate the techniques developed by Transparency International and the World Bank. Here we also describe the seriousness and nature of corruption in India presented by the National Crime Records Bureau.

The Concept of Corruption

Corruption is a heinous crime that unfortunately is also ubiquitous. The year 2011 will be remembered for the protest demonstrations that occurred across the world from India to Athens, from the 'Arab Spring' to 'Occupy Wall Street' phenomena. These public demonstrations were peculiar to each country but corruption was a common denominator everywhere. Indeed, corruption has become a global problem that affects almost all nations across the world. It is also true that corruption has seeped into every aspect of human life. Corruption exists in sports, development, education, health, finance, mineral exploration, security and humanitarian aid, and of course governance and politics, to name a few. While efforts such as the United Nations Convention against Corruption, Right to Information Act and Whistle Blower Protection Act are welcome measures to combat corruption, clearly these have failed to prevent or check corrupt practices. The basic fact is that, 'corruption is universal. It exists in all countries, both developed and developing, in the public and private sectors, as well as in non-profit and charitable organizations' (Myint, 2000, 33).

Since criminological discourses have not dealt with corruption comprehensively, they can be used to provide new insights and help question how, where and why corrupt practices take place and focus upon a wider definition of corruption. This is useful since it helps develop effective preventive mechanisms. Political science, and particularly economics, provides strong methods of measuring corruption but these disciplines limit themselves in taking a rational choice model wherein offenders weigh risks to seek rewards (Brooks, 2016). Opportunity theory of crime, routine activities approach and rational choice perspectives in criminology too have been influenced by this rational choice argument but there are other theoretical perspectives as well that look into deterrence, learning, interaction and even the nature of laws governing corruption. These provide richer and fuller approaches to examine the nature, extent and prevention of corrupt behavior.

Just as crime has been defined as a deliberate act against prevailing laws, corruption has largely been explained in the context of violation of a specific law. However, corruption is also perceived as unethical and even immoral behavior and deemed as serious crime. The term 'corruption' is derived from the Latin verb *rumpere* (to break), which suggests a violation of the law. 'If an official's act is prohibited by laws established by the government, it is corrupt; if it is not prohibited, it is not corrupt even if it is abusive or unethical' (Gardiner, 1993, 7). Such a legal approach seems unsatisfactory, for a corrupt act is looked down in every society as being deviant and iniquitous. Thus, when Scott (1972) states that corruption simply involves the violation of law, it fails to capture the serious consequences that differ from other violations of law, such as being drunk in public. Kaufmann (2006) rightly states that undue emphasis on narrow legalism has obscured subtle yet costly manifestations of misgovernance where 'legal corruption' may be more prevalent than illegal forms. Confining corruption to a matter of law violation does not portray the gravity and the damage that corruption breeds in the individual and the society. *For instance, selling publicly owned natural resources to multinational corporations at reduced prices may be within rules but not in citizen interest and hence, unprincipled and corrupt.* Furthermore, there are numerous acts by government officials that may not have transgressed the boundaries of law but are undesirable or meet social disapproval. Thus, misusing official resources such as telephones, vehicles, personnel and accommodation for personal usage, as seen in every part of India may not be a crime in law but still invites citizen disapproval and are perceived to be corrupt practices.

Moreover, by restricting such acts to the definition of law the remedy is compromised. 'We cannot expect corrupt actors, who control the levers of legislative and executive power, to punish themselves' (Underkuffler, 2005, 7). If the problem of corruption is largely about lawmakers and the public officials, it is unlikely that they will support those legislations and norms that inhibit corrupt practices. We are facing this situation in India where elected politicians and senior bureaucrats are the biggest stumbling block in establishing a strong Lokpal and bringing transparency in public transactions.

One cannot discount that some form of corruption may even be desirable and considered morally good even when it violates the law. An official accepting a bribe from a journalist to leak information about corruption in high places may be forgiven for contributing to the larger good. Therefore, the legal approach diminishes the role of moral discretion and is constrained by clearly defined edicts (Byrne, 2007). Philp (2001) provides a more comprehensive concept stating that corruption occurs when a public official, for personal gain, violates the norms of public office and harms the interests of the public to benefit a third party, who rewards the official to access goods and/or services that this third party could not get otherwise. One could read from this argument that there is no need for the law to be broken for the two could conspire to subvert the just process. 'This is one reason why legal definitions of corruption fail to capture some of the worst cases of corrupt activity' (Philp, 2001, 2).

Corruption remains difficult to conceptualize and as Underkuffler (2005, 70) states, 'efforts by political scientists, economists, legal academics, and others to articulate a politically neutral, methodologically respectable, operational viable definition of public corruption have had little success'. A rather simple interpretation is to define corruption as 'the use of public office for private gain, or in other words, use of official position, rank or status by an office bearer for his own personal benefit' (Myint, 2000, 35). This is well illustrated by bribery, extortion, fraud, embezzlement, nepotism, misuse of public assets and property for private use, and even influence peddling—all seen as various forms of corrupt practices. These common perspectives summarize the concept in simple terms. Even Transparency International defines corruption to be the 'abuse of entrusted power for private gain'. The business dictionary describes it as 'wrongdoing on the part of an authority or powerful party through means that are illegitimate, immoral, or incompatible with ethical standards'. For most people, dishonest behavior by those in positions of power, such as managers or government officials even without personal gain is corruption. But it is clear that such definitions fail to capture the worst aspect of corrupt activity that raises public ire and loss of faith in the government.

A more intuitive way to understand corruption is to examine its various manifestations. Corruption occurs in various forms and may range from 'grass eater' to organized systematic corruption (Sherman, 1978). As Myint (2000) states, the 'low-level' form of corruption is 'need-driven' wherein a clerk with small salary may be induced to seek a monetary gain to expedite the bureaucratic process. Such individual corruption is largely confined to specific bad apples. On the other hand, 'greed-driven' corruption is generally seen at a 'high-level' where it is not economic desperation that makes an official demand more—it is simply greed for money, or power, or equivalent. In general, individual and unorganized corruption is commonly tolerated by the people, but when it becomes so systematic and organized that almost everyone in the unit is engaged in making money it is a serious problem. Such *endemic* or *systemic* corruption occurs when it is an integrated and essential aspect of the economic, social and political system that helps sustain it. Systemic corruption emerges in a situation where individuals and groups use state institutions and functions for personal gain. Sherman (1978) describes how such pervasive organized corruption led to scandals amongst various police agencies in the United States. It is this systematic form of political corruption in India that has corroded the whole society. This kind of widespread corruption is facilitated by political leaders and state agents using their authority to sustain personal power, status and wealth. In such an insidious situation, laws and regulations are abused by the rulers, sidestepped, ignored, or even tailored to fit their interests (Byrne, 2007).

Political economists, who dominate the literature on corruption explain it as a form of economic *rent* (Lambsdorff, 2002). A person having something unique or special in possession can charge more than normal price for its use and earn economic rent or monopoly profit. In the light of this discussion one could refer to bribery, fraud, graft and other shady deals involving misuse of public office as rent seeking activities. This becomes possible when unchecked discretion in exercising options and lack of accountability are coupled in the process. In such a situation, the public official can extract a huge economic rent for his or her services and decisions, and thus it gives rise to systematic corruption. Myint (2000, 38) argues that such a thoroughly corrupt systematic system will emerge in a country if it satisfies the following three conditions:

a. It has a large number of laws, rules, regulations and administrative orders to restrict business and economic activities and thereby creates huge opportunities for generating economic rent, and especially if these restrictive measures are complex and opaque and applied in a selective, secretive, inconsistent and non-transparent way.

b. Administrators are granted large discretionary powers with respect to interpreting rules, are given a lot of freedom to decide on how rules are to be applied, to whom and in what manner they are to be applied; are vested with powers to amend, alter, and rescind the rules, and even to supplement the rules by invoking new restrictive administrative measures and procedures.

c. There are no effective mechanisms and institutional arrangements in the country to hold administrators accountable for their actions.

This argument is based upon the notion that there is a monopoly over the goods and services and a lack of accountability on part of those who hold this power. This is a constricted definition for it suggests that corruption can be prevented by designing methods that force the officials to act in desirable and honest ways in their dealing. As Brooks (2016) suggests, this argument invariably promotes free markets and liberal constitutional systems as the solution and accordingly is ideologically biased too.

Moreover, the economic viewpoint generally explains corruption in the context of specific situations. But it is known that 'incidence of corruption appears to vary strongly across societies even for comparable activities' (Andvig and Moene, 1990, 63). This 'social interactions view' (Goel and Nelson, 2010; Dong, Dulleck and Torgler, 2012) emphasizes that corruption is an outcome of self-reinforcing social processes. The decision of an official to indulge in corrupt practices depends on the social norms that prevail in the organization. Furthermore, individual choices become a function of group level adoptions which can trigger loops of positive feedback and create complementarity between individual action and group behavior. The consequence can be that the same basic fundamental factors and policies can support very different outcomes. As Andvig and Moene (1990) argue, similar socio-economic structures can give rise to different levels of corrupt practices. In such a situation, the causal role of institutions, organizational structures, decentralized decision-making and policy options can only have limited preventive impact.

There are interesting research studies that support this social-interaction perspective. Fisman and Miguel (2007) found that cultural or social norms related to corruption were quite persistent. Diplomats from countries high on corruption indices, would park their vehicles illegally in New York and often would not pay fines citing their diplomatic immunity. This behavior was not seen amongst diplomats representing nations known for low corruption amongst their officials, such as Scandinavian countries. Norms related to corruption are apparently deeply ingrained and factors other than legal ones are important determinants of corrupt behavior. The impact of social interaction on corruption is also substantial. Dong, Dulleck and Torgler

(2012) report that officials participate in corrupt practices when they perceive similar practices amongst other officials. Using official data, Dong and Torgler (2012, 942) find that 'social interaction, both local and global, has a significantly positive effect on the corruption rate in China'.

However, a problem with definitions derived from politico-economic perspectives is that corruption is only seen as being limited to public sector undertakings. If corruption is confined to the abuse of political and or administrative power for personal gain, then collaborative actions of the private sector in instigating and manipulating public officials for profit and violating terms of doing business fall outside the boundary of corruption. Recent scholarship has argued that corruption exists in the private sector too, sometimes without any link to the public sector (Faccio, 2006; Hough, 2015). Today, public–private partnerships and delivery of services by contracting out to the private sector have blurred the distinction between the two sectors. Many forms of corruption such as misuse of power or authority, personal or organizational gains and violation of trust could easily occur in the private sector. Furthermore, the emergence of the new public management reforms (Hood, 1995) has led to the delivery of public services wherein policy decisions are now divorced from policy implementation. In this new form of management, many officials move frequently from public to private sector positions and it is unclear how their responsibilities are to be assessed. In the US, with the election of Donald Trump as President, this conflict has grown wider with many of his family members and friends occupying senior positions or acting as informal consultants to the administration. The exploitation of privileged information by the private sector is an old corrupt practice. The nexus between the political and financial sectors with minimal state regulation seems to be the ideological path for economic development and which blurs corrupt practices as modern management measures.

Hence, the common perception of corruption as 'abuse of power for private gain' is restricted and only describes one of the motives of indulging in dishonesty. Brooks (2016, 8) argues that 'criminology and sociology offer a far more nuanced approach and help place acts of corruption onto a continuum and highlight and analyze all acts of this continuum that range from deviant to non-criminal to criminal acts'. Corruption involves a range of behaviors that may be at the individual, organizational and even the state levels. Such behaviors may emerge from motivation that is rational, calculated or some kind of deviance. Criminology suggests that corrupt practices need to be examined in the situational context in which people interact. This seems a better and more meaningful approach to understanding corruption as we seek ways to combat it in the Indian context.

Criminological Approaches to Corruption

Criminology explains crime and deviance in terms of its public disapproval and notion of punishment as a mean to control it. The discipline also emphasizes social learning and interaction with others as ways in which criminal behavior, including corrupt practices, are understood, learned and adopted. Sutherland, Cressey and Luckenbill (1992) suggest that this learning occurs in a natural manner as part of the growing up and socialization process. This is no different from the natural form of learning except that some find that their behavior is unfavorably defined and is violative of prevailing laws. Subordinate officials learn about malpractices from their colleagues and also see their managers indulging in actions that benefit them personally at the expense of the company or the department. However, they find that their act of taking a paltry sum from the customers is labeled as corruption while the manager's holidays or vacations facilitated by client organizations is a 'perk'. It is this 'differential association' that forms the root of corrupt behavior.

Merton's (1968) strain theory argues that the socially induced pressures to achieve 'success' are generally blocked for many young people growing up in impoverished neighborhoods. They lack the necessary family support, guidance and resources that alone provide access to opportunities to rise up the ladder of success. This situates a set of people to be at a disadvantage for they are unable to accumulate wealth (the notion of success) through the legitimate process. These people perceive 'strain' in their lives finding that what they desire is blocked by socially approved pathways. They end up acting in an illegitimate manner and justifying their corrupt behavior by arguments that 'everyone is doing it'. Sykes and Matza (1957) call these techniques 'neutralization' and suggest that such actors 'drift' in and out of criminal behavior.

A major contribution of criminology in understanding corruption is to focus upon the reasons why many people do *not* indulge in corruption. If rational self-interest is the reason for people resorting to corrupt practices, it is also necessary to examine why individuals decide to resist corruption. There are large examples of people who willingly accept misery, poverty and hardship and never consider any form of gratification. Many junior police officials would stand up to their corrupt bosses at great risk to their career and even physical security but would not let corruption occurr on their watch. All these suggest that together with building an understanding about why corruption happens we should also examine why it does not happen. The reasons why people would not commit crime or act deviant is best explained by control theory that suggests individuals learn to resist temptations and deviant behavior as part of their socialization and through parental or guardian supervision. This perspective is derived from Durkheim (1965) who proposed that the rapid changes in society led to a splintering of social solidarity. Society's foundation was morality rather than economic base and was sustained by strong social bonds that placed the community over self-interest of its members. This provided a sense of purpose and also guide to moral behavior. But weakening of these social bonds loosened the morals and led the people to pursue individual goals and indulge in corruption. This theoretical approach 'did not stress economic inequality and focused on the moral order of society and the role of individual in negotiating and dealing with the desires and disappointments of life' (Brooks, 2016, 131).

This control theory perspective is best illustrated by Hirschi (1969, 31) who argued that since 'we are all animals and thus naturally capable of committing criminal acts' it is unnecessary to explain human motivation in terms of deviance. He suggested that individuals who were tightly bonded to their family, friends, school teachers and guardians are generally less likely to resort to delinquency. This bonding comes from attachment, commitment, involvement and belief, and they are reinforced by the family and also during the schooling period. Later on, Gottfredson and Hirschi (1990) proposed their 'general theory of crime' combining various themes with social control to explain the etiology of crime. For them internal control is an important mechanism and 'low self-control' is the basic cause of criminal action. The control perspective suggests strengthening the bonds to the conventional system where socialization through family members, teachers and extended guardians helps the child to learn to restrain himself and avoid actions that are considered deviant by the elders. Control theory is thus different from the rational choice perspective that has strong economic basis for its etiology.

Control theory has been criticized by other criminologists who have noted that Gottfredson and Hirschi consider white-collar crimes to be trivial (Jones, 2006). Furthermore, this approach puts the blame upon parents for failing to discipline and educate their children, ignoring the wider social and economic factors that hinder parental control. This perspective 'does not fundamentally challenge the structure of the state and inequality' (Brooks, 2016, 135). Since the emphasis is also upon young people, the control theory is also limited in explaining corruption that occurs at later stages of life. Gottfredson and Hirschi (1990) do assert that geographical variations in crime can be explained by variations in opportunities for different forms of crimes. But this adds another dimension—that of opportunity to the control perspective.

The conflict theories of crime (Turk, 1969; Quinney, 1970; Chambliss and Seidman, 1971) focus upon the way crime and its control mechanism are constructed by powerful actors in the society. These theories apply the Marxist perspective to argue that corruption is inevitable in capitalism wherein those who wield power label others as corrupt while enriching themselves. Chambliss and Seidman (1971) argue that legal and administrative sanctions are organized to help the ruling elites and law serves their interests. Taylor, Walton and Young (1973) also argue that existing criminal justice system tends to focus upon actions of the working class while ignoring white-collar crimes.

An implication of such a conflict perspective is that power and official crime rates are going to be inversely related. Those who wield power and authority in any society will not find themselves being treated as violators of law in comparison to those who have less power. This is well understood in India where the jails are full with people from the lower classes, the minorities and the weaker sections of the society who are prosecuted for petty crimes (Dhawan and Thakur, 2015). The demographic profile of under-trial prisoners in 2015 is extremely revealing and supportive of this conflict perspective. In 2015, there were 2,82,076 under-trial prisoners of which 80,528 (28.5 per cent) were illiterate; 1,19,082 (42.2 per cent) did not complete class X and 65.5 per cent belonged to Scheduled Caste (SC), Scheduled Tribe (ST) and Other Backward Class (OBC) categories (NCRB, 2016b). In comparison to 2,22,556 people arrested for the crime of theft, generally belonging to the poorer sections, only 6,657 were arrested for corruption charges in 2015 who invariably hailed from upper classes (NCRB, 2016a, Tables 9-I and 12.1). Lord Acton made an interesting observation that power corrupts and absolute power corrupts absolutely. But it is worthwhile to note that 'absolute power may corrupt absolutely (cited in Lazarski, 2012), but people with absolute power are never officially defined as criminals' (Vold, Bernard and Snipes, 1998, 259).

Some criminological theories find debates about etiology of crime to be unsatisfactory and instead focus upon pragmatic and realistic ways to deal with criminal behavior. Brantingham and Brantingham (1981) suggest that any criminal incident has four dimensions—the law which prohibits such acts; the offender who willfully chooses to commit the act; the victim or target of the act and most importantly, the geographical space in which the first three dimensions come together. This geographical approach has been seen to be very effective in preventing and combating 'street' and predatory crimes (Stark, 1987; Wilson, Brown and Schuster, 2009). Concepts such as 'defensible space' (Newman, 1972), target hardening and other situational factors (Clarke, 1992), 'problem oriented policing' (Goldstein, 1979), and 'predictive policing' (Pearsall, 2010) have all been found to be useful in preventing thefts, burglaries, robberies, riots and wildlife poaching (Verma, 2007; Lemieux, 2014).

The basic tenet of this approach is explained by Clarke (1992) as an opportunity-reducing measure that is directed at highly specific forms of crime; makes it difficult for the offender to commit the crime by increasing the risks of detection and reducing the rewards of crime and finally involves manipulating the environment, the situation which facilitates the commission of these specific crimes. This perspective agrees with the economists that offenders act rationally and operate on the basis of risk and reward. Interestingly, these criminologists do not explain the motivation for choosing to commit crime and accept the arguments of other criminological theories that use sociological and psychological explanations. A large number of specific tactics have been developed to implement these situational crime prevention methods and which have found wide applicability. This situational perspective suggests that incidences of bribes being accepted by police officers enforcing traffic laws may be controlled by a rule that could stipulate such enforcement only under the supervision of a senior officer or by setting competition amongst different agencies (Bertrand et al., 2007). Installation of close circuit television (CCTV) in public offices where citizens deal directly with officials issuing licenses and certificates will provide formal surveillance and hence increase the risk involved in demanding and/or accepting bribes from civilians.

These rational choice and geography-based criminological perspectives are also helpful in combating policies and actions that harm the environment and thus 'fit onto a continuum of corruption' (Brooks, 2016, 191). Many environmental crimes such as pollution, cutting down trees, illegally dumping waste in rivers, illegal mining and encroachment, using banned chemicals and such others are all related to corrupt practices. The illegal mining at Bellary (BBC, 2012); Bhopal gas tragedy (Taylor, 2014); large-scale destruction of forests in Uttrakhand and activities of sand mafia in UP (Rashid, 2013) are all major cases of corruption in the country and can be addressed by situational prevention methods (Huisman and van Erp, 2013; Lemieux, 2014; Mesko et al., 2011).

These criminological perspectives also help explain the genesis and persistence of financial irregularities and political corruption. The monopoly exercised by the state or some organizations invariably involve corruption if there is no public accountability in decision making. Most of the so-called white-collar crimes occur due to the opportunities available to public officials due to their strategic positions and ability of business people to circumvent regulations. Lee (2015) argues that it is difficult to apply criminal law to the corporate sector and that it only provides reactive response to white-collar crimes. Situational prevention methods suggest that regulatory mechanisms such as licensing, certification, performance standards, fines, safety regulations and blacklisting could be more effective in prevention of corrupt practices than invoking criminal laws. We will discuss this further in Chapter 3.

Conceptualization of corruption is important for it encompasses a wide-ranging set of activities and perspectives. What is uncontested is that corrupt acts violate moral norms and are insidious and destructive of human lives and institutions. These 'involve the discard of collective restraints, and the perversion of the apparatus of government' (Underkuffler, 2005, 72). Corruption amongst public institutions destroy confidence and legitimacy of the government. This is a serious consequence and is particularly condemnable as it is a violation of trust reposed in the position held by the official (Shihata, 1997). As Brasz (1978) states, corruption is a stealthy exercise that functions under the pretense of legitimate service but acts to the detriment of the public. For this reason, we support the contention to consider 'corruption as the idea of capture by evil, the possession of the individual by evil, in law' (Underkuffler, 2005, 2).

This may be a strong conceptualization but one that does capture the devastating impact of corruption. It condemns people and destroys the lives of not only those indulging in it but also their family, friends and society. A corrupt police officer, a judge or a political leader not only causes immense harm to their office and individuals, but also to public institutions and the government. Corruption destroys the very legitimacy of public institutions and presents a picture of lawlessness and anarchy. It symbolizes self-involvement, self-indulgence, the loosening and discard of the restraint of social bonds and hence suggests public and personal indolence, excess and, above all, decadence. In an article about rampant public corruption in India, a former Attorney General Soli Sorabjee was quoted stating that corruption spreads like a cancer and suggests a complete breakdown of moral values. It is as if the country's very soul has been irredeemably warped (Gargan, 1992). Corruption is evil since it is marked by immorality and perversion, making the corrupt depraved, venal and dishonest (Parker, 1984).

The above mentioned criminological and other perspectives are useful since these suggest that corruption is not only a crime, a violation of established laws but should also be considered immoral and deviant. Corruption functions as a casual factor by covering illegal actions and getting involved with pervasive organized criminal behavior in public and private institutions. Corruption is also a side effect of crimes of fraud, nepotism, financial shenanigans and political pursuit of power. As such, the deterrent effect of criminal laws or legal sanctions are ineffective since officials and their institutions are affected. This broader criminological approach going beyond legal, economic and political dimensions of corruption is helpful in understanding how, where and why such practices occur. This understanding suggests more effective methods to prevent and combat corruption which we will discuss in subsequent chapters.

Measuring Corruption

While anecdotal evidence about corruption is found everywhere, systematic efforts to estimate the extent of corruption in any society are hard to find. Nevertheless, measuring corruption is important, for without empirical data it is impossible to combat corruption effectively. Measuring corruption offers other benefits as well. It can help to establish priorities for reform by identifying activities and agencies where corruption is concentrated. It educates the public about the economic and social costs of corruption and establishes a baseline against which the successes and failures of reform can later be measured. Until recently it was considered impossible to systematically measure corruption in government institutions and assess its economic and social costs. The data involved general measurements or indices of public perceptions of aggregate corruption in a country. But, recent advances include cross-country analysis of data on perceptions of corruption against institutional and other correlates. The newest frontier in the fight against corruption, is now to survey the parties to corruption directly and simultaneously—including household members, business people and public officials—and ask them about the costs and private returns of paying bribes to obtain public services, special privileges and government jobs. Just as self-reports of criminal behavior were deemed impossible on grounds that offenders will not confess to their crimes, skeptics believed that parties to corruption will either deny or underreport it. But with appropriate survey instruments and interviewing techniques, respondents were found willing to discuss agency-specific corruption with remarkable candor. Even with underreporting and non-responses to some sensitive questions, the results offer meaningful estimates of corruption (Treisman, 2000).

There are several methods that are used for measuring corruption in different regions and countries. Some of the prominent and commonly used methods are:

- Transparency International's Corruption Perception Index (CPI).
- Global Corruption Barometer (GCB): Measuring people's perceptions and experiences of corruption, it is a representative survey of more than 114,000 households in 107 countries.
- Bribe Payers Index (BPI): Measuring the supply side of corruption in international business transaction, this is a ranking of leading exporting

countries according to the perceived likelihood of their firms to bribe abroad. It is based on a survey of business executives capturing perceptions of the business practices of foreign firms in their country.

- Global Corruption Report (GCR): Exploring corruption issues in detail for a specific issue or sector, it is a thematic report which draws on a variety of expert research and analysis as well as case studies.
- Nation Integrity System Assessment (NIS): A series of in-country studies providing an extensive qualitative assessment of the strengths and weaknesses of the key institutions that enable good governance and prevent corruption in a country.
- Transparency in Corporations: The study analyzes the extent of transparency in the reporting on a series of anti-corruption measures by the world's largest companies.
- World Governance Indicators (WGI) and the Business Environment and Enterprise Survey (BEEPS) developed by the World Bank.

Amongst all the methods two units of measuring corruption, the CPI and the WGI have gained recognition in understanding ways in which corruption is facilitated in the country. CPI measures government level of perceived corruption. This index is prepared annually and reflects the perception of corruption within governments from 175 countries scoring from 0 to 10, where 0 is the highest level of corruption and 10 the lowest level of corruption. The CPI scores and ranks countries/territories based on how corrupt a country's public sector is perceived to be. It is a composite index, a combination of surveys and assessments of corruption that is collected by several professional agencies.

The idea behind this index is that corruption is largely a matter of perception that is exposed only through whistleblowing, leading to scandals and persistent investigation. There is no hard data to determine its extent or even nature as it transcends all government functions. Corruption hurts the citizens and common people and it is their perception that suggests the extent of deviance amongst government officials. The CPI includes only sources that provide a score for a set of countries/territories and that measure perceptions of corruption in the public sector. Transparency International (henceforth abbreviated as TI) reviews the methodology of each data source in detail to ensure that the sources used meet their quality standards (TI, 2017). For the year 2016, CPI utilized the following 13 data sources:

1. African Development Bank Governance Ratings, 2015
2. Bertelsmann Foundation Sustainable Governance Indicators, 2016
3. Bertelsmann Foundation Transformation Index, 2016
4. Economist Intelligence Unit Country Risk Ratings, 2016
5. Freedom House Nations in Transit, 2016
6. Global Insight Country Risk Ratings, 2015
7. IMD World Competitiveness Yearbook, 2016
8. Political and Economic Risk Consultancy Asian Intelligence, 2016
9. Political Risk Services International Country Risk Guide, 2016
10. World Bank—Country Policy and Institutional Assessment, 2015
11. World Economic Forum Executive Opinion Survey (EOS), 2016
12. World Justice Project Rule of Law Index, 2016
13. Varieties of Democracy (VDEM) Project, 2016

It needs to be kept in mind that the country with the lowest score is the one where public-sector corruption is perceived to be the greatest *among those included in the list* (TI, 2017) and this score does not suggest an absolute rank. As TI informs, 'the CPI scores and ranks countries/territories based on how corrupt a country's public sector is perceived to be. It is a composite index, a combination of surveys and assessments of corruption, collected by a variety of reputable institutions'. The CPI has become one of the most widely used indicators of corruption worldwide. Such a survey is an appropriate method since corruption involves illegal and hidden activities that are difficult to uncover. Data of officially registered crimes of bribery and their prosecution are tainted by official record keeping systems and invariably leave aside a much larger 'dark figure' of criminal activities. Hence, 'capturing perceptions of corruption of those in a position to offer assessments of public sector corruption is the most reliable method of comparing relative corruption levels across countries' (TI, 2017).

Yet CPI is not without limitations. Since it relies upon the perception and impression of people who encounter corruption, it is 'subject to stereotypical judgments rather than coinciding with reality' (Brooks, 2016, 45). CPI is, therefore, a measure of the impression of corrupt practices rather than the frequency of these acts. This may explain why Switzerland is deemed a country where corruption is minimal and still its banks and financial institutions shelter funds of the corrupt, mafia and politicians (Shaxson, 2007). This impression is also formed largely from experiences of bribery and does not include other forms of corruption.

The second important index is the World Governance Indicator (WGI) developed by the World Bank that relies on the countries' capacity to control corruption. There are six dimensions of governance that are taken into account—voice and accountability, political stability and absence of violence, government effectiveness, regulatory quality, rule of law and control of corruption. These aggregate indicators combine the views of a large number of enterprizes, citizens and expert survey respondents in industrial and developing countries. They are based on 30 individual data sources produced by a variety of survey institutes, think tanks, non-governmental organizations, international organizations and private sector firms (World Bank, 2017).

The WGI draws on four different types of data sources (World Bank, 2017):

- surveys of households and firms (including the Afro-barometer surveys, Gallup World Poll and Global Competitiveness Report survey);
- commercial business information providers (including the Economist Intelligence Unit, Global Insight, Political Risk Services);
- non-governmental organizations (including Global Integrity, Freedom House, Reporters Without Borders) and
- public sector organizations (including the CPIA assessments of World Bank and regional development banks, the EBRD Transition Report, French Ministry of Finance Institutional Profiles Database).

The Global Corruption Barometer conducted by Transparency International has been the largest cross-country survey to collect the general public's views on, and experiences of corruption. In 2013, it conducted a survey of more than 114,000 respondents in 107 countries. The survey addressed people's direct experiences with bribery and presented their views on corruption in the main institutions of their countries. According to the latest Global Corruption Barometer (TI, 2017) corruption is a very real burden, with more than one out of four respondents reporting having paid a bribe when using a public service. India had a high bribery rate with nearly seven in ten people acknowledging paying a bribe. Moreover, the survey revealed that corruption is seen to be running through the foundations of the democratic and legal processes in many countries, affecting public trust in political parties, the judiciary and the police, among other key institutions. Based on its survey, the police force was seen as the most bribery-prone public service. The survey suggests that half of the people in Asia-Pacific believe that their government is ineffective in fighting corruption. Interestingly, according to Global Corruption Barometer, 'people in India were most positive about their government's efforts with over a half saying they were doing well' (TI, 2017, 4).

The major problem with such survey methods is that this may not measure corruption accurately. An interesting technique to measure bribery is to survey bribe givers and use that to estimate the level of corruption in specific situations. The International Crime Victimization Survey or the World Bank Enterprise Survey ask questions about bribes and since these are easy to replicate, they appear to be reliable measures. Many direct observations by researchers in various countries also provide another way to measure corruption in such societies. Public audit of government funds to specific projects provide yet another way to understand leakages and corrupt practices, though this method is tainted by its reliance upon official records which are generally not kept properly to hide corruption. Of course, all these methods have their limitations. 'There are remarkably few reliable estimates of the actual magnitude of corruption and those that exist reveal a high level of heterogeneity' (Olken and Pande, 2012, 3).

Further, 'anecdotal and survey evidence suggests that corruption is rampant in the developing world and more prevalent in developing countries than in rich ones' (Olken and Pande, 2012, 3). But as we all know, corruption is a problem for all the countries. The 2016 CPI ranks 176 countries based on the perceptions of public sector corruption. Not one country got a perfect score and more than two thirds of the countries ranked in the index score below 50 on a scale from 0 (perceived to be highly corrupt) to 100 (perceived to be very clean) implying that levels of bribery and corruption in the public sector of most countries are still perceived to be very high. North American and European countries were relatively less corrupt than countries in South America, Central Africa and Asia. While Denmark and New Zealand were the least corrupt, Somalia and North Korea were ranked as the most corrupt nations in the world. India ranked 79th out of the 176 countries included in the survey (TI, 2017).

An earlier measure developed and implemented by TI was the so-called Bribe Payer's Index that 'rank[ed] the likelihood of companies from 28 major economies to win business abroad by paying bribes'. As TI stated, rich nations let their companies win business contracts by bribing officials and that these nations are complicit in corrupt practices. According to its 2011 report the index shows that there is no country among the 28 major economies whose companies are perceived to be wholly clean and that do not engage in bribery. The Netherlands and Switzerland top the table with scores of 8.8, with Belgium, Germany and Japan following closely behind. Companies from these countries are seen as less likely to engage in bribery than those of the other countries ranked, but there is room for improvement. At the bottom of the table, companies from China and Russia are perceived to be most likely to engage in bribery abroad. The business people surveyed perceived bribery by companies from these countries to be most widespread, resulting in substantially lower scores for China and Russia, than the other surveyed countries (TI, 2011).

Many other institutions and groups have also studied the extent and nature of corruption around the world. Shah (2011) states that corruption 'occurs at all levels of society, from local and national governments, civil society, judiciary functions, large and small businesses, military and other services and so on'. The International Anti-Corruption (IAC) is an organization whose mission is to identify and stop corporate bribery and other corporate corruption. The IAC accomplishes that mission by facilitating the reporting by employees, former employees and other individuals of corporate bribery and other corporate wrongdoings. The IAC seeks to enforce the Dodd-Frank Act that is aimed at encouraging whistleblowers to report corporate bribery and other wrongdoing (IAC, 2017).

The Organization for Economic Cooperation and Development (OECD) too has come to the forefront in fostering anti-corruption measures. It states that integrity is the corner stone of good governance. Fostering integrity and preventing corruption in the public sector support a level playing field for businesses and is essential to maintaining trust in government. The OECD has developed Principles for Managing Ethics in the Public Service and regularly conducts Integrity Framework Reviews to design comparative cross-country benchmarks and indicators in anti-corruption efforts. These Reviews of Public Sector Integrity help policymakers improve policies, adopt good practices and implement established principles and standards. These review processes have been expanded to cover experiences and good practices from both OECD and non-OECD member countries.

Estimation of Corruption in India

Corruption is not a new phenomenon in India. Political corruption has been a fact of life for thousands of years. One of the oldest and perhaps the best systematic and threadbare study of corruption can be found in the treatise *Arthashastra* by the ancient Indian political philosopher and economist, Kautilya, aka Chanakya (3rd–4th century BCE) who believed that men are naturally fickle minded. Honesty is not a virtue that would remain consistent lifelong and the temptation to make easy gains, through corrupt means, can override the trait of honesty any time. Similarly, he compared the process of generation and collection of revenue (by officials) with honey on the tip of the tongue, which becomes impossible not to taste. Based on such assessment of the nature of human beings, he prescribed a strict vigil, even over the superintendents of government departments in relation to the place, time, nature, output and modus operandi of work. Significantly, in keeping with the current trend of exposing corruption, Kautilya also dealt with the concept of whistleblowers. Any informant, *suchaka*, who provided details about financial wrongdoing, was entitled to an award of one-sixth of the amount in question (Kumar, 2012). Undoubtedly, even during this ancient period, corruption was wide-spread across the country.

The Mughal rule was also known for the corruption and extortion by its officials. The term *baksheesh* emerged during this period and since then has been used to pay 'speed money' to officials for getting things done. Mughal emperors had imposed more than forty different types of taxes and zamindars would go to the villages and impose them on the basis of appearance of prosperity. The British simply saw no problem in looting from the land they conquered. Robert Clive faced charges of corruption and Warren Hastings faced impeachment in the House of Commons (Smith, 2008). Cornwall Lewis, a member of the British House of Commons stated, '[N]o civilized Government existed on this earth which was more corrupt, more perfidious and more rapacious than the Government of the East India Company from 1765–1784' (Tummala, 2009, 40).

Systematic studies to measure the extent and nature of corruption in modern India are rather limited. Most of the information is anecdotal and/or has come from external institutions such as TI. The National Crime Records Bureau publishes an annual *Crime in India* that provides data from police and other enforcement agencies about incidents registered under the rubric of 'Economic Offenses'. The latest publication provides data about offenses registered and processed in 2015 and lists 24 different types of economic crimes (NCRB, 2016a). These cover various forms of corrupt practices from tax evasion, smuggling, evasion of excise duty, money laundering, corruption and bribery of public servants, financial frauds, stock market manipulations and company frauds to theft of intellectual property. The common investigators at the local police stations generally investigate crimes such as cheating, counterfeiting and criminal breach of trust as defined by the Indian Penal Code. It may be noted that apart from these corrupt practices there are many specialized agencies that enforce and investigate other forms of economic offenses. Amongst the police agencies are special units for 'Economic Offenses' under the Criminal Investigation Department (CID), the Anti-Corruption Bureau and also the Vigilance Department of the respective states. Some states like Madhya Pradesh have a dedicated Economic Offences Wing (EOW), which also has the powers to investigate corruption cases under the Prevention of Corruption Act. This makes EOW MP one of the most powerful agencies among the Indian states.

Amongst the units functioning under the central government are—the Central Bureau of Investigation, the Central board of Direct Taxes, the Collectors of Central Excise, the Directorate of Enforcement, the Director General of Foreign Trade, and the Serious Fraud Investigation Office. Some have exclusive jurisdiction over specific economic offenses such as tax evasion under the Income Tax Act, which is handled by the Central board of Direct Taxes. The Directorate of Enforcement functioning under the Finance Ministry handles crimes of money laundering under the Foreign Exchange Regulation Act of 1973 and the Money Laundering Act of 2002. For some specific offenses like those under the rubric of 'illicit drug trafficking', are handled by the local and specialized police agencies such as Narcotic Control Bureau at the union level and their counterparts in the states.

Many of the economic crimes described above are defined under special legislations and are enforced by the respective departmental agencies. It is worthwhile to note that not only do these special agencies have legal powers for investigation but also for adjudication, imposition of fines, penalties and even arrest and detention of suspects. These special enforcement officers have the power to summon witnesses, search and seizure of goods, documents and confiscation of proceeds. Not all economic offenses are directly related to corruption. For instance, smuggling, drug trafficking, insurance frauds, theft of intellectual property and such others may prevail due to corrupt officers but the link is only indirect. However, crimes of money laundering, tax evasion and stock market manipulation are obviously entangled with corrupt practices of people both from public agencies and private manipulators.

Unfortunately, the data about corruption is scant and provides only limited evidence of extensive corruption that beguiles the nation. For instance, in 2015, there were only 90 raids reported by the Enforcement Directorate under Foreign Exchange Management Act of 1999 (FEMA) to unearth cases of money laundering that yielded only ₹42.89 crores in actual realization from the offenders. The data on tax evasion reported by the Central board of Direct Taxes presents even more dismal picture. Out of the 669 prosecutions launched during the period 2014–15, only 34 resulted in convictions (NCRB, 2016a, 124–25). The enforcement of the Prevention of Corruption Act, 1988 led to 617 cases being registered by the CBI and 5,250 by the state vigilance authorities. During 2015, the maximum number of cases were reported under Section 13 (accepting remuneration for official duties) that accounted for 62.9 per cent while under Section 7 (seeking gratifications) that accounted for 28.3 per cent of all crimes under the purview of the aforementioned Act. Interestingly, CBI took action against 1,376 gazetted officers and 1,239 non-gazetted officials, while state authorities also took action against 1,261 private persons (NCRB, 2016, 128–29). In the year 2015, in the entire country only 101 officials were dismissed from service for corrupt practices, and 81 were removed from their position while 106 received major departmental penalty (NCRB, 2016a, Economic Offenses).

Further analysis of comparative evaluation of action against corruption by state agencies reveals lack of enforcement by a number of important states of the country. The data, under the Prevention of Corruption Act, 1988, from the Anti-Corruption and Vigilance departments of selected states and for India supports the observation:

Table 2.1 Cases under the Prevention of Corruption Act (1988), 2015

State	Reported	Charge-sheeted	Recovery in lakhs	Convicted
AP	185	133	185	43
Assam	14	1	0	0
Karnataka	259	223	102	65
Madhya Pradesh	634	439	26	145
Maharashtra	1279	1359	450	121
Odisha	456	417	319	78
Punjab	146	127	61	39
Rajasthan	401	338	194	75
Uttar Pradesh	60	30	21	9
West Bengal	18	4	4	0
India	5250	4224	2240	788

Source: NCRB, 2016a, *Crime in India 2015*, Table 9.2.

If all the police agencies could only convict 788 officials across the country in one year then clearly enforcement of corruption prevention efforts is dismal. It may be noted that Assam and West Bengal could not convict even one person and a large state like Uttar Pradesh could do so against nine people only. These numbers are a poor reflection upon a country that has been ranked by TI (2017) 79th on the Corruption Perception Index in 2016 with a score of 40. It is worth pointing out that a score of below 50 indicates a serious corruption problem. Clearly, the performance of anti-corruption agencies of India in pursuing corruption is falling far below expectation.

It was therefore *not* surprising that the movement launched by Anna Hazare against corruption in demand of an independent Lokpal (an ombudsperson) to deal with corruption attracted millions on the streets of Delhi. 'Violations of the community's deeply felt social and moral values […] evoke intense emotions, and call forth a passionate response' (Sunshine and Tyler, 2003, 154). Fed up with corruption, people wanted to see the crooks brought to justice and felt that the government, whose own ministers were corrupt will never let honest investigation proceed independently. But another factor driving the millions to assemble in the humid heat of Delhi was the perception that it was not only a matter of prosecuting the corrupt. The system was plagued and where honesty, probity and integrity were compromised. The Indian state was pursuing policies that corroded moral character while 'the arrogance of the ruling elite' [was seen as if] they can do just about anything they want to do. That kind of power, as Lord Acton wrote years ago, is deeply corrupting' (Walzer, 2008, 11). The Anna movement could galvanize the people because his clean image contrasted sharply against the corruption of the politicians. A prominent public figure whose integrity is well known has the capability to mobilize moral outrage against the abuses of political class (Smith, 2008).

As successive governments have been reluctant in establishing an independent body to handle corruption related complaints and the Supreme Court has castigated the CBI as a 'caged parrot' singing his master's voice (*Times of India*, 2013), the public mood remains frustrated and despondent. There seems little faith in the political parties and their leaders who largely remain tainted and untrustworthy. In such a situation, the wide-spread demand to loosen control over the CBI, provide greater autonomy and establish a Lokpal to handle corruption remain popular and strong.

However, we question if an independent police investigative agency, free from political control, is the best way to control corruption in the country. We believe little thought appears to have been given to the important question—can an independent police investigative agency really be successful in combating corruption? In subsequent chapters, we examine the nature, extent and forms of corruption in India as well as the limitations of investigative agencies. Based on an empirical examination of the efficacy of policing agencies, we will present an alternative that is based upon decentralized accountability, digital transactions and involvement of citizens in public administration and argue that it will be a better method of dealing with corruption.

We will base our arguments comprehensively through a thorough analysis of law, bureaucratic organizations, official data, case studies and a comparative study of international surveys. We theorize that corruption is explained from the perspective of an idealized vision of the state wherein the blame is placed upon an individual rather than the deviant nature of the state itself. The limitations and failures of the institutions in dealing effectively with corruption are overlooked and instead the blame is placed upon some people. The state takes upon itself a major role in controlling public affairs giving extensive discretion to the bureaucrats and politicians. But instead of accepting that unaccounted discretion is routinely misused the state labels some as black sheep to shift the blame from itself. The limitations of such a state structure are unraveled in the course of enforcement and discursive practices employed by anti-corruption institutions. We argue that to control corruption not only is there a need to strengthen investigative agencies but to also evolve decentralized accountability mechanisms that redefine the relations between the individual and the state. Only such mechanisms can prevent corruption at the nascent stage and aid in its speedy investigation.

3

Etiology of Corruption in India

In this section, we look into the history of bribery and other corrupt practices in India. In particular, we present some criminological perspectives that identify the facilitators of corrupt practices in public and political establishments. We suggest that the bureaucratic system with roots in colonial governance bears no local responsibility and functions in secrecy. Moreover, the extensive discretion exercised by public officials is another factor that promotes corruption and misuse of authority. We illustrate this by examining the nature of corrupt practices in the police department and civil administration. We further assert that political shenanigans and criminality is perhaps the biggest cause of corruption in the country. We highlight several cases of political corruption and also examine the role of illegal financing of elections that catalyzes corruption in the country. We argue that the control of the state over natural resources and the lack of transparency in distributing for private exploitation is a major path to corruption. We add that the electronic revolution has also helped build long distance associations that further assist in coordinating actions to siphon public funds. Online banking has opened new avenues wherein financial institutions have become the playground of corruption. This chapter also presents some criminological perspectives to explain the means by which corruption occurs and hides its traces.

Introduction

In independent India, corruption made its presence felt during the period of the Nehru government itself. Starting from the Mundra affairs of 1957 that involved a sum of ₹1.24 Crores (about USD 3.2 million at the time) the current corruption scandals have reached staggering sums of '$40 billion in revenues lost from the crooked sale of 2G telecoms licenses and over $40 billion stolen in Uttar Pradesh alone from schemes subsidizing food and fuel for the poor' (*Economist*, 2011). Independent India started with a socialist stance and the founding fathers led by Nehru saw no problem with the state controlling the commanding heights of economy. Many ministers in Nehru's cabinet were corrupt but the government went out of its way to shield its ministers (*Report on Public Administration*, Planning Commission, Government of India 1951). The Santhanam Committee, appointed in 1962 to examine the issue of corruption commented on the lack of integrity among ministers helping themselves to material profits by illegitimate means and obtaining jobs for family members through nepotism. Over the years, the Indian state has continued to dominate and expand its reach in every sector of the economy. A 'license-permit Raj' strangled the economics of the country and catalyzed corrupt practices in the system. Even today it still takes 'nearly 200 days to get a construction permit and seven years to close a business' which promotes corruption (*Economist*, 2011).

It is not surprising that elected representatives are the biggest cause of corruption in public offices. The former Prime Minister Indira Gandhi famously brushed away allegations against growing corruption in her government by arguing that it is a global phenomenon (Raghavan, 2010). The politicians have also not hesitated to blatantly prevent any investigation into their corrupt practices. The Central Bureau of Investigation (CBI), the premier agency tasked with the responsibility of investigating corruption in the country has been heavily politicized and its authority has been compromised. From Bofors, 2G scam, the coal-gate controversy, Vyapam and in many other corruption-ridden scandals, the CBI investigation has been marred by political considerations. Even when the Supreme Court asserted and required the investigation to be conducted under its supervision the politicians have interfered and attempted to influence the inquiry (Singh, 2013).

While doing business in the country is impossible without participating in corruption, the situation has deteriorated to the extent that public officials routinely extort even when the citizen is not approaching the government. The 'hafta' collection by the police—a practice of collecting weekly bribes from vendors and businesses simply to continue operating in the area governed by the local police—is just one face of this extortion. Bribes have to be paid to provide food to those locked up on false charges, to obtain basic birth, death and even school-leaving certificates. Officials extort bribes from those who seek treatment at government-run hospitals or buy food from public distribution shops. Even minor conveniences such as boarding a train or circumventing the queue to pray in a temple quickly, ahead of others, involves illegal payments to officials.

The subordinate bureaucratic officials extort from the citizens by misusing their authority and discretion in providing basic services. The police patrol officer, the municipal office inspector, the clerks working in registry offices and those processing passport applications are the common faces of extortionist government officials. They are detested and feared for the coercion occurs openly and without seemingly any supervision over their activities. The other form of corruption is somewhat hidden from public view as it provides mutual benefits to the official and the bribe-giver. The trader or the businessperson willingly grease the palms of officers who have the power to grant licences and permission to run their enterprise. In most cases, these officers exercise discretion over allotment of scarce resources controlled by the government. The sale of frequencies for telecom services or coal blocks or mineral resources, all involve transactions where the beneficiaries are willing to pay bribes to get such concessions from the public officials.

Such allotments yield immediate benefits as seen in the 2G scam where Swan Telecom company obtained a licence for ₹15.37 billion (US$280 million) and then it sold 45 per cent stake to the UAE-based Etisalat company for ₹42 billion (US$770 million). Similarly, Unitech Wireless, a subsidiary of the Unitech Group, obtained its licence for ₹16.61 billion (US$300 million) and later sold 60 per cent stake for ₹62 billion (US$1.1 billion) to Norway-based Company Teleno (*NDTV*, 2011). Thus, without even operating their projects these companies reaped substantial profits by receiving the licence from the government. Similar corrupt practices have been seen repeatedly in the defense sector where the discretion to purchase armaments and advanced aircrafts provides enormous dividends to the middlemen who can swing the deal. Thus, in the notorious Bofors' case the Swedish firm allegedly paid a substantial amount of money in order to obtain the contract to the Italian

Ottavio Quattrochi who was reportedly close to the then Prime Minister Rajiv Gandhi's family. The kickbacks were paid to several politicians and government officials and would not have come to light except for the remarkable journalist efforts of Chitra Subramaniam. Another scandal involving the purchase of helicopters from the Italian defense company Finmeccanica is also of similar genre—middlemen receiving kickbacks and paying bribes to ensure contract running in millions of dollars for defense contractors. In these two types of situations corruption is between two mutually accommodating parties—the businessmen and the government officials making the decisions.

A third type is extremely unusual and exists within government offices. Since officials know about the corrupt practices of their fellow officers they squeeze their share by blocking or expediting the concerned decision. For instance, when a licence is being given by one office the related accounts office where the contract is to be routed or the no-objection certificate needed from another office, all wrest their share of the bribe from the front official. In Bihar police headquarters, several officials were charged for extorting money from field police offices that were allotted funds for various projects (Verma, 1999). The understanding was that these field officers will be siphoning the funds allotted for the projects and hence must share with headquarter-based officers who were making the allotment. This corruption appears to run across the country where central and state governments and public-sector officials pay percentages of funds allotted for development to departments controlling the funds and necessary paperwork.

As could be understood, it is only in the case of extortion from the citizen that a complaint is likely to be made. Citizens, forced to pay to ward away officials misusing their authority or to seek relief that is their due, are clearly inclined to protest and lodge a complaint. In case of businessperson and companies seeking discretionary and beneficial decisions from officials, the effort is focused on keeping the matter from being revealed. Of course, in most government offices in-house extortion is almost rarely spoken of or protested against.

Another interesting dimension is the impact of honest officers who make attempts to run the administration according to the rules and seek to prevent corrupt practices. Such officials are universally detested for neither making easy money themselves nor permiting others to make any extra cash. There have been instances where some such honest officers have been killed when attempts to get them transferred have failed because of their good reputation and for being in good books of senior officers. One such case is that of Satyendra Dubey in Bihar (Kapur, 2013). Moreover, an interesting side effect is that such officers generally end up raising the price of bribes. Thus, corrupt officials would claim that they had to be on their guard in exercising favorable discretionary decision and also risked being pulled up by the honest officer. Accordingly, to take these additional risks the price of making the decision goes up! In Patna, the traffic police extorting money from the taxi and bus drivers raised the weekly *hafta* as 'Kunal tax', in name of the Senior Superintendent of Police Kishor Kunal who was strongly enforcing the law.[1] The Indian bureaucracy continues to exemplify the folk tale of 'lehron ka daroga'! There is hardly any government job that does not provide avenues to extort money or receive bribes for discharging public functions. Over the years, even as the state has given up many of its functions and provided entry to the private sector, the corruption within the bureaucracy and the political class has only grown and emerged in new avatars.

A few conclusions can easily be drawn from the above examples. 'the harshness of laws does not result in making the struggles against criminals more effective' (Cheng and Ma, 2009, 176). Greed coupled with unaccountable discretion is a recipe for corruption. Since, even a large number of senior cabinet ministers and bureaucrats are found engaging in corruption this conclusion is not far-fetched. Furthermore, there is little evidence that wages of civil servants are related to the levels of corruption. Thus, in a cross-section of 31 low-income countries, Van Rijkenghem and Weder (2001) find that a doubling of government relative to manufacturing wages is associated with only 0.5 points reduction in ICRG corruption index measured on a scale from zero to six. Despite significant enhancements in pay scales of civil servants in India, there is no appreciable impact upon corruption that indeed has only increased over the years. Many of the recoveries made by the CBI in corruption cases have led to seizure of hundreds of crores in ill-gotten gains. Avarice rather than need appears to be the major motivating factor among officials extorting money or services in discharge of their duties. One minister even protested innocence of a

---

1   Information from one of the authors who worked in the Patna police force at the time.

colleague on grounds that the money alleged in corruption charges was too small and hence allegations were false (*Times of India*, 2012)!

Almost all corruption involves unfettered exercise of discretion. It is such a process of decision making that is unaccountable and unchecked that encourages and enables the official to demand bribes or downright extort the citizens. The law allows discretion and extraordinary powers to the police that are liable to be misused. Most of the legislative language leaves considerable room for interpretation. For example, the Code of Criminal Procedure gives extraordinary latitude to a police officer to arrest any citizen. Thus, Section 54 CrPC states,

> [A]ny police officer may arrest ... without a warrant ... such person who has been concerned in any cognizable [indictable] offense or ... against whom ... reasonable suspicion exists of his being so concerned ... [fourthly] ... in whose possession anything is found which may reasonably be suspected to be stolen property.

In these words, the law has provided extraordinary discretion to the police officer. For, what constitutes reasonable suspicion, even in subsequent clarifications, has not been spelt out and are said 'to depend upon circumstances of the particular case' (AIR, 1950; MB, 83). Thus, the decision of the officer cannot be challenged, for what is 'reasonable' remains vague, ambiguous and depends upon circumstances of the particular case. It is the officer who gets to describe and define these circumstances and there is no authority to dispute it. Only a superior police officer can rescind the decision but it is based on interpretation and not on the judgment of 'reasonable suspicion'. Such powers provide the opportunity to officials to misuse discretion for personal gains. Extortion from suspects and those violating the laws are common forms of corrupt practices within most police stations. Vast discretionary powers and lack of accountability lie at the base of corruption within the police ranks (Verma, 2005).

Social Values and Corruption

As we have stated earlier, corruption should be perceived as evil, one that corrodes basic human and social values. Reducing the notion of corruption to simply an instance of deviant behavior for obtaining tangible personal benefits at public expense 'circumscribes contentious moral questions in favor of creating an actionable consensus' (Smith, 2008, 72). There are some studies that suggest relationship between social norms and corruption. Fisman and Miguel (2007) found that diplomats from high corruption nations such as Nigeria, posted at New York, tend to commit more parking violations as compared to diplomats from low corruption countries such as Norway. They argue that these diplomats follow the social norms of culture of corruption even when they are posted outside their country. Barr and Serra (2006) also report that different levels of corruption across countries is cultural in context, and indulgence or resistance to corrupt practices is embedded in social norms of respective countries. Furthermore, Dong, Dulleck and Torgler (2012) also reiterate that corruption is influenced by the examples and perceptions of corrupt actions by others.

The prevalence and toleration for corruption in India is perhaps explained by the trends in changing values and norms of Indian society. In present day India, consumerism has been unleashed by the opening of the economy and this has promoted values that corrode moral character (Walzer, 2008) and catalyze corruption. The 'I want it now' ethic fueled by 24x7 barrage of advertisements for consumer goods have fueled desire for a lifestyle that is unrestrained and self-oriented. While this may accelerate economic growth, it has also fundamentally changed the social and moral fabric of the Indian society.

The country gained independence under the leadership of Mahatma Gandhi who stressed morality, integrity and community service as the basis of modern India. Gandhiji himself practiced austerity and led a simple life. The message of his life was to control one's desires and live in harmony with nature. He would even write on the margins of paper to avoid wasting paper and cause destruction of trees. Simple living and high ideals were his mantra and he showed this through his exemplary life that not only one can one live such a life but also attain principled ideals. For him, public service was the highest service and that meant living and identifying with the poorest and the downtrodden. India, that emerged in 1947 to attain its 'tryst with destiny' (as famously stated by Nehru) was a nation created on ideals stretching back to the dawn of Indian civilization. All political leaders had participated in the freedom struggle and were inspired by Gandhiji to serve the country.

The policymaking was guided by their lofty principles as reflected in the Constitution that was framed immediately thereafter. The first decade of independent India was unusual in the sense that unlike all other newly emerged nations in Africa and Asia, India alone had a bureaucratic structure that was squeaky clean. Scholars coming to study the new nation were amazed to see this level of morality, uprightness and sense of public service amongst not only the political leadership but also the higher bureaucracy.[2] New institutions were created and major investments were incurred to build new infrastructure and set up 'new temples' of development. Public money was treated with respect and not one scandal touched the first elected government of the country. The same was witnessed in every state and even local governments in most parts of the country. The young nation and its political leaders were driven by principles and adopted simple lifestyles putting the welfare of the state and its people at the forefront. Personal sacrifice was the hallmark of every leader and they took pains to ensure that no impropriety took place.

Unfortunately, these ideals could not be sustained for long. India, in subsequent years drifted from this path of morality and power as wealth and comfort became the guiding norms of leadership. Nehru's second term was rocked by the Mundra corruption scandal and as the freedom fighters' generation gave way to post-independent leadership, public service became the vehicle for corruption and nepotism. The Nehru government was compelled to appoint the Santhanam Committee to examine the nature, extent and problem of corruption in the country. Indira Gandhi's term also saw the scandals of Jagannath Misra selling the railway station and public land in Patna, nepotism symbolized by rise of Sanjay Gandhi and his Maruti enterprise, and the revelation that AR Antulay was collecting funds in her name. The eighties were marked by the Bofors corruption case involving Rajiv Gandhi. A series of high-value corruption cases have emerged after 1991 when the Indian economy was opened to foreign investment. Harshad Mehta, JMM bribery case, 'Coffin-gate', Commonwealth Games scandal, 2G case, Coal-gate, Rail-gate, Helicopter scandal, Vyapam and many others have exposed the shenanigans of senior elected representatives of the country. Corruption cases have been seen in every state and some like the Mumbai housing society or the Reddy mining cases in Karnataka and the Jagmohan

2 Susan and Lloyd Rudolph in private conversation with one of the authors.

corruption in Andhra Pradesh have shaken the public's faith in the government as never before. 'Rising India has been developing much larger and coarser appetites' and the recent scandals 'highlight how some of the most prominent businessmen, politicians, bureaucrats and journalists synergistically plunder natural resources such as land, oil and gas and mines' (Misra, 2011).

These cases also illustrate how opportunities for corruption are being created by the political economy based on concepts of globalization and liberalization to promote growth of capital through the public–private-partnership model. In this design, the state does not control the commanding heights of economy and limit its role in economic activities but facilitates the private sector to assume a greater role. These policies limit the role of the Indian state to sell public assets, natural/national resources to the private sector. Furthermore, by lacking checks and balances, the exercise of discretion by the political leaders in executing these sales is immense and hence misused. Corruption emanates from this collusion of private buccaneers and political shenanigans where the public resources are usurped by connivance and deliberate policy decisions. This unholy alliance is detrimental to public interest as the state fails to regulate the behavior of private entrepreneurs who corner profits through dubious means and connivance of corrupt officials. It is generally believed that the ends of the market process are contaminated by the means of that process (Clarke and Lee, 2011; Phelps, 1975). Indeed, markets function without taking account issues of integrity and morals in public life (Szech and Falk, 2013). These economic policies further promote a culture of consumption and privilege that is fundamentally transforming the Indian society. The earlier norms of Indian ethos—namely, simplicity, social service, self-sacrifice and renunciation—are now ridiculed. In the country where *sadhus, sanyasis* and pursuit of spirituality were admired and revered, a decadent culture of acquisition, greed, individualism and unfettered pursuit of wealth is taking roots. This political economy is based upon individual selfishness and the path to economic growth is creating an unhealthy and rapacious society where corruption has become a natural by-product.

Still, in such a large, diverse and developing country the reasons for corruption cannot only be explained through economic factors. Criminology provides more nuanced explanations as we have discussed in the previous chapter. We do know that there are many factors related to the personality of a common criminal. Most offenders tend to be young males between the ages of 16–30, generally, with poor education and showing deviant behavior at an early age. They tend to associate with other offenders and are risk takers. Specific lifestyle that involves drugs, alcohol consumption and inability to remain committed towards a goal are some other traits. Yet most white-collar offenders tend to negate these characteristics. Many convicted senior public officials, even serving in the coveted IAS/IPS cadres were clearly well educated, had a comfortable lifestyle and a promising career. They had sheltered upbringing and good schooling. Many were not addicted to alcohol, drugs or gambling. Yet why such seemingly educated officials sought out bribes, embezzled public funds and indulged in corrupt practices is a puzzle that remains unresolved.

It is clear that there is no uniform profile of a corrupt official. The offender may be young or old, married or unmarried, educated or with basic schooling and may be serving in any government office. While some offices do provide greater avenues for corruption the ubiquitous reality remains that bribes are demanded and public funds are misappropriated in any public office. The police department may have the reputation of being extremely extortionist but schools, hospitals, welfare centres, sports academies and even the army are affected by corruption. Unfortunately, even women are found to be demanding bribes and siphoning public funds though, their proportion is comparatively small as in the case of corresponding street crimes with respect to their male counterparts.

Perhaps the best way to understand the reasons for perpetuation of corruption in India is to follow the criminological perspective of 'rational choice' (Cornish and Clarke, 1986). As discussed in Chapter 2, this school has argued that opportunity encourages criminal action particularly if the risks are smaller in comparison to the expected rewards. This is applicable to white-collar crimes too for corrupt behavior is similar to criminal act. The offender utilizes his or her unique position to extract a bribe in situations where he has powers for extraordinary discretion and accountability is low. This is largely compounded by the fact that in India the government continues to occupy a large section of the economy and monopolizes the production and distribution of essential goods and services. From natural resources such as coal and iron ore to bandwidth essential for modern communications, the final decision of allotment lies with public officials. Their decisions involve investments and consequent profits running into hundreds of crores of rupees. Furthermore, since there is little accountability and supervision over these decisions, the opportunity to extort money from private companies is immense. Herein lie the causes of major forms of corruption in India. The government holds monopolies over vast sectors of the economy. From power, transport, communication, essential food and water, real estate and education the list is long. A small number of senior bureaucrats functioning under an elected representative, the political master, hold all the major decisions regarding these levers of development and sustenance. The government also collects huge sums of money in taxes and makes large investments in building infrastructure. All these provide lucrative opportunities to make money for personal gain. Additionally, the private sector seeking to maximize profits willingly becomes a partner in vitiating decisions to divert public funds and resources for personal rather than general good. The growth of service sector and new ways of partnership between the public and private sector all create new opportunities and forms of corrupt practices. Today, the essential features of corruption in India can be traced to the opportunities provided by three factors of monopoly, discretionary judgment, and lack of accountability. In such circumstances, it is not surprising that given the likelihood and ease with which personal gains can be made at public expense there is such widespread corruption in the country. This is best illustrated by an examination of some of the major government departments that are known for their corruption.

Corruption in police

Police are perceived by the citizens to be the most corrupt department in the country (TI, 2017). The reasons for police personnel being corrupt are rooted in the structure and role of the organization. Through the Police Act V of 1861, the British designed the police system to be a terror to the citizens and prevent any challenge to their Raj. The police officers were vested with excessive authority, including the power of arrest and detention up to 24 hours on flimsy grounds. The police were also given authority to arrest in the name of prevention of crime. Even the lowest ranking constable had the power to arrest and detain a citizen on grounds of preventing a cognizable crime from taking place (Verma, 2005). These provisions have remained intact even after independence and consequently, there is little change in the police system from 1861.

Thus, Section 151 CrPC even today states, '[A] police officer knowing of a design to commit any cognizable offense may arrest ... the person so designing, if it appears to the police officer that the commissioning of the offense cannot be otherwise prevented'. The Code of Criminal Procedure provides police officers with wide optional powers to exercise discretion when dealing with citizens. The judgment whether a person is likely to commit an offense is, thus, entirely that of the police officer and moreover it is his discretion to decide if the offense cannot be prevented without resorting to arrest. No wonder, even in maintenance of law and order, police make constant use of this provision on grounds that persons concerned are likely to cause affray or rioting, which are cognizable offenses (Verma, 2005). The law, Section 61 CrPC further permits the police to keep a suspect in custody for a maximum period of 24 hours, after which either the person has to be released or brought before a magistrate. Utilizing this provision, Indian police can then arrest a person under Section 151 CrPC and release him late in the night to keep within the boundaries of this legal provision. Such powers provide opportunities to extort money from hapless citizens who fall prey to scrupulous police officers.

The provisions of search are even more discretionary in their nature. Section 165 CrPC states:

> [W]henever an investigating officer has *reasonable* grounds for believing that anything ... may be found at any place ... and that such thing cannot in his *opinion* be obtained without undue delay, ... he may after recording the reasons ... cause search to be made ... even by a subordinate officer, duly authorized by him.[3]

Again, the Indian law merely uses the terms 'reasonable grounds', for providing authority to the police officer who moreover, can conduct this search if in his *opinion* there is no time to seek a search warrant. Clearly, such powers create opportunities for misuse of powers and the officers blatantly extort from citizens threatening to arrest or search their belongings without being held responsible.

No wonder, the Indian police are notorious for making frivolous arrests to browbeat and extort money from the hapless citizens. Perhaps, in view of such complaints the government has brought an amendment where this

---

3 Italics have been added.

power has been restricted. Now the police officer may make an arrest, but he is required to release the accused on bail if the offense for which the arrest had been made carries a punishment less than seven years. However, this too is circumscribed by empowering the officer to deny bail if the detention is required for investigation purposes. The officer is then simply required to record in writing the reasons for denying this bail to the suspect.

Such extraordinary powers, unbridled discretion and absence of any external mechanism of accountability combine to set the stage for blatant extortion and corrupt practices. It is therefore not surprising that the police in India have acquired an unsavory reputation for corruption. From the lowest rank of village watchman (*chowkidar*) to the senior-most police officer of the state—the Director General are known to have been corrupt and receive bribes or other favors. Since most of the police work involves addressing complaints against other citizens, the subordinate rank officers extort money by threatening to arrest or by filing criminal charges. Extortion from citizens on other pretexts is equally common. The constabulary extorts money from hawkers, footpath dwellers, truck and bus drivers and claims a share from the collective earnings made by the police station staff' (Verma, 1999, 267).

What is of serious consequence is the undeniable fact of corruption within the police leadership. The corruption within the IPS is now common and widespread amongst every state and rank. Police leadership of course has greater opportunity for indulging in corrupt practices. Apart from forcing their subordinates to extort from the people and then share part of the proceeds, the IPS officers generally make money from the transfer and postings of subordinate officers. They demand cuts from vendors supplying uniforms, office equipment and vehicles to the department, even extort from the business houses and subvert investigation of cases on pecuniary or political considerations (Verma, 1999). Corrupt practices are now part of the Indian police system and are found in every department, in every rank and in every police institution, including the training schools and colleges.

The officer-in-charge of the police station, called the Station House Officer (SHO), is the most coveted and lucrative office in the department. The SHO enjoys a large measure of autonomy, is the 'gatekeeper' for registering criminal cases, controls most of the criminal investigations and makes the decision to arrest suspects. These powers are stipulated in Sections 154–158 of the

Criminal Procedure Code and have enabled the officers to indulge in extortion and many other forms of corruption. S. K. Ghosh (1978), a retired Inspector General of Police, described the collection of 'hafta' or weekly payments from shopkeepers, hawkers and businesses and of course from the criminal operators within the police station areas as perhaps the most pervasive form of police extortion in India. The posting of officers in police stations that have large markets, shopping malls, industries or transport junctions are greatly coveted for the collections run into large sums. It is believed that even a few months of such postings enable the officers to earn much more than what they could receive in salaries for their entire service. In fact, postings at police stations in Patna's station road, Lucknow's Hazaratgunj shopping road or major shopping centers in any state are seen as extremely lucrative. Reportedly, these postings are at the behest of ministers in charge of police departments since, even the daily extortions from these markets runs into hundreds of thousands of rupees, money that allegedly gets 'shared' right to the top. Similarly, police stations situated in coalfield areas, near large industrial complexes, on highways and border check posts are equally notorious. Such postings are a major source of remuneration for the senior officers too including the chiefs of police who make the decision to post the officers-in-charge of these stations (Verma, 1999). A study by the Bureau of Police Research and Development (Tiwari, 2015) found that more than 50 per cent of the district SPs were transferred in less than one year of their posting. The data presented evidence that the politicians continue to use transfer posting as a tool to keep the police under their control.

Money is extorted from the citizens in variety of ways. Investigation of cases, decisions to arrest a suspect, submit a charge sheet or close some pending investigation, are all processes that are generally influenced by pecuniary considerations. It is usual for the SHO or his officers to demand money to register any citizen complaint and if someone is to be named as a suspect then the charge is naturally more. Furthermore, the complainant has to not only pay for instituting a complaint but also bear the costs of 'entertaining' the officers who come for inquiries. The complainant also ends up paying for the investigative expenses, especially transport as the department provides few vehicles to the investigating officers. Subsequent inquiries, arrest of the offender(s), prosecution in the courts are of course additional costs that the complainant has to bear if he/she is interested in pursuing the matter (Nanda, 1997).

Apart from taking bribes in investigations, the Indian police personnel are also notorious extortionists. Their power to institute criminal cases and arrest anyone on mere suspicion enables them to extort money from businesses. A few examples will illustrate this point. A notorious form of corrupt practice is to check the drivers for their licences and vehicle registrations. Now, the bureaucratic red tape involved in purchasing vehicle registrations and driver licences is immense. Lack of computerization of records has made the process extremely slow and awkward. It takes a couple of days to get the official papers, which also involves high costs. On the other hand, the penal fine is low and the problems of enforcement on crowded Indian roads create easy opportunities to evade checking by the police. Furthermore, for any citizen the problem of going to the courts to settle the matter is a time consuming and costly process that makes them wary of confronting the police. All these factors have forced most citizens to operate their vehicles without registration and proper licences and bribe their way out. Thus, the police power to check the vehicles plying on the roads has become a lucrative form of extortion (Verma, 1999). As we will discuss in the subsequent chapters, police shenanigans are well known and yet the government and political leaders make no attempt to reform the system. The political–police–business nexus is strong and forms the core of corruption in the police organization.

Corruption in civil administration

The opportunities to indulge in corrupt practices within the civil administration are even more extensive and widespread both in terms of avenues and the huge sums of moneys involved. Civilian bureaucrats are petty tyrants who exercise discretion in the provision of a large number of basic services related to food subsidies, health, education, shelter, employment and many other interactive functions of public services. For a long time, the government has been providing subsidized food through 'ration shops' to the poor and low-income people. However, to purchase this food from specific government outlets the concerned citizens have to produce certification of their economic background (Below Poverty Line or BPL cards). The government agents are empowered to survey and examine the claims of each citizen to obtain this certificate and the administrative machinery is just too cumbersome to execute this properly. The agents exercise their own judgement and deny such certification unless palms are greased and bribes are paid. Getting any kind of certificate from any government agency involves bribery and extortion. Whether it is about getting a certificate of birth, death, residency, driver licence or passport, every such application is met with demands for bribes, and failure to pay as much involves delays and unnecessary questions and harassment. In a survey of rural households conducted in 2010, it was found that rural households each paid bribe or were asked to pay bribe 'to get irrigation water' or 'to get the water pipe repaired'. Another reason for which households were asked to pay bribe was for 'installation or maintenance of hand pumps' (Center for Media Studies, 2010, 20).

To serve the large proportion of poor population in the country the bureaucracy has grown big and unmanageable. It is impossible to supervise the thousands of government officials engaged in these functions. As Jayaprakash Narayan (2002) states, '[T]here is a well-developed market for public office in India. Money habitually changes hands for placement and continuity of public servants at various levels'. These public servants in turn have to collect 'rent' from the public. The 'hafta' paid to a policeman, the 'mamool' charged by the excise official, the bribe collected by the revenue functionary or the corruption of a transport officer are all part of a well-integrated, well-organized structure. The widespread and open corruption prevalent in civil services is also facilitated by a lack of system of accountability. Service rules are antiquated and have made it impossible to prosecute a corrupt bureaucrat quickly. Narayan further states (2002):

> The Anti-Corruption Bureau's (ACB) powers are limited, procedures are slow and levels of probity are unsatisfactory. The state government has to approve prosecution and take disciplinary action. Very often political considerations and bureaucratic apathy make it impossible to either launch prosecution or act against erring employees. In case of All-India Services (IAS, IPS and Indian Forest Service), the ACB cannot start an inquiry or investigation without prior permission of the Chief Minister. In most of the cases, a trap cannot be laid without the government's approval. Similarly, heads of the departments cannot be investigated without prior government approval.

Licence permit quota raj

From the beginning, the Nehru government was inclined towards socialist economic policies and a major component was to ensure that the state controls all the commanding heights of economy. The Planning Commission recommended developing domestic markets and emphasis upon 'self-reliance' that blocked foreign investment and entry of multinational corporations in the country. However, the rules to enforce state hegemony in economic matters meant that in almost all major economic functions the permission and approval of the government was made necessary. The Industries Act, 1951 for instance, required all new industrial operations to obtain a licence from the central government. The policy limited foreign investment and stifled competition, and bribery became part and parcel of conducting business. The period up to 1991 was dubbed the 'Permit-Licence-Quota Raj' as a result of the government's excessive oversight of the economy. 'Historically, the roots of India's corruption came from the proliferation of licences', said noted economist Jagdish Bhagwati. 'The idea was to ensure economical use of resources, so you would not waste foreign exchanges. To this day, this is what Indians have been very aware of: that the institution of licences and permits was responsible for creating corruption on a massive scale' (cited in Xu, 2014). This policy enabled public officials to exercise discretion over distribution of scare public resources and control the licence to operate industries, all creating and encouraging the incentives for bribery and corruption. Rose-Ackerman (1997, 1) states, 'Corruption occurs at the interface of the public and the private sectors'. Undoubtedly, licence-quota-raj came from unchecked discretionary powers with little accountability that encouraged public officials to extort and private individuals and businesses to exploit and steal public wealth by paying bribes to the officials.

The politicians exercised their own discretion in the transfer and posting of officials after quickly realizing the importance of officials in exercising such similar discretionary measures. By posting specific bureaucrats in key positions, the politicians got the control to determine their judgements. A lucrative market emerged for such important positions in ministries and associated departments that generated large bribes. Furthermore, the nexus between the politician, bureaucrat and the businessperson developed from this situation where the three conspired to cooperate and loot public funds. Thus, in the allotment of 3G spectrum, coal-blocks, purchase of guns, helicopters and submarines, the political executive and bureaucrats took bribes from company executives to take decisions favoring that particular company. The Bofors case, Agusta Westland Italian helicopter manufacturing company case, the allotment of 3G spectrum and coal mines all exhibit this phenomenon where the companies allegedly paid bribes to win the contract from the government. This is not limited to defense and major projects but to everyday dealings and almost all public schemes. A study of irrigation projects in India suggested that large percentage of the public funds were wasted in corruption and malfeasance (Ward, 1982).

'A fast-growing economy, especially one that needs to invest heavily in infrastructure, is a magnet for corruption' (N. Singh, 2014, 4). Bureaucratic corruption as seen in India has also been reported from Thailand wherein infrastructure construction projects involved leakages ranging from 30–40 per cent of project costs; in public projects in Brazil under President Fernando Collar de Mello and in sales to privileged insiders at below market price in Russia and Eastern Europe (cited in Rose-Ackerman, 1997). From Italy to Ghana to Venezuela corruption has led to scandals and arrest of senior politicians (Rose-Ackerman, 1997).

The demand for bribe and corrupt practices in India is further related to the nature of secrecy surrounding government functions. The monopoly of licensing and quota system is exercised by the bureaucracy that also controls vital information and takes decisions not open for public scrutiny. Such a system creates the incentives for corruption and bribery as traders need to pay in order to be included in the list of qualified bidders, to structure favorable bidding specifications and to dilute quality as cost saving measures. Often the government sells goods such as food grains and kerosene oil at below market price to help the poor. But this creates the incentives for private operators to buy these goods and sell them at the market price making a sizeable profit. Moreover, the officials get to decide who is poor and qualified to receive these subsidies. This further introduces bribery that even the poor must pay in order to receive essential food and fuel for their sustenance. The recent attempts to digitize the record system and make direct payment to the beneficiaries is meant to control these corrupt practices. However, these are limited measures as we will discuss in subsequent chapters.

Similarly, after nationalization of the banks, the supply of credit and rate of interest came under the control of the government. Private individuals then had to bribe bank officials to get loans and credit on affordable interest rates. In cases where the applicants far exceeded the amount of benefits sanctioned by the government, corruption became inevitable. For example, many states in the country adopted the populist policy of providing pension to the poorest people. However, the number of qualified people was far more than the government could afford to pay and the officials were, therefore, empowered to select these beneficiaries. This discretion and poor governance ensured that all such schemes were steeped in corrupt practices.

A variety of laws and regulations that the state imposes to control the economic activities also results in corruption. Officials get the power to delay or harass the companies and can impose additional costs in ways that can affect productivity and profitability. Where the governments introduce public regulatory programs such as hiring and retention of labor or controlling emissions from factories the companies seek access to the inspectors to interpret rules favorable to them or get discretionary judgements in case of gross violations. The 'inspector raj' is symbolic of this system that has made corruption endemic in the country. Everyone seeks to lower the taxes or avoid paying them. Businesses and private individuals collude with tax collectors to minimize their payments through corrupt practices. Moreover, the enforcement officials soon begin to misuse their position and power to extort from other businesses as well. Nexus between corrupt regulators and businesses also leads to a strange situation where money is paid to restrict or damage other businesses that may be competitors in order to build monopolies.

Delay is an important factor that affects economic enterprises adversely. This incentivizes businesses to pay officials in order to seek quick decisions about their transactions. This occurs frequently in accounts offices where the officials would delay payment to the vendors even when all the bills have been cleared and funds made available for payment. For a long time in India, payments had to be made to obtain telephone, gas and power and water connections. Deliberate delays in granting passport or driving licences or birth–death certificates were practiced to extort money from the applicants. In view of the scarcity of many of these items before the Indian economy opened to global trade, such essential services were available only to the corrupt and those willing to pay significant amounts in bribery. Newspapers openly published a list of 'fees' for a range of routine public services that could be obtained only through bribery ('Bribe Index', *Times of India*, 1995).

The amount of corruption and extortion indulged in by public officials is a function of the honesty and integrity of both public officials and private individuals. The size and incidence of bribes are determined by available benefits, exercise of discretion, risks of taking bribes and relative bargaining power of the bribers and bribe (Rose-Ackerman, 1997). Opportunity created by monopoly of state undertakings, excessive discretion to public officials and lack of transparency and accountability stir the pot of corruption. The control over the licence-quota-raj undoubtedly ensured abundant money to the party coffers and one where the opposition party found themselves to be at a disadvantage. 'Today, black money is considered a "legitimate" way of financing politics, as witnessed by the broad consensus that emerged in the Parliament—across party lines—to exclude political parties from the purview of the Right to Information (RTI) Act' (Maiorano, 2014).

Politics and corruption

'There are two things that are important in politics', Mark Hanna, the great Republican kingmaker of the late nineteenth century, once said. 'The first thing is money, and I can't remember what the second one is' (*cited* in Kirkpatrick, 2010) . Politics and political party funding lies at the root of corruption in every society. 'Politics is to a large extent, a combination of business projects run by powerful oligarchs enjoying political immunity and individuals using office as a means for gaining wealth' (Walecki, 2003, 4). Politicians use their hold over the state and its functionaries to fill their own pockets and to raise funds for fighting elections. It is a common belief that the financing of political parties provides fertile ground for the development of corrupt practices. This is a problem that is not confined to India but even established democracies such as Germany, France and Italy have been plagued by corruption scandals relating to political finance. The USA is notorious for its extravagantly expensive electoral campaigns, which regularly breed accusations of corruption or illegitimate funding practices.

Politicians indulge in corruption by controlling the transfer and posting of bureaucrats enforcing administrative and policy decisions for personal gain. This is not limited to individual bureaucrats but to entire public institutions that become subservient to the wishes and shenanigans of corrupt politicians. 'Political corruption is therefore something more than a deviation from formal and written legal norms, from professional codes of ethics and court rulings. Political corruption is when laws and regulations are more or less systematically abused by the rulers, side-stepped, ignored or even tailored to fit their interests' (Inge, 1999, 3).

In developing economies like India where economic liberalization is occurring with institutions compromised by political interests, corruption spreads even more across competing interests. Thus, local politicians and ambitious entrepreneurs, brokers and middlemen and unscrupulous businessperson all seek and find opportunities to loot the public funds and resources. Loosening state control and supervision also provides new incentives for corruption, in particular in the mounting of electoral campaigns, in the struggle for senior political and civil service offices, in the lucrative possibilities of formerly state-owned property and businesses up for privatization, and in securing both political and economic gains (Inge, 1999).

Problems of political finance are at the heart of the debate on political corruption (Walecki, 2003). Contesting elections in a large country such as India requires huge funds without which much of political activity simply cannot run. Most of the laws regulating election expenses are weak and set limits on how much individuals can spend upon campaigning. India's laws stipulate that individual candidates can spend only ₹ 70 lakh on their campaigns; this amount does not even cover the poster printing costs in important contests. Sources in parties say a 'big fight' between star candidates cost between ₹ 75-300 crore for each person. Lesser contests cost between ₹ 15-50 crore and marginal ones between ₹ 1-10 crore (Pocha, 2014). All political parties organize huge rallies where lakhs of people are summoned to cheer their candidates. Such rallies cost close to ₹ 3 crore and every major party holds at least one major rally a day. Further, there is also the cost of sending thousands of workers out in cars, trains, planes, rickshaws, bicycles, bullock carts, tractors, camels, horses and boats to woo voters with speeches, street plays and songs. These party workers set up makeshift stages and carnivals in the farthest corners of the country and seduce voters with liquor, currency notes and all-night parties (Pocha, 2014). Money matters for democracy because much of the political activity simply could not occur without it (Walecki, 2003).

However, laws do not govern political parties and their fund-raising activities. Accordingly, political parties collect money from dubious sources and donors seeking quid pro in terms of favorable policies. All this money is of course not reported to the Election Commission and is utilized in assisting the campaigns of specific leaders. The manner in which the money is channeled into electioneering is simply difficult to monitor. It is therefore impossible to prevent malpractices. Parties report funds received in a formal manner but do not describe funds diverted to individual politicians and candidates. Every candidate and political party needs huge funds to run all-India campaigns and hire thousands of workers to push the political agenda. The most visible expenditures are for transport, billboards, seats and refreshments for rallies. Moreover, hiring of thugs paid by parties for capturing voting booths is also common phenomenon of India's elections. This implies that a nexus between the politicians and the business houses must occur to finance the campaigns.

A new phenomenon is the corruption of newspapers and TV channels that give local candidates coverage only in return for payment, called 'paid news'. A sting conducted by a TV channel even showed how parties pay pollsters to stack surveys. Several channels and newspapers, as also individual editors and reporters, are also reported to have received millions in dark funding from political parties and/or wealthy candidates (Pocha, 2014).

A study by the Association for Democratic Reforms (2014) and National Election Watch suggests that a large chunk of the funds raised by the six national parties between 2004–05 and 2011–12 came from sources labeled as 'unknown'. The election laws provide that political parties are not obliged to reveal funds below ₹20,000. This provides the loophole that is taken advantage of by all political parties in the country. The laws also permit business houses to set up trusts through which donations can be made without any restriction in exchange for disclosing the amount donated to specific parties.

An estimate by the Centre for Media Studies in Delhi (2010) puts the total cost of the campaigns for seats in India's Parliament and State Assemblies at $4.9 billion. That would make it the second-most expensive in world history, trailing just behind America's of 2012, which cost $6 billion (*Economist*, 2014). The Election Commission sets the limit of 70 *lakh* rupees per campaign for a parliamentary seat whereas a candidate must spend 50 to 100 times more money than that, if he or she hopes to win.

Moreover, most of the money spent in India is in the form of untraceable cash and significant amounts are brought back into the country from tax havens, such as Switzerland, where industrialists and politicians stash their illicit fortunes. In fact, just prior to elections in India the rupee usually strengthens as it has in the last few weeks because money stashed illegally in Swiss banks is brought back into the country through the *hawala* route and havens such as Mauritius (Pocha, 2014). 'The secrecy in political finance systems often results in: 1) funding from undesirable sources; 2) improper influence of the money over policy outcomes and 3) financial barriers for average citizens against standing for political office' (Walecki, 2003).

Since the costs of funding political campaigns are increasing rapidly, there is growing reliance on funding from private sources. This apparently appears to be associated with greater vulnerability of political systems to corruption. However, while the pundits of course raise this alarm of the pernicious influence of politics over corruption in state affairs, in reality the evidence seems marginal. Reports from the US suggest that after tightening of electoral finance laws big corporate donors found that their stock prices were unaffected after they stopped giving to the parties. However, there is no evidence that stricter campaign finance rules reduce corruption or raise positive assessments of government. Based on a sample of 50 old and young democracies, Krishnan (2010) explored whether high levels of perceived corruption in politics is associated with an absence of, or weaknesses in, key measures to regulate political party funding. He concludes that it is difficult to make any categorical statements about whether the absence of, or weaknesses in, such measures is a good predictor of higher levels of perceived corruption in political party funding systems.

Why business houses give money to politicians is unclear, for the benefits can be hard to measure. It is interesting to note that Australia barely regulates money given to political parties. Individuals and corporations can give without limit and the political parties are permitted to spend freely. There is not much disclosure about who gives what to whom and yet political corruption has not threatened the island nation's democracy. In the United States, studies comparing states like Virginia with scant regulation against those like Wisconsin with strict rules have not found much difference in levels of corruption or public trust. 'Campaign financing as an excuse for corruption won't wash—good economic and social outcomes trump expensive political marketing, bribes and pandering to voters' base instincts as drivers of political success' (N. Singh, 2014, 4). Nevertheless, in India the stipulated election expenses are unrealistically small in comparison to the actual expenses incurred and hence, invariably lead to corruption. Business houses pour money into party coffers and individual campaigns to build high level contacts in the elected government. These are cashed by way of getting concessions, licences, contracts and favorable treatment. Funding election campaigns are good insurance cover for the private sector and as seen in numerous scams come in handy when even the enforcement agencies are constrained to act against people in high places. Quraishi (2014) cites elections as the root cause of corruption in India.

Corruption in financial sector

Corruption emanates from financial institutions where secrecy of transactions is geared towards malpractices and lack of accountability to the public. White-collar crime is an underbelly to modern economy based upon stockholdings where structural factors promote corporate fraud and wrongdoing. The distance between shareholders who invest their hard-earned money and the directors who control these companies is vast. Directors hold a large sum in trust for investors but lack of accountability and proper supervision induces temptations to misappropriate and steal that money. Indian regulators continue with outdated accounting practices that make proper auditing of global transactions impossible to conduct. Furthermore, the complexity of modern financial transactions blurs the boundary between public good and private gain.

Loans on forged documents are the main component of losses to financial institutions. Bankers for instance, exceed their discretionary powers and give loans to unscrupulous borrowers on fake or forged documents. After getting the money, the borrower escapes causing huge loses to the banks. 'Public sector banks have cumulatively lost a massive sum of ₹ 22,743 crore due to cheating and forgery in the last three years (2011–14) alone. Indian Overseas Bank is the worst hit with a loss of ₹ 3,200 crores as against State Bank of India (SBI), which lost ₹ 2,712 crore. Between April 2010 and September 2013, the number of bank fraud cases has shown a slight decrease yearly but the amount of money lost has been increasing year on year (Pai and Venkatesh, 2014).

Since most citizens are unaware of banking rules and regulations, unscrupulous offenders easily cheat them. Such offenders for instance, have even cheated major trust funds, developmental societies and cooperatives by opening fixed deposits with public sector banks on the promise of higher rates of interest. Once the fixed deposits were opened, the perpetrators gave a fake FD receipt to the entities and retained the original receipts with themselves. This fixed deposit money was later siphoned off through the original receipts. In another twist, cashing fake fixed deposit certificates in connivance with bank officials dupes many financial institutions. The depositors pledge these fake receipts to take out large loans and then vanish with the money. Sometimes, the funds are surreptitiously transferred out of the bank by creating fake overdraft facility, resulting in a fraud on the bank and the concerned entities or even government organizations.

Collusion of bank officials and corrupt practices adopted by senior managers lies at the heart of most irregularities and corruption in the finance sector as the recent cases of diamond merchant Nirav Modi and ICICI CEO Chanda Kochhar suggest. In 2010, the CBI had busted a racket in which executives from large banks and finance companies like LIC, Housing Finance of LIC, Central Bank of India and Punjab National Bank were arrested for allegedly accepting bribes in return for sharing confidential information (Inamdar, 2013). A study conducted by the Reserve Bank unearthed fraud of staggering ₹15,677 crores as of September 2013, and 88 per cent of this fraud worth ₹13,766 crores was perpetrated at nationalized banks alone. This involved 197 accounts and took into consideration only large value fraud that was above ₹50 crores, so the total amount will be much larger in reality (cited in Inamdar, 2013). Many reasons were given in this study for the growing corruption in public sector banks and financial institutions. For one, time taken for cases to be ascertained as fraud is very high. It took over 10 years for 45 per cent of the cases and between 5 to 10 years for 67 per cent of the cases, creating a great disconnect between the punishment meted out and the offence. Moreover, the delays in bringing fraudsters to book aggravated transgressions and the fact that public sector bank employees enjoyed a great degree of impunity further emboldened those committing the fraud. Most of the officials found liable were let off with minor penalties—caution, warning, censure and stoppage of increments for limited period that sends out a wrong message—a message about passive tolerance rather than active intolerance towards misconduct. The study furthermore highlighted the 'skewed' nature of the vigilance process, which tended to focus on lower level functionaries even though the sanctioning of advances is usually at the level of senior executives/Board. Out of 719 officers who were found accountable in 230 large value fraud accounts in the banks over a period of time, 426 officers were up to the rank of Senior Manager, 196 officers were Chief Managers and Assistant General Managers, 94 officers were of the rank of Deputy General Manager, General Manager and Chief General Manager and 3 officials were from the top management and Board of Directors (cited in Inamdar, 2013). One of the consequences of this collusion by senior bank managers is that huge loans are sanctioned without scrutiny and then defaulted by the recipients. Recently, the demonetization of ₹ 500 and ₹ 1000 notes was an attempt to unearth black money and control corrupt practices. However, a number of bank officials themselves colluded with scrupulous people to exchange old notes with new ones without proper documentation (*Times of India*, 2017).

Corruption is not just about ethics, it is also about how the government is set up and managed. Tavares (2007) suggests that economic liberalization creates bountiful opportunities for corruption, because when a country is open to international trade state-owned public sector companies are privatized that generates new sources of rents. 'Opportunity drives the thief' is an idiom that equally applies to corrupt practices. As the above discussion suggests, corruption can occur in many situations. It is more likely, however, where some of the following occur:

• Policies and procedures are absent, unclear or not adequately enforced.
• Employee training is inadequate.
• Checks such as audits are lacking.
• Communication and reporting lines are unclear.
• Employee supervision and performance management are inadequate.
• Employees have high levels of discretion in their decision-making.
• Employees develop close relationships with external stakeholders.
• Accepted ethical standards are lacking.
• The corporate culture condones rule breaking and short cuts.

(Independent Commission against Corruption, 2017)

Corruption in India has undergone a qualitative shift from the days of licence raj to the era of liberalization. The economic policies and opening of the Indian economy to external trade have unlocked various opportunities for making money in new ways. Corruption has taken a new turn since the advent of liberalization in the early 1990s from 'retail to wholesale', in words of the former Central Vigilance Commissioner N. Vittal (2004). Earlier, doling out licences and awarding government contracts were the primary sources of corruption, done on a piecemeal basis, post-liberalization, formulating policies that benefit select players and discretionary distribution of natural resources create an abundance of rent-seeking opportunities for the politicians.

Political shenanigans

While the above explanations hold true, in the Indian context, political shenanigans and criminalization of politics seems to be *the* major cause of corruption. The politicians are not only indulging in large-scale loot of public funds but also seeking devious ways to make quick gains with impunity. Amongst the top listed scams of the previous few years almost all involve involvement of senior politicians. Thus, the wrongful allotment of coal deposits by the Manmohan Singh government without resorting to competitive bidding caused an estimated loss of ₹ 1.86 lakh crore—perhaps the biggest in Indian history. The 2G-spectrum scam involved allocation of valuable unified access service licences. A. Raja, the minister-in-charge, carried out this dubious award and led to a loss of ₹ 1.76 lakh crore to the nation. The Supreme Court recently acquitted Raja stating that Prosecution failed to substantiate the charges. The Karnataka Wakf Board that controlled around 27,000 acres of land allocated it illegally or misappropriated to the tune of ₹ 1.5–2.0 lakh crores. It is alleged that politicians and board members misappropriated nearly 50 per cent of the land owned by Wakf Board in conjunction with real estate mafia at fraction of actual land cost. It is estimated that almost 50 per cent of the ₹ 70,000 crore spent on the Commonwealth Games has been misappropriated by Kalmadi and other officials. The Central Vigilance Commission has found discrepancies in tenders—like payment to non-existent parties, willful delays in execution of contracts, over-inflated price and bungling in purchase of equipment through tendering and misappropriation of funds. The fake stamp sale by Abdul Telgi caused a loss of an estimated ₹ 20,000 crores and was apparently facilitated by government departments that were responsible for the production and sale of high security stamps. The Bofors scam was a major corruption scandal in India in the 1980s when the then Prime Minister Rajiv Gandhi and several others were accused of receiving kickbacks from Bofors AB for winning a bid to supply India's 155 mm field howitzer (*Economist*, 2014; Pai and Venkatesh, 2014; Pocha, 2014; Xu, 2014).

Politicians in power accumulate more wealth compared to those who are out of power. Studies conducted by the Association for Democratic Reforms, or ADR (2014) have found that politicians who win Parliamentary and State elections grow their wealth at a significantly higher rate over the next five years of being in office when compared to the runners-up who lost the election. This clearly provides an empirical yardstick at the possibility of misuse of political power for personal gain. Moreover, the growth in the assets of ministers is 13 per cent to 29 per cent higher than non-winners. Another analysis done by ADR shows that average assets of MLAs of Maharashtra have increased from ₹ 4.99 crore in the 2009 assembly elections to ₹ 10.87 crore in the 2014 assembly elections. This suggests that candidates contesting the elections are now largely coming from rich backgrounds and may be a reason for their nomination by respective political parties. More disturbingly, according to Election Commission data, 34 per cent of the sitting Lok Sabha MPs and 31 per cent of all MLAs in October 2014 have criminal cases against them. In the 2014 Maharashtra assembly elections, the ADR scrutinized 2,336 candidates and 798 of them have criminal backgrounds, which is 34 per cent. Among them, 23 per cent have serious charges like murder, attempt to murder, abduction, communal instigation and so on leveled against them. Thus, criminalization of politics is the biggest reason for corruption and other problems of the country. 'With substantial numbers of such individuals now present in public life, few political parties have an interest in weeding out those with checkered pasts because of the significant collective-action problems that such an enterprise would entail' (Ganguly, 2012, 145).

While Nehru's party also was not unfamiliar with khadi-wearing criminals, it was during Indira Gandhi's reign that vitiated the political landscape in the country. She openly encouraged unsavory elements led by her son Sanjay to find strong roots in the political system. The Indira Gandhi era also saw attacks on established institutions and erosion of their ability to check executive excesses. Lack of accountability of the political leaders became a hallmark of the Indian system and decision-making became arbitrary and unashamedly for personal gain. Politicians acquired control over illicit funding and used this brazenly to make wealth at the expense of public good. 'Booth capturing' perhaps illustrated the extreme perversion of the political system and its degradation in the country.

Since politics and political power became the key to making huge gains and increase personal wealth, money was needed in enormous quantities to keep the system stable and functional. This is best illustrated by the Jharkhand Mukti Morcha bribery case in which the former Prime Minister Narasimha Rao was accused of bribing MPs for winning a parliamentary vote and saving the government from being voted out of office. In several states, even the departments seeking passage of their budgets gift lavishly to the MLAs to help pass their budget (Jha, 2016). Beyond generating resources to service the vested interests within the system, politicians have also begun to dabble directly in economic activities resulting in the emergence of a new class of politician-entrepreneurs. Ministers and lawmakers sit on top of immense wealth created by corrupt practices and blatantly use political power for personal profiteering.

The situation seems dismal and difficult to reform. Electoral reforms and controlling for unaccounted money flowing in to finance political campaigns can improve the situation. More transparency in the engagement between the industry and politics is also called for. In India, citizens are generally obsequious to the politicians because of their exalted high status and position even if involved in criminal acts. The failures of investigation and delayed trials further allow corrupt politicians to get away with their crimes—perhaps a major reason for continuing corruption in the country.

Yet it is imperative to place corruption in proper perspective. Inefficiency in government functions is immense and leads to proportionately greater loss of public revenue than through corrupt practices. Bandiera, Prat and Valletti (2009) make a distinction between 'active' and 'passive' waste by government whereby only the former is the one that is profitable for politicians and bureaucrats and part of corruption. Their analysis suggests that in government programs 83 per cent is passive waste and even, 'in an OECD country, the elimination of corruption would only eliminate 17 per cent of the overall waste' (cited in Kelkar and Shah, 2011, 29). The inefficiency and waste in public offices is blatant and cause of more widespread citizen grievances than from corrupt practices. The challenge, then, in obtaining an effective government is that of finding mechanisms of public administration through which both passive waste and active waste are controlled. This is a truly daunting challenge in India (Kelkar and Shah, 2011).

Part II
Combating Corruption in India

4

Anti-Corruption Machinery

This chapter describes the existing anti-corruption machinery in India, both at the central and state levels, and examines in detail their functions and limitations in the country. We describe the nature, structure and role played by the CBI and the CVC. Their charters are evaluated in terms of a large number of case studies to illustrate the strengths and weaknesses of these two organizations in handling corruption in the country at the federal level. The major argument we make is that the efficacy of investigative agencies is affected due to their lack of autonomy. The political leaders and bureaucrats tightly control the funds as well as personnel in terms of their transfer, posting, promotion and disciplinary matters. These are often misused to 'tame' recalcitrant officers and make them fall in line to ensure that political considerations are not affected by these investigation agencies. We present strong evidence about the misuse of power of the politicians to grant approval for inquiring into or registering cases against senior bureaucrats. A number of cases are presented to illustrate how corrupt officials have thwarted attempts of investigators to inquire into their questionable activities. On the other hand, we also examine why immunity granted to the senior levels of bureaucracy, drawn from the All India Services, including the Indian Administrative Service (IAS), Indian Police Services (IPS) and Indian Foreign Service (IFS), under Article 311 of the Constitution has failed to shield them to work independent of political, bureaucratic and other pressures. We also argue that the Anti-Corruption Bureaus (ACBs) in this country are mainly concerned with the detection and prosecution of corruption and economic crimes and there is little by way of prevention in their functions. These agencies step in only when the damage is done.

Structure of Anti-Corruption Machinery

The jurisdiction and set up of the anti-corruption machinery in India is based on the mandate that 'police' is a state subject, being in List II Entry 2 of the Seventh Schedule of the Constitution of India and hence police agencies are distributed between the union and state governments. At the level of the union government, there are specific agencies to deal with cases of corruption under the Prevention of Corruption Act, 1988 against officers and employees of the central government. There are different anti-corruption units functioning under each state government to deal with state officers and employees.

At the union government level, the primary anti-corruption machinery comprises: (1) the Lokpal, created through an Act of Parliament, the Lokpal and Lokayuktas Act, 2013; (2) the CVC, given the statutory status through the CVC Act, 2003 and (3) the CBI that derives its power from the Delhi Special Police Establishment (DSPE) Act, 1946. There are other agencies such as the Enforcement Directorate, the Income Tax department and units functioning under the Finance Ministry that are also engaged in dealing with specialized type of corrupt practices. This chapter will primarily deal with the functioning and efficacy of CVC and CBI. At the state level, the agencies are: The Anti-Corruption Bureau (ACB), Economic Offences Wing (EOW), CID/Vigilance, Lokayukta and of course the District Crime Branch (DCB)/Police Station. Few states like Madhya Pradesh have empowered its EOW to deal with corruption cases also. As a representative anti-corruption agency, EOW Madhya Pradesh is examined in great detail in Chapter 5, while the Lokpal and Lokayuktas are discussed in Chapter 6. A typical diagrammatic representation of anti-corruption machinery in India is depicted below in figure 4.1:

Figure 4.1 Anti-Corruption Machinery in India

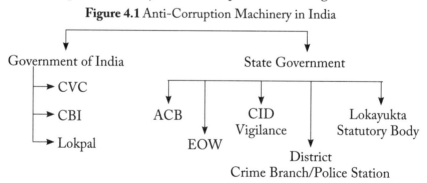

Anti-Corruption Agencies in India

The structure and organization of anti-corruption agencies in India is complex and embedded with obstructions. There are multitude of rules and regulations that bind the powers of the investigation agencies and inhibit their independent functions. The government not only controls the recruitment and service conditions of all officials, but also controls many aspects of the investigation and subsequent prosecution. Corruption charges against senior officials and ministers cannot be investigated without the permission of the government. Even after the investigation establishes specific charges, the prosecution cannot be launched unless the concerned head of the unit gives administrative sanction where the official may be functioning. More significantly, the government controls the transfer and posting of investigators and this power is often 'used' to protect suspect politicians and officials or to slow down the investigation (Tiwari, 2015).

Furthermore, there is systematic failure to prosecute the offenders even in cases where investigation provides cogent evidence of wrongdoing. A large number of cases illustrate how a significant number of prosecutions against politicians and senior officials remain pending for years due to delay and indifference to grant official sanction for prosecution. The matter is exacerbated by the fact that the officers from the three All India Services—IAS, IPS and IFS, require the sanction of the union government, being the appointing authority. All these bottlenecks are compounded by problems of years of litigation in the Trial Courts, High Courts and even the Supreme Court. Several well-known cases such as that of Late Jayalalithaa—the former Chief Minister of Tamil Nadu, dragged on for 18 long years at the trial stage itself. And by the time the final judgment was delivered by the Supreme Court on 14 May 2017, after 21 years of the registration of the offence, maintaining the Trial Court conviction, the appeal against her was abated because she had expired. However, fines were levied on her properties. This is a classic example wherein political connivance, compromised investigative and prosecution agencies and powerful battery of lawyers exploited the loopholes in the system to keep the case pending for more than two decades.

Conspiracy of the police with the accused for monetary considerations result in summons not being served on witnesses and hence leads to constant adjournments with long gaps for the next hearing. Meanwhile, the investigating officers (IOs) get transferred out of the region and leave the current IO to follow up the case in the court with hardly any motivation. The advocates are also happy for they get to earn without work for adjournments of the case. The one who suffers the most in this game is the victim complainant for whom all the laws and the criminal justice system have been put in place. In many cases by the time the conviction finally comes through, one or more of the accused is even dead in this long drawn out process; as in the aforementioned case of late Selvi Jayalalithaa. It is clear to any unbiased examination of the criminal justice system in India that systematic failures in investigation, prosecution, and latitude granted to the accused and political/bureaucratic shenanigans combine to prevent any meaningful and timely action against corruption in the country. This is borne out by the dismal performance of anti-corruption units in the country. A brief examination of the *Crime in India 2015 Statistics*, published by the National Crime Records Bureau (NCRB), responsible for maintaining the crime figures of the entire country on behalf of the Government of India, helps bring out this in ample measure. According to these statistics (Table 9.2), a total of 13,014 cases under the Prevention of Corruption Act and related Sections of IPC were taken up for investigation by the Anti-Corruption and Vigilance departments of all the states and union territories in 2015. However, of these only 5,250 were new cases registered all over India and 7,764 were those pending investigation from previous years. Maharashtra (2,328); Rajasthan (1,956); Orissa (1,197); Madhya Pradesh (1,099) and Karnataka (1,020) were the states with the highest proportion of registered cases. Large states like Uttar Pradesh (118), West Bengal (36) and Delhi (238) barely investigated any cases. While Maharashtra (165,269,031); Karnataka (7,251,762); Chhattisgarh (406,274,112); MP (442,400,000) and Orissa (345,778,644) could recover such vast amounts of illegally acquired property (all figures are in thousands of rupees) it is incredulous that large states like Assam (841,970); Delhi (11,220) and Uttar Pradesh (155,800) could recover so little property! It is also disheartening that only 788 cases ended in conviction in the year 2015 even when 24,800 cases were tried in different judicial courts around the country. This leads to a meager and dismal 3.18 per cent of conviction rate in corruption cases and speaks volumes about the poor concern of the state governments and its police to combat corruption effectively. This is also suggested by an examination of the functions and performance of the CVC of India.

Central Vigilance Commission (CVC)

Origin and formation of CVC as statutory body

On the recommendations of the Santhanam Committee, the Government of India set up the CVC on 11 February 1964 by a Government of India resolution as an apex body for prevention of corruption in central government institutions. It functions through a well-established vigilance administrative set up, guidelines and manuals. However, it was not till 1997, more than two decades later, that the CVC moved towards becoming a statutory body due to the historic judgment of the Supreme Court in the Vineet Narain Case, popularly known as Jain Hawala Case or the Vineet Narain Case.

In this landmark judgment towards the evolution of an autonomous and non-partisan anti-corruption machinery, the Hon'ble Supreme Court struck down the 'Single Directive' (4.7[3] [i]) of the central government. This Directive stipulated seeking prior approval/sanction of the government by the CBI to initiate even a preliminary enquiry or register a regular case against decision making level of officers of the rank of Joint Secretary and above. The clause was issued to protect the senior echelons of bureaucracy from the threat and ignominy of malicious and vexatious inquiries/investigations and to relieve them of the anxiety from the likelihood of harassment for taking honest decisions. The Supreme Court held that the directive was violative of the guarantee of equal treatment and equal protection of the law under Article 14 of the Constitution. It was this directive that had come in the way of enquiry and investigation of allegations against officers of Joint Secretary and above in Jain Diary Hawala Case. In addition, the Supreme Court, by way of 'Directions of the Court', outlined the structure, powers and functions of the CVC and the CBI to ensure greater independence, insulation and objectivity in their functioning. Excerpts of some such specific directives to the central government (covering both the CVC and the CBI) are given below:

1. The Central Vigilance Commission (CVC) shall be given statutory status.

2. Selection for the post of Central Vigilance Commissioner shall be made by a Committee comprising the Prime Minister, Home Minister and the Leader of the Opposition ... This shall be done immediately.

3. The CVC shall be responsible for the efficient functioning of the

CBI. While Government shall remain answerable for the CBI's functioning, to introduce visible objectivity in the mechanism to be established for overviewing the CBI's working, the CVC shall be entrusted with the responsibility of superintendence over the CBI's functioning. The CBI shall report to the CVC about cases taken up by it for investigation; progress of investigation; cases in which charge-sheets are filed and their progress. The CVC shall review the progress of all cases moved by the CBI for sanction of prosecution of public servants which are pending with the competent authorities, especially those in which sanction has been delayed or refused.

4. The Central Government shall take all measures necessary to ensure that the CBI functions effectively and efficiently and is viewed as a non-partisan agency.

5. The CVC shall have a separate section in its Annual Report on the CBI's functioning after the supervisory function is transferred to it.

6. Recommendations for appointment of the Director, CBI shall be made by a Committee headed by the Central Vigilance Commissioner with the Home Secretary and Secretary (Personnel) as members.

7. The Director CBI shall have a minimum tenure of two years, regardless of the date of his superannuation. This would ensure that an officer suitable in all respects is not ignored merely because he has less than two years to superannuate from the date of his appointment.

8. The transfer of an incumbent Director, CBI in an extraordinary situation, including the need for him to take up a more important assignment, should have the approval of the Selection Committee.

9. The Director, CBI shall have full freedom for allocation of work within the agency as also for constituting teams for investigations. Any change made by the Director, CBI in the Head of an investigative team should be for cogent reasons and for improvement in investigation, the reasons being recorded.

10. Selection/extension of tenure of officers up to the level of Joint Director (JD) shall be decided by a Board comprising the Central Vigilance Commissioner, Home Secretary and Secretary (Personnel) with the Director, CBI providing the necessary inputs.

11. Proposals for improvement of infrastructure, methods of investigation, etc. should be decided urgently. In order to strengthen CBI's in-house expertise, professionals from the Revenue, Banking and Security sectors should be inducted into the CBI.

12. The CBI Manual based on statutory provisions of the CrPC provides essential guidelines for the CBI's functioning. It is imperative that the CBI adheres scrupulously to the provisions in the Manual in relation to its investigative functions, like raids, seizure and arrests. Any deviation from the established procedure should be viewed seriously and severe disciplinary action taken against the officials concerned.

13. The Director, CBI shall be responsible for ensuring the filing of charge-sheets in courts within the stipulated time-limits, and the matter should be kept under constant review by the Director, CBI.

14. A document on CBI's functioning should be published within three months to provide the general public with a feedback on investigations and information for redress of genuine grievances in a manner which does not compromise with the operational requirements of the CBI.

15. Time-limit of three months for grant of sanction for prosecution must be strictly adhered to. However, additional time of one month may be allowed where consultation is required with the Attorney General (AG) or any other law officer in the AG's office.

16. The Director, CBI should conduct regular appraisal of personnel to prevent corruption and/or inefficiency in the agency.

(*Source:* http://cbi.nic.in/dop/judgements/excrpts.pdf)

In compliance with the directions of Hon'ble Supreme Court in the above judgment, the government promulgated an Ordinance in 1998. The Ordinance of 1998 conferred statutory status to the CVC and the powers to exercise superintendence over functioning of the Delhi Special Police Establishment (DSPE), and also to review the progress of the investigations pertaining to alleged offences under the PCA, 1988 conducted by them. In 1998, the government introduced the CVC Bill in the Lok Sabha in order to replace the Ordinance, though it was not successful. The Bill was re-introduced in 1999 and remained with the Parliament till 12 September 2003. After being duly passed in both the Houses of Parliament and with the President's assent, the CVC Act 2003, came into being.

Single directive given legislative cover

However, while following most of the Supreme Court Directions in the Vineet Narain Case while legislating the CVC Act 2003, the government brought back the earlier struck down Single Directive by making the following provision in the Act:

> In the Delhi Special Police Establishment Act, 1946,... (c) after section 6, the following section shall be inserted, namely:

> 6A. (1) The Delhi Special Police Establishment shall not conduct any inquiry or investigation into any offence alleged to have been committed under the Prevention of Corruption Act, 1988 except with the previous approval of the Central Government where such allegation relates to—

> (a) the employees of the Central Government of the level of Joint Secretary and above; and

> (b) such officers as are appointed by the Central Government in corporations established by or under any Central Act, Government companies, societies and local authorities owned or controlled by that Government.

However, the constitutional validity of this 'insertion' was challenged on the same grounds of being arbitrary and violative of Article 14. A Constitution bench yet again struck down (6 May, 2014) the legislative protective shield of Section 6A and observed:

> It seems to us that classification which is made in Section 6-A on the basis of status in the Government service is not permissible under Article 14 as it defeats the purpose of finding prima facie truth into the allegations of graft, which amount to an offence under the PC Act, 1988. Can there be sound differentiation between corrupt public servants based on their status? Surely not, because irrespective of their status or position, corrupt public servants are corrupters of public power. The corrupt public servants, whether high or low, are birds of the same feather and must be confronted with the process of investigation and inquiry equally. Based on the position or status in service, no distinction can be made between public servants against whom there are allegations amounting to an offence under the PC Act, 1988.

Further,

> The essence of police investigation is skillful inquiry and collection

of material and evidence in a manner by which the potential culpable individuals are not forewarned. The previous approval from the Government necessarily required under Section 6-A would result in indirectly putting to notice the officers to be investigated before commencement of investigation. Moreover, if the CBI is not even allowed to verify complaints by preliminary enquiry, how can the case move forward? A preliminary enquiry is intended to ascertain whether a prima facie case for investigation is made out or not. If CBI is prevented from holding a preliminary enquiry, at the very threshold, a fetter is put to enable the CBI to gather relevant material. The CBI is not able to collect the material even to move the Government for the purpose of obtaining previous approval from the Central Government ...

Current status

As of date, the CBI does not need any prior approval for enquiry or investigation of officers of the level of Joint Secretary and above. Still, an alternate mechanism was created to circumvent the directives of the Supreme Court. The CBI tweaked its investigation guidelines by making it obligatory for the investigating officers to take permission of the Additional Director in such cases. It is significant that this insertion in the CVC Act was made during the NDA regime in 2003. It can thus be seen that regardless of political ideologies of the party/alliance in power, whether it be the UPA or the NDA, there is concurrence in shielding the higher echelons of the bureaucracy and the government in corruption cases.

CVC overview

After the enactment of the CVC Act, 2003, the Commission became a multi-member body consisting of a Central Vigilance Commissioner (Chairperson) and not more than two Vigilance Commissioners (Members), to be appointed by the President (CVC, 2017). The total sanctioned staff strength of the Commission is 296. As on December 31, 2016, the total staff strength in position in the Commission was 243 (2017, Para 1.7 and 1.20). The Commission is entrusted with powers to inquire or cause inquiries, call for any information/documents from the central government and exercise superintendence over the functions of CBI for offences related to PCA, 1988

(2017, Para 1.7). The Commission has been empowered through the Lokpal and Lokayuktas Act, 2013 to conduct preliminary inquiry into complaints referred by the Lokpal to it. The Act also has a provision for a Directorate of Inquiry to be set up in the Commission. All departments/organizations under the Commission's jurisdiction have vigilance units headed by Chief Vigilance Officers (CVOs). The CVOs act as an extended arm of the Commission. There are 200 posts of full time CVOs and 512 posts of part time CVOs (2017, Para 1.24 and 1.25).

The Commission claims that transparency and objectivity in governance hold the key to combating corruption. In its endeavor for ensuring transparency, fair play and objectivity in matters related to public administration, the Commission as part of a multi-pronged strategy to tackle corruption, has been stressing on punitive, preventive and participative vigilance measures. It has proactively reached out to ministries, departments, and other organizations using a variety of interventions in order to achieve these goals. (2017, Para 2.3).

Functions and powers of CVC under CVC Act, 2003

1. Exercise superintendence over the functioning of the DSPE (CBI) insofar as it relates to the investigation of offences under the PCA, 1988 —Section 8(1)(a).

2. Give directions to the DSPE (CBI) for superintendence insofar as it relates to the investigation of offences under the PCA, 1988—Section 8(1)(b).

3. To inquire or cause an inquiry or investigation to be made on a reference by the central government in respect of a public servant being an employee of the central government and its organizations has allegedly committed an offence under the PCA, 1988—Section 8(1)(c).

4. To inquire or cause an inquiry or investigation to be made into any complaint alleging commission of offence under PCA, 1988 received against any official belonging to such category of officials specified in Sub-Section 2 of Section 8 of the CVC Act, 2003—Section 8(1)(d).

5. Review the progress of investigations conducted by the DSPE into offences alleged to have been committed under the PCA, 1988—Section 8(1)(e).

6. Review the progress of the applications pending with the competent authorities for sanction of prosecution under the PCA, 1988—Section 8(1)(f).

7. Tender advice to the central government and its organizations on such matters as may be referred to it or otherwise—Section 8(1)(g).

8. Exercise superintendence over the vigilance administration of the various central government ministries and its organizations—Section 8(1)(h).

9. Shall have all the powers of a Civil Court while conducting any inquiry —Section 11; Proceedings before the Commission to be judicial proceedings—Section 12.

10. Call for reports, returns and statements from central government/ organizations under its jurisdiction—Section 18.

11. Respond to central government on mandatory consultation with the commission before making any rules or regulations governing the vigilance or disciplinary matters relating to the persons appointed to the public services and posts in connection with the affairs of the Union or to members of the All India Services—Section 19.

By exercising superintendence over the CBI, under the PCA, 1988, the CVC now asserts vigilance over all the top officials of the country and has powers to inquire any kind of alleged corrupt practice in public administration. Similar vigilance units have been set up in all bodies of the central government.

Performance of CVC

According to the CVC (2017), the Commission has been very active in pursuing corruption related complaints against public officials. It tendered advices in 3,804 cases during the year 2016. These include the Commission's advice of initiation of major penalty proceedings in 460 cases and minor penalty proceedings in 183 cases as its first stage advice. Similarly, it advised imposition of major penalty in 206 cases and minor penalty in 153 cases as its second stage advice. The Commission recommended grant for sanction of prosecution in 62 cases involving 85 officials during 2016. The Commission received 51,207 complaints (including brought forward) during 2016 out of which 48,764 complaints were disposed. Complaints received in the

Commission are processed electronically through IT enabled core processes to ensure speed and transparency. It accorded vigilance clearance for 395 board level appointments and for 2,037 officials for empanelment to the post of Joint Secretary and above, in the central government. As per the Annual Reports received from CVOs, 18,541 penalties, both major and minor, were imposed on all categories of public servants, as a result of punitive action during the year 2016. Major penalties were imposed against 5,716 officers and minor penalties were imposed against 12,825 officers.

The question, however, to ask is whether all the changes in the statutory status and streamlining of the functioning of the CVC through legislations and the Supreme Court Judgments and the aforementioned self-report card of the CVC have actually ensured independence of CBI and effective combating of corruption in central government organizations? The answer is obviously and unfortunately in the negative, as evidenced by the series of scams, including the likes of the 2G scam, Commonwealth scam and Coalgate scam and the now oft quoted observation of the Supreme Court about CBI being a 'Caged Parrot' and 'Its Master's Voice' while hearing the Coalgate scam case in 2013 (*Times of India*, 2013). All the reforms mandated by the Supreme Court in 1997 in the Jain Hawala Case to define the status of the CVC and CBI and insulate the investigation powers of the CBI, it would seem, had turned a full circle and matters are back to square one.

Limitations of CVC

What is significant is that the CVC is not an investigative agency per se and must operate through the CBI or other vigilance units. Furthermore, CVC is only an advisory body and central government departments are free to either accept or reject CVC's advice in corruption cases. It cannot register corruption cases by itself and must refer the complaint to the CBI that generally initiates a 'preliminary' inquiry into the complaint. Only after some prima facie evidence is procured, is a criminal case registered and the formal investigation begins. Thus, inordinate delay and possibility of interference from external vested interests is in-built in the structure of these agencies. A significant limitation is that the CVC cannot direct the CBI to initiate inquiries against any officer of the level of Joint Secretary and above on its own. Such permission has to be obtained from the concerned department, a process likely to delay the proceedings. CVC has supervisory powers over the CBI but it cannot direct the CBI to investigate any case in a particular manner.

Controversy over appointment of CVC

CBI is under administrative control of the Department of Personnel and Training (DoPT) and the powers to appoint, transfer and suspend CBI officers lie with the DoPT. While a procedure has been enacted for the appointment of members of the CVC, the government too could tamper with them. Thus, appointments to CVC are indirectly under the control of the Government of India, though the leader of the opposition in the Lok Sabha is a member of the committee to select CVC and VCs. However, it is important to note here that the committee considers only those candidates who are put up before it, pre-selected by the government (DoPT). This came to the fore when P. J. Thomas was appointed the Chief Vigilance Commissioner in 2010, on the recommendation of a High-Powered Committee (HPC) headed by the Prime Minister. But Sushma Swaraj, the then leader of the opposition in the Lok Sabha, and member of the three-person committee, objected to this appointment citing a pending case of corruption against him. One Public Interest Litigation (PIL) was also filed in the Supreme Court of India against his appointment. The Supreme Court in 2011 quashed the appointment of Thomas as the Chief Vigilance Commissioner, noting that the HPC did not consider the relevant materials on the pending charge sheet. Subsequently, Mr Thomas resigned from the body. None other than the Supreme Court had to intervene to upturn the appointment. It is a sad state of affairs when the highest court of the land has to often intervene to set aside vested interests in the very appointment of the CVC.

CVC powers in Lokpal Act

The Lokpal and Lokayuktas Act, 2013 has made provisions (Section 20 of the Act) wherein the Lokpal can refer a complaint received in respect of a public official belonging to Group A, Group B, Group C or Group D to the Commission to inquire or cause a preliminary inquiry to be conducted. While the CVC has to submit the inquiry report in respect of Group A or Group B to the Lokpal, CVC shall proceed in accordance with the CVC Act, 2003 in respect of Group C or Group D public officials.

Central Bureau of Investigation (CBI)

Origin

The major investigative police unit in the country at the union level is the CBI which traces its establishment to the decision of the British government during World War II to create a special investigation unit for dealing with corruption in war supplies. Bribery, extortion, nepotism and siphoning of public resources were known to occur even during the medieval period and corruption indulged by public officials was frequently reported from Mughal courts. During the British rule this scourge became institutionalized and in particular, the police department attained extraordinary notoriety. A Police Commission appointed by Lord Curzon in 1902–03 found that 'the police force is far from efficient; it is defective in training and organization; it is inadequately supervised [and] it is generally regarded as corrupt and oppressive' (Gupta, 1979, 201). However, the British did little to reform the system as a corrupt and brutal force helped them in subjugating the people while simultaneously posing as guardians who alone could provide relief from the local marauders.

But the corruption threatened British interests when supplies to the military fighting the World War II were compromised through black marketing, and siphoning of public funds became the norm. Self-interest pushed the colonial government in 1941 to create a special unit in the supply department to investigate corruption amongst its officials. An executive order in 1941 established the Special Police Establishment (SPE) under a DIG within the Department of War to investigate cases of bribery and corruption in materials and supplies being procured for the war. In 1943 a special police force was created to deal with war-related corruption cases amongst central government employees. This unit was seen necessary to continue even after the end of the war and the Delhi Special Police Establishment Act (DSPE Act), 1946 was enacted to provide with legal powers to investigate and prosecute corruption cases. It is this Act that is the backbone and genesis of the CBI.

After independence, the superintendence of SPE was transferred to the Home Ministry and its jurisdiction was extended to all the central government employees, union territories and even to the states with the permission of the respective state governments. Gradually, with its reputation for good investigation, the SPE was entrusted with cases under other acts such as Import and Export (Control) Act and various sections of the Indian Penal Code. As the need to investigate cases of violation of different 'Central fiscal laws, major frauds relating to departments under the Central government, Public Joint Stock Companies, Passport frauds, crimes on the High Seas, crimes on the Airlines and serious crimes committed by organized gangs and professional criminals' became urgent, the Government of India set up the CBI by a Resolution No. 4/31/61-T dated 1 April 1963.

Evolution of divisions

Initially, the following six divisions were created within the CBI: (1) Investigation and Anti-Corruption Division (DSPE); (2) Technical Division; (3) Crime Records and Statistics Division; (4) Research Division; (5) Legal and General Division; and (6) Administration Division. The CBI was further strengthened by addition of an Economic Offences Wing by a Government of India Resolution dated 2 February 1964. Now CBI has two investigation wings: one called the General Offences Wing, which deals with cases of bribery and corruption involving employees of central government/PSUs and the other EOW, which deals with cases of violation of fiscal laws (Section 1.7, Annual Report, 2013).

Good reputation sometimes leads to the detriment of the institution. The CBI earned the reputation of being the premier investigation agency and became burdened with major crimes committed anywhere in the country, even when these were not corruption related. Citizens and even politicians would not trust their own local or state police investigators and demand the case to be transferred to the CBI. The annual report informs that beginning in the 1960s many 'conventional crimes, like assassinations, kidnappings, hijackings, crimes committed by extremists, violation of Official Secrets Act, large-scale banks and insurance frauds, etc., and other complicated cases, like Bhagalpur Blinding, Bhopal Gas Tragedy' were referred to CBI. Since early 1980's, Constitutional Courts also started referring cases to CBI for enquiry/ investigation on the basis of petitions filed by the aggrieved persons in cases of murders, dowry deaths, rape, etc. In view of these developments, it was decided in 1987 to have two investigation divisions in CBI, namely, Anti-Corruption Division and Special Crimes Division, the latter dealing with cases of conventional crimes as well as economic offences. Banking Frauds and Securities Cell was created in 1992 to investigate cases related to banking frauds and securities scams (CBI, 2013, 4).

Faced with such demands the CBI established the special investigation units within the organization to handle other types of crimes. A good number of murder cases, for example, were entrusted to the CBI in view of controversies surrounding the accused people. The allegations surrounding the involvement of dentist parents in the murder of their young daughter, Arushi, led to the demand for the CBI to take up the investigation from the UP police. Similarly, the rape and murder of two young teenagers at the village, Badaun, in UP with caste issues in the foreground again led to vociferous demands to hand the case over to the CBI.

The growing need for specialization and additional responsibilities has led further restructuring of the CBI to establish three investigation divisions within the organization:

1. Anti-Corruption Division deals with cases of corruption and fraud committed by public servants of all central government departments, central public-sector undertakings and central financial institutions.

2. The Economic Crimes Division deals with bank frauds, financial frauds, import-export and foreign exchange violations, large-scale smuggling of narcotics, antiques, cultural property and smuggling of other contraband items.

3. The Special Crimes Division deals with cases of terrorism, bomb blasts, sensational homicides, kidnapping for ransom and crimes committed by organized groups. While this has helped the agency develop professional expertise, growth of specialization and retain its reputation amongst the citizens and the judiciary, it has certainly added to its substantial load.

In this context the creation of another specialized investigation agency, the National Investigation Agency (NIA), to handle all terrorism and extremism related cases is yet another attempt to build specialization in police units. Furthermore, in-house specialization has also been a continuing focus within the agency. A 'Technical Forensic and Coordination Zone' (TFC) headed by IG/DIG has been created at CBI Headquarters in 2010. This unit is assisting in building technological support within the CBI as also those of Technological and Forensic Support Units (TAFSUs). The IG, as a senior officer, is also able to assist the Director in strengthening inter-branch, inter state and international cooperation and coordination. This has helped improve efficiency by reducing one level of decision making and streamlining resources for investigation.

Current divisions

To sum up, the current divisions and their functions, as of date, in the CBI are:

1. Anti-Corruption Division: The Anti-Corruption Division is responsible for collection of intelligence with regard to corruption, maintaining liaison with various departments through their vigilance officers, enquiries into complaints about bribery and corruption, investigation and prosecution of offences pertaining to bribery and corruption and, tasks relating to preventive aspects of corruption. The Anti-Corruption Division investigates cases against public servants under the control of the central government, public servants in public-sector undertakings under the control of the central government and cases against the public servants working under state government entrusted to the CBI by the state governments and serious departmental irregularities committed by the above mentioned public servants.

2. Special Crimes Division: The Special Crimes Division handles all cases of economic offences and all cases of conventional nature such as offences relating to internal security, espionage, sabotage, narcotics and psychotropic substances, antiquities, murders, dacoities/robberies, cheating, criminal breach of trust, forgeries, dowry deaths, suspicious deaths and other IPC offences as well as offences under other laws notified under the DSPE Act. It is also responsible for investigation of interstate and international rackets, large-scale frauds affecting the property or revenue of the government and crimes of national importance.

3. Economic Offences Division: The Economic Offences Division investigates financial crimes, bank frauds, money laundering, illegal money market operations, graft in public sector undertakings and banks.

4. Technical Advisory Units: The Technical Advisory Units provide expert guidance and assistance in banking, taxation, engineering and foreign trading/foreign exchange matters during enquiries and investigations

taken up by the CBI. The technical advisory units are:

- Banking Company Law/Insurance Advisory Unit
- Engineering Advisory Unit (Civil/Electrical matters)
- Taxation Advisory Unit (Direct/Indirect Tax matters)
- Foreign trading/Foreign Exchange Advisory Unit

5. Directorate of Prosecution: The Directorate of Prosecution was established in pursuance of the orders of Supreme Court in Vineet Narain Case. The Directorate provides legal advice besides conducting prosecution in CBI cases. The Directorate also attends to matters relating to legal matters raised in the IGPs/DGPs conference, matters relating to interpretation of laws, appointment of special counsels, statutory rules and regulations and amendments thereof, preparation of notes on Legal matters for publication in CBI Gazette, etc.

6. Policy Division: The Policy Division deals with all matters relating to policy, procedure, organization, vigilance and security in the CBI, correspondence and liaison with ministries and implementation of special programs for vigilance and anti-corruption, etc.

7. Administration Division: The Administration Division of the CBI looks after all matters relating to personnel, establishment and accounts of all the Divisions of the CBI and is headed by an officer of the rank of Joint Director/IG.

8. Systems Division: The Systems Division looks after the information technology needs of the CBI. It generates data required for answering parliament questions, CBI clearances for appointments/awards of medals, etc. This division also monitors the current ongoing comprehensive computerization plan of the CBI. The CBI Command Center consisting of Strategic Communication Center and Network Monitoring Center functions under the Systems Division.

9. Co-ordination Division: The Co-ordination Division comprises of

   a. The Co-ordination Unit takes part in the organization of Directors General of Police, CID and other conferences and is also in-charge of the publication of the CBI Bulletin.

   b. Interpol Unit is the Secretariat of the National Central Bureau

(NCB) and assists the Director CBI in his capacity as the Head of the NCB. The INTERPOL Unit, in its capacity as the Secretariat of the NCB, liaises with the International Criminal Police Organization (INTERPOL) and is required to maintain liaison with the member countries of the INTERPOL. It handles and follows up the correspondence relating to requests for investigation to be carried out abroad in cases under investigation with the CBI or the state police. Similarly, requests received from foreign countries for investigation in India are forwarded by the INTERPOL Unit to the state police and then followed up.

10. Central Forensic Laboratory: The Central Forensic Science Laboratory (CFSL) provides Expert Opinion on various aspects of forensic science concerning crime investigation. Apart from Delhi Police and the CBI, it assists central government departments, states, state forensic science laboratories, defense forces, government undertakings, universities, banks, etc. in criminal cases. The laboratory has a research and development set up to tackle special problems. The expertise available at the CFSL is also utilized in teaching and training activities conducted by the CBI, ICFS, police training institutions, universities and government departments conducting law enforcement courses. The cyber forensic laboratory and digital imaging center functioning under CFSL assist enforcement agencies in the collection and forensic analysis of electronic evidence. CFSL experts are summoned for appearing before courts. Their services are also utilized by investigating agencies for the inspection of scenes of crime.

11. Training Division: The CBI Academy at Ghaziabad is a modern police training center and imparts specialized knowledge and skills that make a modern crime investigator. Residential foundation courses are conducted for freshly selected deputy superintendents, sub-inspectors and constables. Refresher courses and courses on specialized subjects are also offered to officers of CBI and state police, as well as to vigilance officers of various departments.

Mandate

The CBI, functioning under Department of Personnel, Ministry of Personnel,

Pension and Public Grievances, Government of India, is now the premier investigating police agency in India. It is also the nodal police agency in India which coordinates investigation on behalf of INTERPOL member countries. CBI investigations have a major impact on the political and economic life of the nation. The following broad categories of criminal cases are handled by the CBI:

1. Cases of corruption and fraud committed by public servants of all central government departments, central public-sector undertakings and central financial institutions.

2. Economic crimes, including bank frauds, financial frauds, import–export and foreign exchange violations, large-scale smuggling of narcotics, antiques, cultural property and smuggling of other contraband items, etc.

3. Special crimes, such as cases of terrorism, bomb blasts, sensational homicides, kidnapping for ransom and crimes committed by the mafia/ the underworld.

Jurisdiction of CBI with respect to state police

Law and order is a state subject and the basic jurisdiction to investigate crime lies with state police. CBI may, however, investigate:

1. Cases which are essentially against central government employees or concerning affairs of the central government.

2. Cases in which the financial interests of the central government are involved.

3. Cases relating to the breaches of central laws with the enforcement of which the Indian government is mainly concerned.

4. Big cases of fraud, cheating, embezzlement and the likes, relating to companies in which large funds are involved and similar other cases when committed by organized gangs or professional criminals, having ramifications in several states.

5. Cases having interstate and international ramifications and involving several official agencies where, from all angles, it is considered necessary that a single investigating agency should be in charge of the investigation.

6. Cases directed by High Courts to be investigated.

7. Cases that the state government wants to be investigated by the CBI in the interest of fairness and objectivity.

Organization and strength of CBI

The CBI is headed by a Director who is one of the senior most IPS officers of the country. The other police positions in CBI are the Special Director/ Additional Director, Joint Director, Deputy Inspector General of Police, Inspector, Sub-Inspector, Assistant Sub-Inspector, Head Constable and Constable. The total sanctioned police strength including all ranks is 4,078. The sanctioned strength of administrative staff is 1,284. In addition, CBI also has a sanctioned strength of 230 law officers, 155 technical posts, 144 Group D posts and 171 posts of scientists in CFSL.

Superintendence over CBI

As per the CVC Act, notified on 12 September, 2003, the superintendence over CBI so far as it relates to investigation of offenses alleged to have been committed under the PCA 1988, shall vest with the CVC.

Performance of CBI: An examination

According to the annual report (CBI, 2013), a total of 1,131 regular cases/ preliminary enquiries were registered. 50 of these were taken up on the requests of state governments/union territories and 190 on the directions of the Constitutional Courts. 836 regular cases and 234 preliminary enquiries were finalized during the year. At the end of year, 922 cases/enquiries were pending investigation/enquiry. During 2013, charge sheets were filed in 666 cases and judgments were received in 1,225 court cases. The conviction rate for this period was 68.62 per cent. There were as many as 9,366 cases (court cases) pending in various courts at the end of year (Section 2.1, 20). The sanctioned strength of the agency is 6,674 of which only 5,796 were currently available with 878 vacancies. Significantly, the vacant positions in the ranks of Deputy Superintendent of Police, inspector and sub-inspector are 319, around 36 per cent. Nevertheless, although the ratio of investigators to the caseloads is still much better than the ones handled by ordinary police officers serving at the police station level, it is far below the desirable level for the much-burdened premier investigating agency of the Government of India.

The data of CBI cases under the PCA for the year 2015 points to a dismal performance. The total number of cases registered under the PCA by the CBI was 617, for which only 434 persons were arrested during the year 2015. The performance of all the states combined was no better. A total of 5,250 cases were registered across the country and which led to the arrest of 6,223 people (NCRB, Crime in India, 2016a, Table 9-I).

It is worth recalling that in a written reply in August 2013, Minister of State for Personnel, Public Grievances and Pensions, V Narayanasamy, told the Lok Sabha that the agency registered a total of 2,283 cases of corruption between January 2015 and June 2013. Of these, 650 such cases were registered in 2010, followed by 600 in 2011 and 703 in the year 2012. Of the total registered cases, charge sheets were filed in 1,317 and closure reports were filed in 208 others, he said. The Minister also mentioned that out of the total of 758 cases under probe, 34 were registered in 2010, 88 in 2011, 348 in 2012 and 288 filed in the first six months of that year (2013). Thus, in a span of three years that is, 2010, 2011, 2012 and up to June 2013, as many as 758 cases (32 per cent) were pending investigation out of a total of 2,283 cases registered. It is also significant to note that the number of cases under probe has progressively increased from 34 in 2010 to 88 in 2011, an increase of 258 per cent, from 88 in 2011 to 348 cases in 2012, an increase of 395 per cent.

The situation regarding pending trials in CBI Special Courts is equally gloomy. In reply to a Lok Sabha unstarred question number 3231 on pending corruption cases in CBI Courts asked by SR Jeyadural, Minister of State in the Ministry of Personnel, Public Grievance and Pensions replied that 9,910 cases investigated by the CBI are at different stages under trial in CBI courts in the country as on January 31, 2011. The Minister further stated that the central government has decided to set up 71 additional special courts for CBI cases in the country. However, subsequently even though sanction order for setting up 54 courts were issued by the central government, only 10 courts had started functioning by 2013. It must be noted that setting up of these special courts requires a long bureaucratic process in which the state governments too have to take steps for their operationalization. Many of the newly sanctioned courts are still yet to become operational.

The question that arises once again is whether these 71 additional special courts would suffice to dispose of 9,910 cases pending trial. And if so, what about the growing deluge of complaints? How would the courts deal with the phenomenal increase in the number of cases being registered, investigated and sent for trial? Are more courts the answer? Are more investigation officers the solution? Considering the phenomenal increase in the number of complaints, how long and to what extent can we match the voluminous increase of numbers?

In absence of latest comparative data in the public domain on the performance of the CBI, the reply by the Minister of State of the Ministry Personnel, Public Grievances and Pensions to the Rajya Sabha Starred Question No. 45 by Dr KVP Ramachandra Rao on December 8, 2016 speaks for the large backlog of cases pending investigation and trial. Dr KVP Ramachandra Rao presented the following questions (a) whether CBI has a huge backlog of cases, if so, the details thereof, state-wise; (b) how many of these cases are a decade old; (c) what factors have contributed to delay in disposal of these cases and (d) whether courts have passed strictures on CBI in this matter, if so, the details thereof?

The Minster's response says it all: 'The number of cases pending under investigation and trial, as on October 31, 2016, is 1297 and 9347 respectively. Of these, 7 and 2555 cases are pending for more than 10 years for investigation and trial respectively'. Regarding disposal of cases, it was stated:

> The Government had earlier set up 46 courts of special judge and 10 courts of special magistrate exclusively for trial of CBI cases all over the country. Subsequently, in order to speed up disposal, it was decided to set up 92 additional special courts out of which 88 are functional.

Further, during the last two years, 80 public prosecutors and 22 assistant public prosecutors in CBI have been appointed. The central government has also taken various initiatives to improve the training infrastructure and capacity building of the investigators and prosecutors in CBI to increase their efficiency. Besides, rigorous monitoring of investigation of cases is done by CBI and CVC as mandated by CVC Act, 2003.

Nevertheless, the reasons for delay in disposal of cases are (1) complex and voluminous nature of cases and large number of witnesses; (2) large number of cases referred by state governments, Hon'ble Supreme Court and High

Courts; (3) delay in handing over the cases to CBI for investigation after initial investigation by local police; (4) non-traceability of accused persons; (5) delay in getting expert opinion; (6) stay by courts; (7) delay in execution of letters rogatory with foreign countries; (8) non-appearance of accused persons and adjournments taken by them on different grounds, etc.

To sum up, while at the end of 2012, 598 cases (47 per cent) were pending investigation, the number climbs up to 922 cases at the end of 2013 and reaches the number 1297 till October 30, 2016. Similarly, while the number of cases pending in various courts at the end of 2013 was 9,366, the latest figures of cases pending trial at the end of October 2016, as per the minister's reply, stood at 9,347. Thus, in a space of about three years, cases pending trial virtually remained at the same levels, despite the government's efforts to reduce pendency by sanctioning and operationalizing additional courts.

Description of some important corruption cases handled by the CBI

Some illustrative cases against prominent officials are:

1. Against an income tax officer, for demanding and accepting a bribe of ₹ 7,500,000 for settling his income-tax dues from ₹ 30,000,000 to ₹ 10,000,000 (RC0282013A0016).

2. Against a superintendent of customs at Kolkata for possession of disproportionate assets to his known sources of income to the tune of ₹ 57.64 crores (RC2182013A0003).

3. A preliminary enquiry against a prosecutor of CBI, representing CBI in 2G Spectrum case and private person for colluding with the accused person and sharing strategy of the prosecution with him and advising him to devise strategy to defend himself in the case (PE2182013A0001).

4. Against a retired Air Chief Marshal, his 3 cousins and 15 other accused persons/suspect firms for entering into a criminal conspiracy and engaging themselves into alleged unethical dealings with a firm of Italy in the matter of procurement of 12 VVIP helicopters (RC2172013A0003).

5. Railway bribery scam where charge sheet was filed against relative of the then Minister of Railways, a senior member of railway organization and other persons for entering into a criminal conspiracy in the matter of seeking appointment of such member to the post of member (electrical) with additional charge of general manager Western Railway.

6. Against the then Chief Managing Director, the then Executive Director, Director, General Manager and others of Bharat Dynamics Ltd. for committing several irregularities in awarding the contract worth ₹ 575.51 crores to M/s Tata Power Company Limited pertaining to Akash Weapon systems for two regiments of Indian Army (PE0352013A0004).

7. Food grain scam where a charge sheet has been filed against 109 accused persons, including ex-MLA, the then District Magistrate and other public servant and private persons for diversion of food grains of Public Distribution System (PDS) to other countries, like Bangladesh and other places.

8. Against a Member of Parliament (Rajya Sabha) and other private persons for entering into a criminal conspiracy for cheating the Government of India by claiming undue reimbursement of expenditure incurred upon performing purported air journeys along with companions during the year 2012 (RC2182013A0009).

9. Against a former minister, a Member of Parliament, members of 35 Screening Committee and other companies/private persons for entering into a criminal conspiracy and showing undue favor to these companies in the matter of allotment of coal blocks. In lieu of favor to these companies, the accused person paid ₹ 20,000,000 to the minister through investment in one of his company (RC2192013E0006).

10. The Cyber Cell of CBI charge sheeted two cases in which the offenders fraudulently transferred, online, an amount of around ₹ 12.50 crores and ₹ 29.50 crores from two different accounts maintained at State Bank of India (SBI) by intruding into the systems of SBI through Wi-Fi device, accessed the Core Banking System of the bank and managed the transactions using Real-Time Gross Settlement (RTGS) facility.

The variety of graft cases handled by the CBI suggest widespread corruption amongst public officials in the country. Corrupt practices are seen not only in financial institutions, bureaucracy and public-sector undertakings but also disturbingly in the armed forces, scientific community, elected representatives and within the CBI itself. Interestingly, a good proportion of the cases are downright extortion by officials misusing their positions but a number of them also occur due to the unchecked discretion and opportunities provided by the growing economy. It is also clear that the CBI is barely able to touch a few illustrative cases that do not seem to make any dent in the on-going corruption in the country (Chowdhary, 2013). Every annual report of the CBI for the past years describes similar cases and transactions that involve discretion. Further, many institutions like public-sector banks, specific bureaucratic positions and procurement processes frequently figure in the list of cases. It is unknown if the CBI has made any effort to reach out to the policymakers and managers to find ways to plug these loopholes that offer opportunities for corruption.

Some important CBI cases in 2016

We list a few illustrative cases handled by the CBI for the year 2016 to inform the readers about the nature and extent of activities of this anti-corruption agency. The various categories of public officials and the varied nature of their corruption is something to be noted:

1. Arrest of then Chief of Air Staff and two other accused in an on-going investigation of a case involving corrupt practices in a defense deal.
2. Filing a charge sheet against then Union Minister of Communication, A. Raja and others for causing loss to government exchequer in the ill-famous telecom case.
3. Arrest of five directors of a private firm in an on-going investigation of a chit fund case.
4. Filing a charge sheet against then three directors and a private company in an on-going investigation of a chit fund case.
5. Registering a case against the Principal Chief Commissioner of central excise and four superintendents in bribery.
6. Arrest of then principal system analyst and then assistant programmer in an on-going investigation of a case related to Vyapam.
7. Filing charge sheet against three candidates in a case related to Vyapam.
8. Registering a case relating to alleged spiking of banned substances/drugs in the meal of an international wrestler.
9. Registering a case against then MD of REPCO Bank and others.
10. Registering a case against Executive Director, Central Bank of India.

11. Arresting a senior Civil Judge of Delhi including an advocate acting as local commissioner in a bribery case.

12. Arresting an official of Haryana police in a bribery case.

13. Registering a case against two directors of Delhi-based private firm and others for causing an alleged loss of ₹ 4,138 lakh (approx.) to the Indian Overseas Bank.

14. Registering a case against CMD of United Bank of India and others and recovering assets worth crores during searches.

15. Arresting a senior Divisional Finance Manager of Railways for accepting a bribe of ₹ 1 lakh.

16. Arresting Managing Director of Odisha-based private group of companies in a chit fund case.

17. Registering a case against three promoters/director of Chandigarh-based private company for causing an alleged loss of ₹ 33.79 crore (approx.) to the SBI.

18. Filing a charge sheet against Chief Manager of Syndicate Bank and four private persons in a case relating to an alleged loss of ₹1000 crore (approx.) to the bank.

19. Registering a case against Vice Chancellor and three others of Vishwa Bharti University, Shantiniketan for committing alleged irregularities in appointments.

20. Registering a case against an Under Secretary in Ministry of Home Affairs.

21. Recovering cash of ₹ 1.37 crore (approx.) and investment of ₹ 9 crore (approx.) during further searches from the premises of Deputy GM in an alleged bribery case.

22. CBI's special court convicts then Chairman and MD of Jharkhand-based private firm in a case relating to allocation of coal block.

23. Conducting searches at 82 locations including Jharkhand, Bihar, Odisha, West Bengal and Andhra Pradesh in an on-going investigation of two cases related to the alleged chit fund.

24. Filing charge sheet against then Chief Engineer of Noida/Greater Noida/Yamuna expressway authorities (UP) and 13 others for causing an alleged loss to the government exchequer in awarding various contracts.

25. Arresting an Income Tax Officer, a Senior Tax Assistant and a Branch Manager of Syndicate Bank in separate cases of bribery.

26. Filing a charge sheet against Rajendra Sadashiv Nikalje aka Chhota Rajan, a dreaded mafia gangster and three others for allegedly obtaining passport on forged documents.

27. Arresting a sub inspector of Delhi Police for accepting a bribe of ₹ 2.5 lakh and two private persons in another case of bribery.

28. Filing a charge sheet against two Directors of a private firm and then two Executive Directors of UCO bank and others for causing an alleged loss of ₹ 36 crore (approx.) to the bank.

(CBI Press Releases for 2016)

Enforcement Directorate

There are other specialized anti-corruption agencies too functioning under economic and finance ministries. Amongst these, a prominent one is the Directorate of Enforcement which is a multi-disciplinary organization mandated with the task of enforcing the provisions of two special fiscal laws—Foreign Exchange Management Act (FEMA), 1999 and Prevention of Money Laundering Act (PMLA), 2002. The Directorate recruits some personnel directly but largely depends upon officials drawn on deputation from other units such as customs and central excise, income tax, police and others. On March 11, 2011, after the approval of the government, the Directorate underwent a massive restructuring becoming a force of 2,064 officers/staff from the earlier 758, simultaneously raising its number of offices from 21 to 49 across India. However, the process in order to have a full contingent of work force and to get all the 49 offices to become functional is still underway. The officers of the Directorate are empowered to conduct enquiries to locate; provisionally attach/confiscate assets derived from acts of scheduled offences besides arresting and prosecuting the money launderers.

The origin of this Directorate goes back to May 1, 1956, when an 'Enforcement Unit' was formed, in the Department of Economic Affairs, for handling exchange control laws violations under Foreign Exchange Regulation Act, 1947 (FERA, 1947); this Unit was headed by a legal service officer, as director of enforcement, assisted by an officer drawn on deputation from RBI, besides three inspectors of special police establishment; besides Delhi Headquarters, to start with, there were two branches—at Bombay (Mumbai) and Calcutta (Kolkata). In the year 1957, this Unit was renamed as 'Enforcement Directorate', and another branch was opened at Madras (Chennai). The administrative control of the Directorate was transferred from Department of Economic Affairs to Department of Revenue in 1960. With the passage of time, FERA, 1947 was repealed and replaced by FERA, 1973. For a short period of four years (1973–77), the Directorate remained under the administrative jurisdiction of Department of Personnel and Administrative Reforms.

With the onset of the process of economic liberalization, FERA, 1973, which was a regulatory law, was repealed and in its place, effective June 1, 2000, a new law—Foreign Exchange Management Act (FEMA), 1999 (FEMA) came into operation. Further, in tune with the International anti-money laundering regime, Prevention of Money Laundering Act (PMLA), 2002 was enacted, and entrusted for its enforcement to the Directorate.

Carved in the role of a multi-dimensional organization, the Directorate enforces two laws; FEMA, a civil law having quasi-judicial powers, for investigating suspected contraventions of the exchange control laws and regulations with the powers to impose penalties on those adjudged guilty and PMLA, a criminal law, whereby the officers are empowered to conduct enquiries to locate, provisionally attach/confiscate assets derived from acts of schedules offences besides arresting and prosecuting the money launderers. The existence of a predicate offence is necessary for the ED to register its own offence.

Some important ED cases

1. The ED has been pursuing Vijay Mallya to recover a huge sum of money, following the collapse of his Kingfisher Airlines in 2012. Reportedly, ED has attached properties and assets worth ₹ 9,700 crores held by Mallya and his companies.

2. The ED issues fourth summon to Zakir Naik, February 28, 2017. The ED has issued fresh summons, also possibly the last, to controversial Islamic preacher Zakir Naik in connection with its money laundering

probe case against him and others.

3. ED files PMLA case against Karti Chidambaram, others, May 19, 2017. The CBI, carried out searches at the homes and offices of Karti across four cities for allegedly receiving money from the media firm owned by the Mukerjeas to scuttle a tax probe.

4. Louis Berger case: ED attaches assets of Kamat, Alemao in Goa, March 30, 2017. It also attached 8 apartments in Varca village worth ₹ 75 lakh (book value) of Alemao, the lone NCP MLA. The ED had registered a PMLA case in 2015, based on a Goa police FIR.

5. ED attaches ₹ 263 crore assets of the *Deccan Chronicle*, March 29, 2017. ED had booked a case under the PMLA against the company and others based on a CBI FIR and charge sheet.

6. ED summons Air Asia India's ex-chief Mittu Chandilya, March 6, 2017. The ED investigation followed a complaint by BJP leader Subramanian Swamy in which he accused the carrier of 'money laundering'.

7. ED attaches ₹ 21 crore assets of arms dealer Sanjay Bhandari, June 1, 2017. This is the first attachment of assets order (provisional) issued by the central probe agency under PMLA, which is based on the new Anti-Black Money Act notified by the government in 2015.

8. ED asks top Bollywood actor to share details of foreign currency remittances, May 1, 2017. The person in question will have to disclose offshore investments under the RBI approved liberalized remittance scheme and his expenses abroad.

9. ED attaches ₹ 2.77 crore assets of former IAS and CPT Chairman, February 8, 2017. ED had slapped money laundering charges against Suresh and others based on a CBI FIR and charge sheet against him on charges of possessing alleged disproportionate assets.

(Compiled from various newspaper reports.)

Performance of ED

Table 4.1 Enforcement Directorate: Performance from 2012 to 2015 under PMLA, 2002

Action	2005–12 Jul–March	2012–13	2013–14	2014–15	Total–2015
No. of cases registered	1,437 (Pending)	221	209	178	1,326 (Pending)
No. of cases disposed	—	100	277	342	—
No. of Provisional Attachment Orders (PAOs) issued	131	65	130	166	492
Value of assets under attachment (₹ in crores)	1,214.66	2,358.1	1,773.4	3,657.1	9,003.26
No. of PAOs confirmed	108	52	57	138	355
Value of assets under PAO confirmed by Adjudicating Authority (₹ in crores)	960.77	325.98	1,395.4	2,150.8	4,832.91
No. of persons arrested	22	3	7	19	52
No. of prosecution complaints filed	38	11	55	69	173

Source: Enforcement Directorate website of 2017—performance.

Analysis

Examination of the above data makes it clear that from July 1, 2002 to March 31, 2015, out of the 2,045 cases (1,437 + 221 + 209 + 178) pending with the ED, only 719 (100 + 277 + 342) could be disposed off, leaving at the end of the period under review with a pendency of 1,326 cases, thus leading to the conclusion that the ED was able to dispose of only 35 per cent of its cases while 65 per cent cases still remain pending. This analysis speaks for itself and shows that the agency remains rather ineffective in dealing with PMLA cases.

However, the success rate in terms of PAOs and their confirmation presents a much healthier picture. Out of 492 PAOs issued during the period July 1, 2002 to March 31, 2015 involving ₹ 9,003.26 crores, as many as 355 were confirmed involving assets worth ₹ 4,832.91. The confirmation percentage of PAOs works out to be a healthy 72 per cent. However, on deeper examination it is seen that out of the 2,045 cases registered, only in 492 cases PAOs were issued and only 355 cases were confirmed. When translated in percentage terms, POAs were issued only in 24 per cent cases and ultimately only 17 per cent of the cases were confirmed. Similarly, though the confirmation percentage of 72 is encouraging, in terms of the confirmation of attachment of assets comes to only 54 per cent, that is ₹ 4,832.91 out of ₹ 9,003.26 crores. This suggests that the ED has not been able to make any appreciable dent in the anti-money laundering efforts.

Table 4.2 Under Foreign Exchange Management Act (FEMA), 1999

ACTION	Pendency (March 31, 2012)	2012–13	2013–14	2014–15	Pendency (March 31, 2015)
No. of investigations initiated	5,823	1,722	1,041	915	4,776
No. of investigation disposed	—	1,471	1,678	1,576	—
Show cause notices (SCNs) issued	1,560 (pending adjudication)	647	573	654	1,304
SCNs adjudicated	—	532	780	818	—

Source: Enforcement Directorate website of 2017—performance.

Analysis

In terms of investigation of FEMA cases by ED during the period July 1,

2002 to March 31, 2015, the disposal is 50 per cent and the pendency as on March 31, 2015 is also 50 per cent. With respect to final adjudication on SCNs, while the disposal is 62 per cent, the pendency remains as high as 38 per cent. Besides all other reasons for the ineffectiveness of the ED in putting an effective curb on money laundering, including its lack of autonomy, one of the major issues is also the lack of personnel. The statistics provided later in this chapter, makes this assertion amply clear.

Staff position in ED

The sanctioned strength of the ED is 2,064 while the working strength for the past few years has been as given below:

Table 4.3 Staff Position in Enforcement Directorate

As on March 1, 2012	570
As on March 1, 2013	656
As on March 1, 2014	691
As on March 1, 2015	682

Source: Enforcement Directorate website of 2017—performance.

If we consider the available strength of 682 of the ED as on March 1, 2015 out of a sanctioned strength of 2,064, the vacancy works out to be 67 per cent and an unpalatable fact comes to light that ED is actually working on only 33 per cent of its strength. The Directorate is largely dependent upon officers on deputation from other units. The fact of the matter is that officers are not inclined to go on deputation to ED due to lack of any incentive allowance unlike CBI that has both special incentive scheme and a reward policy. Repeated requests by the ED to the Ministry of Finance on this count have, however, yielded no results. How serious are successive governments in curbing money laundering and FEMA violations, is quite evident from the above examination.

Ineffectiveness of Anti-Corruption Agencies (ACAs)

Based upon the above mentioned examination of the leading anti-corruption agencies functioning under the union government we can assess their functions and performance in terms of their capability to handle corruption in public offices. Sousa (2010) argues that independence is an important factor in the effectiveness of such agencies.

> Under their statutes, all ACBx are 'independent', but in practice degrees of operational autonomy vary considerably from one agency to another. Some of these agencies act as window dressing institutions or at best they function as a governmental anti-corruption discourse mechanism. (2010, 13)

The independence of CBI has been a major contentious issue and topic of agitated discourse in public domain for decades.

While responding to the CBI Director Ranjit Sinha's second affidavit filed on May 6, 2013, stating that Law Minister Ashwani Kumar and senior officials of the PMO and Coal Ministry had made changes in the 'Colagate' probe report, pertaining to the alleged irregularities and corruption in the coal mines allocation, the Supreme Court expressed strong displeasure at the government's interference and observed, 'the heart of the report was changed on the suggestions of the Government officials'. Raising questions on the independence of CBI, the Apex Court called it a 'caged parrot speaking in its master's voice'. Further expressing its exasperation, the Court observed, 'It's a sordid saga that there are many masters and one parrot'. It further ruefully observed, 'We gave CBI a structure of stone (in the Vineet Narain case) but 15 years later it seems CBI is all sand' (*Times of India*, 2013).

Indeed, after the land mark judgment in the Vineet Narain case in 1997 and Supreme Court's historical specific directives to make the CVC and the CBI autonomous, discussed in detail in the earlier part of this chapter, while the CVC was given a statutory status by the CVC Act 2003, no legislation was brought forward to make the CBI independent and autonomous either by the UPA government or subsequently by the NDA government in its term so far. What is most unfortunate is that no such Act is being envisaged even now! It is clear that regardless of which party is in power, there is no political will to grant autonomy to the CBI. By adding layers of CVC and the Lokpal, the levers controlling the investigation unit have been strengthened enabling indirect and camouflaged authority to be exercised upon the agency.

Thus, while an independent CBI still remains a far cry, even the basic issue of correcting the defective institutional mechanism of the formation and powers of the CBI through a separate law remains elusive. Even now, there is no independent statutory act to govern the functions of the agency and it still derives its power to investigate cases under the old colonial DSPE Act, 1946. The CBI is completely dependent on the government (DoPT) for funds, infrastructure, personnel and even administrative matters. The bureaucratic red-tapism and vested interests involved in getting approvals from the DoPT often dampens initiatives when taken by the directors CBI, to improve the efficiency of the Bureau in terms of strengthening manpower and technical resources, capacity building to enable swift investigations and prosecutions. Furthermore, all police agencies in the country also lack financial independence. Their budget is made and approved by the Home Ministry and for most expenses the Director/Chief has to go to the ministry to seek approval. Purchasing equipment and technology to improve performance are all outside the purview of the police chiefs and through such mechanism the government and bureaucracy create fissures into the management of investigation of important cases. As well understood, these cases are the ones involving politicians, senior bureaucrats, business leaders and their associates.

The functions of the ACAs in the country are also affected by a lack of basic resources—both personnel and material. A large number of vacancies exist and persist in these agencies. According to the CBI's annual report 2013, the organization had a shortage of 878 officials at the end of 2013. Alarmingly, the posts of 69 law officers and 92 technical officers (including 38 technical officers working on contract basis) was lying vacant. The same is true for most ACBx and EOWs while a general shortage of police personnel in the country has reached an alarming proportion. The latest data from the Bureau of Police Research and Development (BPR&D) (2017) informs that there is one police personnel to 729 people in the country. The reported vacancies as of January 1, 2016 were a staggering 24.07 per cent (2017, 1). Scandals involved in the recruitment process and delays in giving sanction to hire more personnel have been other reasons for shortage of personnel. The budget for procuring material resources such as new technologies and forensics is also tightly controlled by the ministry. There is no systematic policy planning to build the capacities of ACAs and provide them with necessary tools to combat corruption effectively.

This is a significant problem, as the organizational leadership needs flexibility and operational freedom to carve creative and effective solutions to the organizational problems without having to go through slow bureaucratic approval and contentious legislative processes. The mobilization and utilization of resources and funds should not be held hostage to vested interests operating in the ministry and elsewhere. Recruitment of motivated individuals, training to build in house expertise and specialization as well as modern management practices that build professional competency and pride in their work are matters requiring urgent attention for any meaningful assault on corrupt practices. However, this cannot come about unless there are determined efforts to combat corruption and a pragmatic honest attempt by the political leadership. 'Political commitment has been particularly important for the successful institutionalization of the Singapore CPIB and the Hong Kong ICAC' (Sousa, 2010, 19) and unless that transpires in India the struggle against corruption will be in vain. Unfortunately, in India there appears to be hardly any political and bureaucratic will or urgency to strengthen and empower these agencies (Chowdhary, 2013).

Also, till recently, CBI could not even take up a preliminary inquiry against bureaucrats of the rank of Joint Secretary and above as also ministers without permission from the government, as discussed in detail in the earlier part of this chapter. Similar such approvals were needed from the government for filing of FIRs, launching prosecutions and seeking appeals against court acquittals. To be precise, the CBI has to depend for its functioning upon several ministries in the central government, primarily the DoPT, followed by the CVC, Ministry of Law and Ministry of Home Affairs.

Moreover, the CBI does not have its own investigators and must depend largely upon other police units to send their officers on deputation, which could be anywhere from five years to ten years. Besides affecting the continuity in the investigation of offences due to change in investigating officers, the prospect of having to go back to the parent state/cadre, loom large upon their decisions. It is unlikely that the officer will be strong enough to carry out investigation in cases affecting the big wigs of the state.

The autonomy of the Director CBI is also often eroded by the government, irrespective of political formation in power, through the lure of post-retirement jobs. A good number of CBI directors have been appointed as governors or given other lucrative posts such as membership in the National Human Rights Commission (NHRC) or the Union Public Service Commission (UPSC).

This is an old practice stretching back to several decades and many retired CBI directors have been bestowed high offices by political rulers. These practices unambiguously confirm allegations of allurements to keep the CBI favorably disposed towards the ruling establishment. Therefore, there is an urgent need to ensure that there is a provision whereby the CBI Director follows the cooling off period of a suitable duration before accepting any employment under the government.

The need for independence is acute as political and vested interference can be exerted directly or indirectly upon the investigators. The power to transfer and post officials is a crucial weapon that is used regularly to 'tame' officers. The problem is grave in state governments, where action against the chief minister or ministers/bureaucrats are seldom taken to their logical conclusion while they are in power (Tiwari, 2015). In the CBI and in the state anti-corruption agencies this becomes significant as it has diluted the efforts to combat corruption and destroyed the credibility of the organization.

The specialized anti-corruption agencies such as the CBI, ACBx and EOWs are also hampered by the organizational, bureaucratic and legal hindrances existing in the system. For instance, the modes and processes of inter-institutional cooperation with other state agencies were not thought well in advance before their creation. The Constitution has stipulated that policing will be a state subject and in the federal system prevailing in the country this has become a contentious issue. Since opposition parties are in power in many state governments, they see any attempt by the central government to restructure police functions, including anti-corruption efforts, as interference in their autonomy and functions. The states have strongly resisted any attempt by the Parliament to make laws that could compromise their control over the police. Even in inter state crimes and those affecting multiple states, the central government agencies do not have the power to conduct independent investigations. They need permission of the state government in order to function in their region. While center–state conflict seriously affects anti-corruption efforts, the absence of policies governing inter-agency cooperation is another important factor in weakening corruption related work. Intelligence agencies generally do not work with the investigation agencies and at best provides general intelligence that needs investigation. However, in the global economy where terrorism, organized crime, drug trade and money laundering are all inter-related and even involve the same set of offenders and gangs, the lack of institutionalized cooperation between intelligence agencies and crime investigators is a serious limitation. Yet the laws, rules, regulations, organizational culture and bureaucratic turf battles persist and no viable mechanism has evolved where a concerted effort to combat corruption is made.

Sousa (2010) further argues that specialized knowledge on corruption is essential to the role and performance of ACAs. Investigation of corruption cases requires wide knowledge of rules, procedures and finance. Corrupt officials are well versed with the intricacies of their organizations and use insider knowledge to make illegal gains. To unearth such corrupt practices and gather sufficient evidence to prosecute them successfully requires the investigators to be as knowledgeable, if not more than, their suspects and understand the internal decision-making mechanism of the organization.

The recruitment to anti-corruption agencies is generally limited in the country. Even when it is held the selection follows the general and traditional procedures based upon recruitment to traditional police organizations. While academy training and experience of investigation does help prepare them to investigate corruption cases but in most incidents evidence must be gathered about financial transactions. There is little training in such subjects and most investigators are generally poorly equipped to investigate corruption in public offices. As mentioned above most personnel are brought to the agencies through deputation from other police organizations. There are little requirements for being deputed to these agencies except willingness and years in service. While the CBI and ACBs have improved in-service training for their investigators, there is still much desired impetus required in this domain. Setting up of central and state training academies to empower the officers with the requisite skills to investigate corruption and economic crime cases will go a long way in professionalizing the anti-corruption agencies to combat corruption effectively.

As well understood, the efforts to combat corruption requires that the authorities do not limit themselves to simple legal, enforcement and administrative processes. To combat corruption effectively, it is necessary that management practices, systems of accountability, opening data sources and ensuring in-house supervision be done as well. Unless, opportunities and facilitating working environment for corrupt practices are blocked through new laws, procedures, rules and regulations as well as administrative measures, motivated offenders will continue to exploit the system and make illegal gains.

Corruption exists in many forms and hides under the blanket of privacy, financial transactions, involvement of offshore safe heavens and connivance of higher echelons of society. An investigative agency alone cannot curb this menace as by its own functions it can at best prosecute a few of the guilty people. The only effective and long-term solution is to examine the basis of corruption. There is an urgent need to carry out research about the etiology of corruption and white-collar crimes; techniques and modus operandi adopted by the offenders; rules and regulations that leave loopholes to be exploited and the political economy that encourages corruption and exploitation rather than compliance and public service. The CVC, CBI, ACBs, EOWs and other agencies not only need to cooperate but also promote research and data sharing so that corrupt practices are targeted and prevented in the first place.

The CBI has created a research division within its organization and has also signed an MOU with the National Law School of India University to 'research in all mutually agreed areas of law enforcement, including criminal procedure, anti-corruption laws, laws and procedures relating to investigation, prosecution and trial' (CBI, 2014, 13). Similar MOUs have been signed with NIMHANS for application of psychology and training officers in the art of interrogation as also with IIMs to 'facilitate collaboration for mutual interest'. While the intent may be honest but it is clear from the annual reports that the CBI is doing nothing to conduct research that translates into strengthening its efforts in combating corruption.

Unfortunately, CBI publishes limited and selective data, generally for a year only in its annual report. Even these do not appear to be available on its website for the year 2016. In the absence of statistics related to corruption cases for a period of several years pertaining to number of complaints received each year, PE registered, FIR registered, enquired/investigated, charge sheeted, filed, referred to other agencies and pending enquiry/investigation each year, external researchers are unable to explore the nature of corruption and its control in the country. While there are a large number of studies that have examined the etiology of corruption and failures to deal with it (see Chapter 3) the agencies themselves have been lukewarm in using research as a tool to fight corrupt practices.

As Sousa (2010) suggests it will be fruitful for the CVC, CBI and other agencies to conduct original empirical research, provide research support for major investigations, monitor and assess anti-corruption initiatives, create databanks of reported cases, affected public offices and modus operandi of corrupt officials, on corruption trials, on crime statistics and also undertake attitude surveys. By processing and transforming raw data into relevant, ready-to-use information and serving as an interface for other researchers in the field, these agencies can begin to expand preventive methods by involving concerned citizens and develop effective strategies. Research is the key to successfully combat corruption in the society (Verma, 2010).

An area that has hampered the growth and performance of ACAs in India is the apprehension of decision makers, bureaucrats and politicians about the abuse of powers by these agencies. In the contentious democratic polity of India, it is not unusual for political parties to misuse power to frame and involve political opponents for personal interests. The prevalence of 'false' cases being lodged against opponents is common and wide spread. Police powers have been misused to throw opponents in jail as seen in the infamous emergency era. The opposition parties after attaining power in the 1977 elections then took revenge by putting Mrs Gandhi in jail on vague charges. The failures to prosecute politicians stems from deliberate interferences in the functions of the investigative agencies but it is also true that a number of motivated, ambiguous of even false cases appear to have been instituted to target opposition political leaders by the political party/alliance in power, be it UPA or NDA.

Such a reputation of the CBI has given rise to apprehension about its role and doubts about its impartial functioning. There is genuine fear that giving it more powers or making it independent may make the agency unaccountable. 'One of the legitimate fears is that special prerogatives can be abused for personal vendetta or political purges' (Sousa, 2010, 16). Despite being under the control and supervision of the CVC, the CBI has not functioned in an objective professional manner. It has pursued or delayed investigations to suit political expediency as seen in the disproportionate wealth cases of Jayalalitaa, Mayawati and Mulayum Singh—all three major political leaders in the country. The mechanism whereby the ACAs can be independent of political control and function in accordance with the due process is obviously desirable.

But at the same time methods to make it accountable to some external system and transparent in its operations is also very much the necessity of the day. How this can be achieved in the country remains unanswered and a dilemma.

The assumption that mere provision of funds and enacting new laws can handle corruption is equally misplaced.

> If there is one lesson to be learnt from the history of anticorruption activity, it is that there are no individual solutions but a cocktail of measures, no silver bullets but a mixture of successes and failures and no quick fixes but a long and hard learning process. (Sousa, 2010, 19)

The inability of anti-corruption agencies comes from a variety of internal factors such as the lack of resources, organization dynamics, management limitations, weak leadership, lack of competency and poor motivation of the personnel.

The major limitation with anti-corruption efforts in India has been the short sightedness in the legal framework of the agencies themselves. As already discussed, the CBI is yet to get a proper legislation that can provide it the requisite powers and guide its functions. It was created to address corruption in war efforts of the British India government and then the independent India government extended this executive action. Due to this limitation, there have been questions about the power of the agency to investigate in accordance with the provisions of CrPC (Mazumdar, 2013). The Supreme Court (November 8, 2013) had to stay the judgment of the Guwahati High Court declaring the CBI unconstitutional. Hence, the matter about the establishment of the CBI and its powers to investigate corruption must be determined in coming days. Now, with passing of the Lokpal Act, the new Lokpal will also share the control of the CBI. How this will affect its performance remains to be seen. However, given the lack of political will to provide for an independent anti-corruption agency in India and the recent history of tussle between the executive and the judiciary, the former bent on retaining its control and the latter determined to give the agency its autonomy, the future does not appear bright.

5

Evaluating Efficacy of Anti-Corruption Agency
Case Study from Madhya Pradesh

Case Study of EOW Madhya Pradesh

We conduct an important empirical case study about a major anti-corruption and anti-economic offences unit and its functions from one of the largest states of India. Our objective is to present statistical evidence that even when an anti-corruption agency is run professionally and efficiently, it is not able to curb corruption to any significant extent. The Madhya Pradesh (MP) government, over successive decades, took a number of innovative and promising steps to strengthen the Economic Offences Wing (EOW), empowering it with progressive legislations, administrative measures and providing resources of personnel, technical support and requisite infrastructural facilities. We examine the structure, powers and enabling legislations and assess the ability of such an empowered unit to combat corruption in the state. A major part of this examination is done through specific case studies to illustrate its success and limitations. Furthermore, a detailed empirical examination of the assiduously collected unique official data for 13 years (2000–12) has been carried out to assess the nature and problems of investigation and prosecution of corruption cases. Such a detailed examination of real and comprehensive data provides an *in-depth* understanding of what one can term the functioning of a representative anti-corruption agency and the extent of its ability in tackling and curbing corruption effectively.

Evolution of EOW MP

Long before the anti-graft movement came into focus in India and at a time when there were still plenty of admirable, honest and committed political leaders and bureaucrats around in the 1970s, Madhya Pradesh was a pioneer state in visualizing and conceiving a single specialized agency to combat corruption and economic offences simultaneously. The police leadership proposed for a single agency on grounds that a majority of the economic offences under the Prevention of Corruption Act (PCA), 1988, other relevant sections of the IPC and other minor Acts involved similar modus operandi and set of offenders. Accordingly, it was prudent to combine the various roles performed by a single agency. BM Shukla, a former IPS officer and then advisor to the Government of MP, had earlier conceptualized a 'Special Wing' of the police under the Home Department with the avowed objective of collecting intelligence and investigating serious type of such offences against society. It was clear to the administrators that the regular police stations were not equipped and trained to handle economic offences, frauds of particular nature, concealment of wealth, evasion of government taxes and dues, etc. Consequently, the EOW combined the dual roles of investigation of economic offenses as well as of corruption crimes, the latter falling within the purview of ACB in most of the other states.

The politics of the Emergency era also played an important role in forcing the Congress government in power in MP to declare its determination to fight corruption and take more effective action against the corrupt officials. Soon, the Governor, on behalf of the government informed the Legislative Assembly (Vidhan Sabha) on February 4, 1976, the intent to establish a specialized organization to combat corruption and other economic crimes. Consequently, in May 1976, the then Chief Minister of Madhya Pradesh, Shyama Charan Shukla, envisaged a special cell to combat economic offences and trap corrupt officials through flying squads with powers to carry out on-the-spot investigations. In 1976, with the setting up of the Special Investigating Cell (SIC) under police headquarters, the journey of evolution of the current EOW began. In 1977, this Cell was declared as a police station and named: C.I.D. (EOW) and empowered to take action under certain Acts. In 1983, the nomenclature went another change and the agency was rechristened: State Bureau of Investigation of Economic Offences (SBIEO).

To ensure freedom of decision-making, as way back as in 1990, EOW was taken out of the superintendence of the Home Department/PHQ and put under the administrative control of the General Administrative Department of the Government of MP. Under this dispensation, Director General EOW reported directly to the Chief Secretary and the Chief Minister of the state. This arrangement enhanced the importance and significance of the agency both in the administration as well as before the people at large. The message was that the government was determined to combat corruption and economic crimes. By functioning directly under the Chief Minister and the Chief Secretary, the EOW DG acquired ready access to the executive heads of the government; an accessibility coveted within the large corridors of the hierarchical power system. In the bureaucratic round table of status and connections, this signaled a significant feature of anti-corruption measures.

In 2000, EOW was declared as a part of the 'General Police District' and in respect of all purposes, its senior police officers, executives and ministerial officers were ordered to follow the powers and rules, in the same manner as police officers of equivalent rank and denomination of the general police district. The DG EOW, headed by a senior IPS officer in the rank of Director General of Police (DGP)/Additional Director General of Police (Addl. DGP), was vested with the same powers as those of the IG and DG of Police, under Section 4 of the Police Act, 1861. This was an important step, for it vested equal powers to the unit to function independently and also for the prevention of corruption within public organizations. The unit had the authority to undertake surveillance, register criminal cases and investigate without seeking permission from any other unit. The nomenclature SBIEO was seen to be awkward, cumbersome and long and so it was changed back to its original name, Economic Offences Wing (EOW).

The leadership was cognizant that a good number of bureaucrats and even police officers themselves have vested interests and can influence the investigation in their or their protégé's favor. Accordingly, the government established the norm of putting a known independent, honest and committed senior officer to spearhead the EOW, thereby blocking in-house office shenanigans from obstructing investigation of corrupt officials. The high status and backing by the Chief Minister could also ensure greater operational freedom and capability to pursue even the highest offices suspected of corruption. In order to maintain judicial standards in investigating and charge sheeting of corrupt officials, a post of law officer, of the rank of an additional district judge, was also created by the state government. This legal assistance was necessary to examine cases and advise the investigating officers and the senior officers of the EOW about quality and value of evidence and proper procedures.

Thus, thanks to the MP government and a series of Chief Ministers, a powerful investigation agency, on the lines of the CBI, headed by a DGP/ Addl. DGP, with powers of investigation of both economic offences and corruption crimes against the high and mighty in the government as well as members of the public, took roots. It needs to be acknowledged that such a powerful and comparatively independent police unit could be a double-edged sword; depending on the political and administrative will and the inclination of the highest authorities in the state, it could strike in either direction. Unwarranted persecution of political rivals or lack of action against the real culprits is certainly inherent within such a system. The Vyapam case is a good example when political considerations took precedence over probity and raised doubts about the intentions and willingness of the political leaders to combat corruption. However, as far as the personal experience of one of the co-authors is concerned, fair and just investigation was not interfered during his tenure and he received the support of the highest authorities in the state.

Legal Sanctity of EOW

It is important to inform that the EOW was created through a Government Executive Order of May 1977, duly published in the Gazette. According to this notification, the state government of MP declared the CID (Economic Offences Wing) of the police, MP, Bhopal to be the police station having jurisdiction over the entire state of MP for the purposes of offences punishable under various sections of the IPC (relating to corruption and economic offences), the PCA 1988 and several other state and central laws and minor Acts. This was significant since it empowered the agency to act independently of state police organization which could change priority of its efforts to pursue specific cases.

It needs to be also mentioned here that unlike EOW, that functions on the basis of executive orders, the institution of Lokayukta in the state has been created under the 'Lokayukta Evam Up-Lokayukta Adiniyam' (the Lokayukta and Up-Lokayukta Act, 1981). It is noteworthy that the MP state government, as way back as 1981, had again showed vision and determination to curb corruption by legislating for an ombudsperson (Lokayukta) completely free from executive control. A committee comprising the Chief Justice, the Chief Minister and the Leader of the Opposition, from a panel of retired Supreme Court Judges or Chief Justices/Judges of the High Courts, selects the Lokayukta from a panel. Unlike in many other states, the Lokayukta in MP has its own investigation wing headed by a rank of DGP/Addl. DGP.

Streamlining of EOW

In order to streamline the functioning of the EOW, the state government Home ('C' Section) Department vide circular of August 1988 issued instructions regarding referring of cases to the SBIEO, now renamed as EOW. According to this circular, eight categories of cases were listed which need not be taken up by or referred to the Bureau (EOW). These exceptions included cases relating to departmental irregularities, negligent loss, minor service matters concerning reimbursement of bills, information/complaints containing vague/general allegations against public servants, cases involving forged documents like school, caste and birth certificates, ordinary/individual cases of fraud and other economic offenses that were to be dealt with by the local police/CID, while ordinary/individual complaints of bribery and misuse of official position by public servants that could be handled by the local police/Special Police Establishment (Lokayukta). These exclusions further included injudicious application of discretionary powers by public servants where mala fide was not apparent and complaints were of civil nature. The order laid down the types of cases that could be taken up by or referred to the EOW and included abuse of official position leading to heavy loss to the public exchequer and cases involving corruption/abuse of official position relating to large undertakings/projects, abuse of fiscal policies of financial institutions by private businessman and cases of exploitation of citizens by organized white collar offenders.

Accordingly, six various steps were outlined as to how the cases should be referred to the EOW by various government departments. It was made clear that all the references were to be routed through the then Home Department and now the General Administration Department (GAD) as per the executive order of April 1991. The circular went on to empower the EOW to take up offences under IPC and various minor Acts of the state. The concluding part of the circular further empowered the EOW to take up cases on its own, based on information/intelligence collected or received by its officers.

Operation of EOW

From the aforementioned circulars, the government clearly narrowed down the scope of operation of EOW to cases of large and wide spread dimensions that could not be dealt with by the local police or the CID. It is pertinent to note that the CBI and various other state vigilance and anti-corruption agencies also follow the same procedure. From the Government Circular of 1988, it was made clear that the EOW:

1. Can take up cases referred to it by various departments through the GAD.
2. Can take up cases based on information and/or complaints received from the public at large.
3. Collect its own intelligence for enquiries and investigations and registration of a case if need be.

In the light of foregoing paragraphs, following processes took root.

Cases from GAD

With regard to cases referred by the government departments, it was stipulated that the cases could be referred to the EOW only through the GAD with a self-contained note with/without any documents. It was also directed that once the EOW took up the enquiry/investigation, the departments must cooperate and provide the necessary documents.

This made it imperative upon the EOW to conduct a *preliminary inquiry* (PE) based upon the GAD reference and collect relevant documents from the concerned departments or register an FIR if a criminal case was made out. The process was to ensure that solely based on the collected evidence a conclusion must be drawn if prima facie case was made out as per EOW's charter. Depending on the content of the reference and various parameters within which the EOW was expected to operate, EOW headquarters would need to take a final decision whether: a PE or an FIR was to be registered. It is significant to remember that a PE may not lead to full investigation while an FIR, according to Section 154 CrPC initiates a formal investigation of a criminal act. The following discourse also highlights the elaborate steps and bureaucratic processes when dealing with issues of corruption. As we will discuss later, these processes invariably delay the proceedings and adversely affect combating corruption. Of course, these steps are necessary to prevent abuse of authority by the state functionaries and protect the rights of the individuals. However, the lesson is important—that combating corruption is not a quick fix mechanism. All institutions need to follow the due process even if it is time consuming and aids the offender.

Following two case studies illustrate as to when the EOW registers a PE or an FIR:

Case study to show registration of PE on GAD reference

In July 2011, the GAD forwarded a brief to the EOW in which it was alleged that the officials of the Department of Tribal Welfare embezzled state funds meant for the development of tribal and backward classes worth several crores. Some documents were attached with the briefs. On examination of the brief, a PE was registered in July 2011 since complete and entire facts of the case were not clear from the attached documents. Subsequently, on the basis of evidence collected in the PE, an FIR was lodged in December 2011.

Case study to show registration of an FIR on a complaint received from GAD

In September 2012, the EOW received a brief from the government in which it was alleged that an executive engineer of the Irrigation Department had cleared bills of construction works that were not carried out. The irregularities reported were to the tune of more than ₹ 7 crores. The brief was accompanied by a complete set of supporting documents. On examination of these documents, it was clear that a prima facie case was made out. Hence, the EOW registered an FIR in December 2012 straight away to begin criminal investigation against the engineer.

The same principles of ample facts/evidence/supporting documents, as given in above case studies, applied to complaints from the public, non-governmental institutions as well as intelligence received or collected by EOW on its own. Following scenarios indicate the action to be taken by the EOW when a complaint is received from some other source than the GAD:

1. If the complaint contains specific allegations, well supported by documents where prima facie case is made out, FIR was registered.

   Case study: In November 2011, the Managing Director of the Cooperative Bank of MP presented a complaint to the EOW alleging that some officials of bank had conspired to obtain a loan of thousands of crores from an overseas agency without due permission of the government and the Reserve Bank of India (RBI). A guarantee on behalf of the bank to return the sum at zero percent interest rate was furnished by the conspirators to the private overseas financiers. The complaint was accompanied by supporting documents and prima facie a cognizable case was made out. Consequently, an FIR was lodged on the same day and taken up for investigation.

2. If the contents of the complaint are not so specific and some documents have been provided, yet large numbers of relevant documents are still to be procured, a PE is registered.

   Case study: In a complaint received from a member of the public from the city of Indore, it was alleged that an officer of the commercial tax department had amassed movable and immovable property disproportionate to his income. The allegations were specific but necessary supporting documents were not furnished. Therefore, a PE was registered in December 2009.

3. However, if a complaint is vague and general in nature and hits any of the eight exceptions specified in Para 3.1 of the 1988 circular, it would be referred to the concerned department for necessary departmental action, relevant police agency, police station, SP of a district, CID or SPE (Lokayukta) as the case may be. For example, cases relating to criminal offences but not related to the EOW Charter, economic offences involving two members of the public were such cases that were not to be taken up by the Wing as laid out in the 1988 circular.

   Case study: In June 2006, a member of the public presented a complaint to the EOW alleging that a forest guard posted in the Raisen district had resorted to purchase and sale of immovable property without the due permission from the Forest Department. The matter was enquired into by the EOW and it was found that the forest guard had indeed not obtained due permission to purchase and sell a dwelling house situated in Katni, although the transaction was valid. The allegations pertained to the violation of service rules and therefore did not require action from the EOW. Consequently, the case was referred to the forest department to take appropriate departmental action against the errant forest guard.

4. If allegations are such that the comments of the concerned department are required regarding the actual action taken by it, the cases are referred for enquiry to the department or sent to the concerned agency. In trivial, vague and general complaints, the inquiry is referred to the relevant department. Rarely is the complaint filed at the examination stage in the EOW headquarter. A decision regarding the registration of FIR or PE or complaint or its filing is taken by the EOW on the basis of the report received and its further scrutiny from the evidence point of view.

Case study: In September 2011, the members of a housing society belonging to the municipal corporation in Ujjain presented a complaint to the EOW regarding illegal sale and diversion of land of a housing society in contravention of the rules laid down by the District Administration and Town and Country Planning Department. The complaint required comments from the local administration regarding action taken by them. Hence, it was forwarded for enquiry to the Commissioner, Ujjain Division in April 2012. The Commissioner submitted a report in July 2012 in which it was found that misappropriation of the mentioned society's land and money had occurred, with regard to the said diversion. Hence, the report further merited enquiries at the ground level and for collection of specific documents. Based on the Commissioner's report a PE was registered in July 2012 and taken up for enquiry. Subsequently, based on inquiries and evidence collected, an FIR was registered in April 2013.

5. Complaints which are of great magnitude and affect public interest and yet contain no documents, though the allegations are specific and not roving in nature are inquired into by the EOW.

Case study: In August 2013, the EOW received a letter from the DGM, of SEBI, Indore through which the EOW was informed that 10 private companies located at Bhopal, Indore, Jabalpur, Betul and Katni were accepting unauthorized investments from the public at large. It was also made clear in the letter that the investments accepted by the 10 companies were unauthorized. On the basis of the above letter, a complaint was registered in October 2013 and was taken up for enquiry.

6. On completion of such a PE and depending on the evidence gathered, EOW may either register an FIR directly or file the complaint for lack of substantiation depending on the content and the extent to which criminality is being made out.

Case study: In March 2011, a member of the public presented to the EOW a complaint alleging that a builder/promoter in Bhopal was illegally selling plots of land to people without requisite permissions from the District Administration, the Town and Country Planning, etc. and causing loss to exchequer. A complaint was registered in March 2011 and was taken up for enquiry. On the basis of enquiry conducted by the EOW a case of fraud, forgery and misuse of official position was clearly made out. Subsequently, an FIR was registered in July 2011.

Legal Sanctity of PE

Apart from this established procedure, the Supreme Court has also upheld the practice of enquiry before registration of an FIR in several cases pertaining to public servants. The following observation of the Supreme Court in the case of *P Sirajuddin etc. vs. State of Madras* in its judgment dated March 9, 1970 is relevant and often quoted in support of the practice of conducting enquiries before the registration of FIR as stipulated under section 154 CrPC:

> Before a public servant, whatever be his status, is publicly charged with acts, of dishonesty which amount to serious misdemeanor of misconduct of the type alleged in this case and a first information is lodged against him, there must be some suitable preliminary enquiry into the allegations by a *responsible* officer. (Italics is our emphasis)

Further,

> The lodging of such a report against a person, specially one who like

the appellant, occupied a top position in a department, even if baseless, would do incalculable harm not only to the officer in particular but to the department he belonged to, in general. If the government had set up a vigilance and anti-corruption department, as was done in the state of Madras, and the said department was entrusted with enquiries of this kind, no exception can be taken to an enquiry by officers of this department but any such enquiry must proceed in a fair and reasonable manner.

The enquiring officer must not act under any preconceived idea of guilt of the person whose conduct was being enquired into or pursue the enquiry in such a manner as to lead to an inference that he was bent upon securing the conviction of the said person by adopting measures which are of doubtful validity or sanction. The means adopted must be impeccable.

In ordinary departmental proceedings against a government servant charged with delinquency, the normal practice before the issue of a charge sheet is for someone in authority to take down statements of persons involved in the matter and to examine documents which have a bearing on the issue involved. It is only thereafter that a charge sheet is submitted and a full-scale enquiry is launched.

When the enquiry is to be held for the purpose of finding out whether criminal proceedings are to be resorted to, the scope thereof must be limited to the examination of persons who have knowledge of the affairs of the delinquent officer and documents bearing on the same to find out whether there is prima facie evidence of guilt of the officer. Thereafter the ordinary law of the land must take its course and further inquiry be proceeded with in terms of the Code of Criminal Procedure by lodging a First Information Report.

At present, the enactment of the Lokpal and Lokayuktas Act, 2013, has laid to rest any dispute over the legal sanctity of a PE. The following quote from the Act is self-explanatory:

Chapter VII: Procedure in Respect of Preliminary Inquiry and Investigation

20. (1) The Lokpal on receipt of a complaint, if it decides to proceed further, may order—

(a) preliminary inquiry against any public servant by its Inquiry Wing or any agency (including the Delhi Special Police Establishment) to ascertain whether there exists a prima facie case for proceeding in the matter; or

(b) investigation by any agency (including the Delhi Special Police Establishment) when there exists a prima facie case: …

We wish to reiterate that the functioning of any anti-corruption agency requires various forms of empowerment to enable it to function effectively. We will discuss next some important steps of empowerment that were carried out in MP.

EOW MP: An Empowered Agency

EOW is at present an independent investigation agency, which can take up cases on its own or those referred by the state government as also those received from people at large. DG EOW has been empowered by the state government to be the final authority in all decisions relating to the verification and registration of complaints/FIR as also investigation and disposal of cases after an internal process involving examination of the case by EOW IGs and the Law Officer. Unlike other anti-corruption agencies, the permission of the government is not required to register FIRs and investigate the complaints. However, the charge sheet of senior levels of political and bureaucratic hierarchy require a formal prosecution sanction from the government. The DG EOW also has to seek prosecution sanction against public servants, of any rank, facing corruption charges before presenting the charge sheet in the court.

The EOW has been empowered in terms of personnel too. The agency functions through five investigating units, located in Bhopal, Indore, Gwalior, Jabalpur and Rewa, each headed by a Superintendent of Police rank officer with requisite number of investigation officers. All sub-units function from newly built buildings, generously funded by the government to provide modern facilities and improve working conditions of subordinate officers. This is a significant issue for, in most states, the subordinate field offices are generally neglected which in turn affect the effectiveness of operations. These units in MP have been provided with requisite manpower, technical equipment, transport, as well as a portable cyber forensic kit, to investigate various kinds of economic and corruption crimes and collect digital leads/evidence.

In keeping with the provisions of the *United Nations Convention against Corruption (Article 17, UNCAC)*, the state government also took a large number of initiatives to empower the EOW, the prosecuting agency and the judicial system to effectively combat corruption and economic offences. A few significant steps were the new laws conferring greater power to the investigating agencies in a wide array of circumstances. In particular, confiscation of property derived from ill-gotten gains was a prominent feature of laws enacted in the state of MP.

Enabling Legislations

The MP Special Courts Act, 2012 (Vishesh Nyaylaya Adhiniyam, 2012)

One of the most progressive and effective steps taken by the Government of MP in combating corruption in the state was the enactment of the Madhya Pradesh Special Courts Act, 2011 that provides for 'freezing, seizure and confiscation of property', derived from proceeds of corruption crimes, within six months, for cases pending investigation or trial. Except for a couple of other states, MP has been the pioneer in legislating such a deterrent law in keeping with Article 31 of the UNCAC.

This law came into force on February 22, 2012. The government showed equal alacrity and determination to curb corruption effectively by creating special courts in the four major cities of the state including Bhopal, Indore, Gwalior and Jabalpur, in double-quick time, within a couple of months. The EOW, on its part, too, on priority investigated nine cases of disproportionate assets under the PCA, 1988, obtained approval of the government and put them up before these special courts: Bhopal (two cases), Indore (two cases), Gwalior (three cases) and Jabalpur (two cases). Consequently, between this period of February 2012 to October 2013, the special courts ordered confiscation of the disproportionate assets in all the nine cases amounting to a staggering sum of ₹ 7 crores. This speedy investigation, prosecution, trial and forfeiture of disproportionate assets boosted the anti-corruption efforts of the nascent agency to a great extent.

MP Vinirdisht Bhrashta Nivaran Adhiniyam, 1982

This Act provides for punishment in cases of corruption in public works, such as violation of contract, lack of supervision by an officer in charge, preparing of false muster rolls, submission of manipulated tenders, etc. The onus of burden of proof has also been placed upon the supervisory officers of the concerned departments for the acts of commission or omission that lead to financial loss to the government and public exchequer, and to prove that such acts or omissions are *not* acts or omissions of willful corruption.

MP Niveshakon ke Hiton ke Sanrakshan Adhiniyam, 2003 (Protection of Interests of Investors Act)

This is an Act to protect the deposits made by the public in financial establishments and matters connected therewith or incidental thereto. A number of crimes committed through the so-called Chit Funds which were disguised ponzi schemes are specifically covered under this Act and meant to protect the general public making investments in good faith. EOW is not empowered under this Act and this law has been quoted only for the purpose of showing the overall anti-corruption efforts of the state government.

The main objective of this act is to safeguard the interests of the investors of the state making investment in different private financial institutions or finance companies.

1. The act provides for attachment of property of financial establishments, which intend to defraud the depositors.

2. As per the act when the competent authority is satisfied that a financial establishment is not likely to return the deposits, then in order to protect the interest of the depositors, the competent authority can pass an order forfeiting the money or attaching other property alleged to have been procured through depositors. If such money or other properties are not available for attachment or not sufficient for repayment of depositors then the property of the promoters, partners, directors, managers or members of the financial establishment can be attached.

3. The state government may, by notification, appoint any authority not below the rank of a Collector as competent authority.

4. In MP, the state government has appointed the District Collector as the competent authority.

    Case study: A company known as the Dairy and Allied Businesses accepted deposits from the general public in the Chambal Division of MP in the year 2010. The company accepted deposits as term deposits for the periods ranging from a month up to 10 years. The company promised the investors to allot residential and agricultural land in lieu of the term deposits. The company had no registration as an NBFC with the RBI and it was seen to be violating the Companies Act 1956. Upon the receipt of a complaint against the Company, the EOW enquired into the case and forwarded its findings to the Collector of Gwalior (competent authority) in the year 2010 to take action under Madhya Pradesh Niveshakon ke Hiton ke Sanrakshan Adhiniyam (2003). In December 2010, the Collector presented the case before the Judicial Court in Gwalior, leading to the freezing of the bank accounts of the company. The whole process prevented the company from misappropriating depositors' monies and put an end to their illicit activity.

MP Public Services Guarantee Act/Lok Seva Adhiniyam, 2010

Though, this Act has little to do with the charter of EOW, it has been cited here to show the overall efforts of the government to prevent corruption in providing essential services. This law has the laudable objective of providing and ensuring time bound services to the public, failure of which would result in payment of fines by the concerned public servant. Services *guaranteed* under the Act included: birth certificate, caste certificate, domicile certificate, tap water supply connection, *khasra* copies and death certificate. Efforts are afoot to bring more and more services within the ambit of this Act.

Setting Up of Special Courts

The state government U/S 3 of the Prevention PCA, 1988 has appointed the first Additional Session Judge in each of the 51 districts of MP as the judge of a special court for expeditious trial of cases under the PCA, 1988 and corruption/economic crimes under the IPC and other Acts in the charter of the EOW. Through this simple step, the objective of the state government was to make the courts readily available for the EOW cases to expedite trials, without having to go through the lengthy process of creating special courts.

Appointment of Special Public Prosecutors in District Special Courts

In another effort to facilitate a speedy trial, to virtually provide 'justice at door steps' and simplify problems of jurisdiction of judicial courts, the state government in 2011 appointed the District Prosecution Officers (DPOs)/ Deputy Prosecution Officers of each of the 51 districts of MP to plead and conduct the trials on behalf of the EOW in the District Special Courts. Qualitative improvement in presentation of cases by the Prosecution Officers resulted in convictions in few important cases in the years 2012 and 2013. The following two cases are worth mentioning that resulted in convictions due to good pleading by the special public prosecutors:

1. In the case of a leading public-sector bank, involving embezzlement of funds to the tune of ₹ 50 crores, the Jabalpur District Special Court, within a year, in August 2012, convicted the 10 accused in the case with imprisonments in the range of five to eight years and a fine starting from ₹ 5 lakhs up to ₹ 60 lakhs.

2. In another prominent case, due to the availability of a designated prosecutor, an All India Service lady officer was convicted by the Mandla District Special Court for a period of five years and fine of ₹ 45 lakhs in a corruption case.

However, since the DPOs hold only the additional charge of prosecuting EOW cases and their main function is to plead the large number of district police cases, this provision has not worked so well in a majority of cases as was expected. According to the collated statistics from 2001 to 2012, unfortunately, the average time taken to bring a trial to its conclusion was eight years.

Special Prosecutors for High Courts/Supreme Court

Similarly, in order to ensure the proper pleading of cases in the High Courts and Supreme Court the state government, on the recommendations of the EOW, appoints special prosecutors from a panel of eminent advocates in all the three High Courts of MP at Jabalpur, Indore and Gwalior. The appointment of such senior advocates/prosecutors has improved the rate of success/convictions in cases of EOW before the High Courts. For example, in a case concerning a housing society situated at an exclusive and expensive locality at Bhopal, EOW filed the charge sheet against the main accused and others in the district court. The main accused approached the High Court to quash the FIR in the said case on August 22, 2013. As a result of outstanding pleading of the case conducted by the special prosecutor at Jabalpur, the case of the accused was dismissed by the High Court in merely four days on August 26, 2013.

Provision Relating to Public Documents

The state government directed in 1993 all the departments to furnish relevant documents to the EOW for investigation and enquiries whenever the records were summoned. Most of the corruption cases relating to public officials involve large number of official documents and department files/note sheets where specific decisions are noted and recorded. For example, there may be an order to purchase an item without following the established procedures; or to release public funds without authorization and proper account keeping. These documents form the basis of proving the guilt or complicity of the suspect official. However, procuring these documents to help investigate or provide evidence in the court could be hampered by the suspected corrupt officials under investigation who could use their administrative network to delay and hinder the procurement of these documents. The requests/summons to procure these documents now have the backing of the government. This has naturally helped investigators and empowered the EOW to procure the relevant documents to proceed against the corrupt officials and their collaborators in other departments.

Prosecution Sanction

To facilitate the speedy grant of prosecution sanction, the state government, through an executive order in 1998, made the Law Ministry, the Nodal Ministry to provide prosecution sanction of public servants being charge sheeted under section 197 of the IPC and section 19 of the PCA 1988. The mechanism prescribed is that the Law Ministry will decide on the grant of prosecution sanction request by the EOW after seeking the comments of the concerned department and examining them in the light of the materials and evidence furnished by the agency. This provision has removed the inconvenience of chasing various departments and subsequent delay in obtaining prosecution sanctions.

Suspension of Charge-Sheeted Officials

Again, as early as 1985, through an executive order, the state government has made mandatory for all departments to suspend their employee(s) against whom a charge sheet has been filed in the court by the EOW. This has taken care of the absurd situation where a connected or influential official could continue functioning in his capacity despite the initiation of prosecution in a special court. In many cases, such corrupt officials could/would even continue in the same offices where they had misused their authority to indulge in corrupt practices. Clearly, they would also be in a position to frustrate the investigation or prosecution by virtue of the access they continued to enjoy by being in the same office. Despite the absurdity of one government agency launching prosecution and another shielding the public servant, these situations were occurring regularly and making a mockery of anti-corruption measures. Such a change in policy has paid dividends by ensuring that the prosecution of a corrupt official can now proceed without hindrance and interference of the accused employee(s).

Disciplinary Action against Accused Public Servant

It has been made mandatory by the state government by a decree in 1989 to initiate departmental action when a report of misconduct or irregularity has been forwarded by the EOW to the concerned department. This is in addition to the suspension and launch of prosecution. The idea is to ensure that an official found indulging in corruption and being prosecuted for his criminality should also be punished administratively as per the service and conduct rules. This measure helps to ensure that the corrupt official, even if not convicted in a court of law, is at least punished administratively and loses either her/his job or promotion or an increment in the departmental inquiry initiated against her/him. Thus, adverse and deterrent consequences of corruption have been enhanced by such administrative measures.

Empowerment through Appointment of Experts

Well aware of the necessity of experts to assist in investigation of corruption and economic crimes, the state government also empowered the EOW to hire them with approval from the GAD. The GAD order dated January 30, 2006 has laid down guiding principles for appointing of experts in broadly two categories:

1. Experts in government departments, public-sector undertakings, government engineering colleges, retired officers of PWD/Irrigation, nationalized banks cooperative and panchayat departments as also MP State Electricity Board.

2. Experts in various fields with minimum eight years of experience in the relevant area. These include experts such as chartered accountants, tax advisors/auditors, government or income tax department appointed experts in evaluation of properties, computer software experts with a computer degree or Masters in Engineering as also law experts.

All these appointments are made by the GAD on recommendations of the EOW as per the case requirements.

Examples of appointment of experts

1. In order to head the technical wing and cyber forensic lab, on the recommendations of EOW, in April 2012 the general administration department of the state government appointed a Deputy General Manager (DGM) of the Telecom Department of the Government of India as Director Technical/ System Analyst in the EOW. This appointment has facilitated setting up of the cyber forensic lab with all its hardware and software. Due to the technical expertise of the officer, EOW now possesses a state of the art functional cyber lab, which has been extremely useful in providing leads for investigation, gathering evidence and corroborating gathered evidence from the analysis of seized computers, laptops, mobile phones and other IT equipments.

   Case study: In a case registered on July 20, 2012 of an accused opening a savings bank account and taking loan from the bank on the basis of forged documents, the hard disk and pen drives seized from the possession of accused were forwarded to the Director Technical for Cyber Analysis. The examination confirmed that the accused had misused the proof of residence of a person and had made it his own residential address on his computer. The analysis also revealed that the accused created a forged demand draft on the computer. Further investigation revealed that the accused had created a large number of forged insurance policies and mark sheets of various persons by substituting the photos and names of clients over the photos and names of the original certificate holders. On the basis of the vital evidences provided by the Director Technical, a charge sheet was presented in the court in May 2013 with concrete digital evidence.

2. Similarly, to facilitate investigations and obtain expert opinion in various engineering departments including the PWD, Public Health Engineering (PHE), and Irrigation, a retired Superintendent Engineer of PHE was appointed in the EOW by the government. The Director Engineering has provided valuable advice on complex technicalities of various cases relating to different engineering departments.

Case study: In August 2009, a member of the public from Gwalior presented a complaint to the EOW alleging that the Superintending Engineer, the assistant engineer of the PWD and others misused their official position and caused financial loss to the exchequer in the construction of a river bridge. The technical examination of the case by the Director Engineering revealed that the errant Superintending Engineer, the Assistant Engineer and others did not provide the necessary base level measurements to the contractor in the process of construction of a river bridge in the district of Ashok Nagar. As a result, the construction of the bridge was stalled. Yet the errant engineers disbursed a sum of nearly ₹ 5 lakhs to the contractor. On the basis of technical examination of the case carried out by the retired Superintendent Engineer, an FIR was registered and taken up for investigation in June 2013.

With regard to the appointment of experts in fields other than the government departments as envisaged in Para 1 (b) above, a large number of experts have been made available to the field units to assist the officers in their enquiries/investigations as per the case requirements. **Case study:** In a case of disproportionate assets by a Superintending Engineer (SE) of the Madhya Pradesh Electricity Board (MPEB) posted at the Rajgarh District in MP, the EOW enlisted the services of an experienced Chartered Accountant (CA) to look into the earnings and expenses of the accused in November 2012. The CA helped the investigator in estimating the total movable and immovable properties acquired by the accused SE. On the basis of findings, a case of confiscation of property of the accused SE was presented in court in April 2012. In March 2013, the court ordered confiscation of the properties worth ₹ 1.01 crores of the accused SE. The CA was instrumental in bringing about this quick success.

Empowerment through Resources

Infrastructure

In another landmark step to bolster the infrastructural set-up of the EOW to effectively combat corruption, the state government sanctioned ₹ 7.5 crores for a new fully furnished state of the art modern glass building for the EOW in 2009. The MP government sanctioned another ₹ 4.5 crores for establishing a modern cyber forensic laboratory on the lines of the CBI Lab. State governments are generally cash strapped and reluctant to sanction funds for basic infrastructure. In particular, the police station buildings, housing for personnel and even many newly created units within the police organization remain starved for funds and lack basic amenities. The MP government is to be credited here since it deemed it necessary to empower and equip the EOW and thereby displayed its commitment to its objectives of combating corruption effectively.

Personnel

As part of the same package and the political will to tackle corruption, the government also sanctioned 148 new posts of various ranks for the four new units: investigation, anti-corruption, economic intelligence and technical support unit.

Impact

The above detailed description of organizational and administrative resources suggests strong efforts by the government to empower investigative and prosecution wings of this unit. Over the decades, the MP government, *irrespective* of the political party in power, displayed strong determination to deal with corruption. Yet these efforts and political support appear to have produced only limited results. While many senior administrators, including All India Service officers and current/former Ministers/MLAs were investigated and prosecuted, these cases did not provide the requisite and desirable deterrence to corrupt practices. In the following section, we analyze the data about investigation and prosecution to measure the performance of this specialized anti-corruption wing of the MP government

Corruption by Public Servants Related to Public Work Projects

1. Purchase: Public servants/officials causing loss to the exchequer by buying goods/services for the government at costs exceptionally higher than the actual prices.

2. Sale: Public servants/officials causing loss to the exchequer by selling goods/services of the government at costs exceptionally lower than the actual prices.

3. Misuse of official position: Officials misusing their official powers to provide undue favors to contractors like giving grants for big construction or service contracts for personal gains, thereby causing loss to the exchequer.

4. Deliberate non-performance: Officials deliberately not performing their official duties (acts of omission) in order to overlook illegal activities. For example, not stopping a company from illegally mining excessively more than the authorized amount or turning a blind eye to illegal mining without permits or felling of forest trees, etc. This causes huge losses to the exchequer in terms of royalties.

5. Manipulation of tenders: A very common form of crime, this entails conspiracy with a particular contractor or supplier in order to grant him a contract and in the process, receive huge kickbacks.

6. Seeking bribes/gratifications: An official forcing a beneficiary or a claimant to pay bribes in order to get the work done. For example, an officer in charge of giving permission for construction of a commercial building does not issue the obligatory permission until he has received a bribe. Bribes can be voluntarily given and received as facilitation or speed money or favoring one over the other to make personal gains at the cost of the government.

7. Embezzlement: It is another commonly occurring economic/corruption

crime in which public officials siphon off public money or government properties for their own gains.

8. Falsification of records: Public officials conspiring to falsify official records to favor someone for some gain, causing loss to the rightful claimant. For example, entering the name of the co-conspirator in land records instead of the rightful owner.

9. Disproportionate Assets: Public officials amassing wealth and properties several times more than their legal income, that is, assets disproportionate to known sources of income.

10. Dispensation of undue loans/grants: Public officials granting loans grants/deposits/insurance payments to parties which do not qualify for these benefits. For example, providing compensation for loss of crops en masse to hundreds and thousands of recipients who are not the intended beneficiaries.

11. Providing benefits of welfare schemes to non-deserving: Public officials providing monetary benefits or benefits in kind to persons who do not deserve these benefits. For example, providing good quality seeds of a cash crop for personal gains, free of cost to traders and businessman and not to the farmers for whom they have been sanctioned.

Analysis of EOW Statistics: 2000–12 (13 years)

In the previous pages, it has been outlined in great detail, how the EOW of MP is a unique institution and the extent to which the Wing was empowered by several successive governments, both in terms of human, material and technical resources as well as legislative and administrative orders and circulars. During the tenure of one of the authors as the chief of the EOW for around three years (2011–13), focus upon professional investigation and prosecution helped transform the agency into an efficient and professional organization that combated corruption with determination. The co-author's experience suggests that this anti-corruption agency was not only fully equipped and empowered but also overtly supported by the government. The functioning of the agency was the siren call about the determination of the government to deal with corruption seriously. However, a detailed analysis and examination of the EOW statistics helps to understand to what extent actually the Wing has succeeded in tackling corruption and related economic offences. As mentioned previously, the objective of this analysis is to assess the ability of a fully functional and empowered police agency to deal with corruption. For this purpose, crime statistics pertaining to corruption and economic crimes of 13 years from the year 2000 to 2012 have been analyzed and examined thread bare to arrive at objective inferences. These statistics and their analysis can be safely considered as representative of any other anti-corruption agency in India, including the CBI. It is noteworthy to point out here that such large data with so many parameters *have never been compiled and analyzed* before by any anti-corruption agency of India. Moreover, compilation of such statistics requires extensive professional knowledge about the system of record keeping followed in various public offices. It will be almost impossible for any non-police officer unfamiliar with the police organization and its functions to determine relevant data and compile it into a meaningful format.

Analysis of the statistics, clearly shows that the EOW peaked in its professional efficiency during this period of 2010–12. The EOW was at its professional best in terms of the disposal of cases and charge sheets put up between 2010–12 as evident from the following data analysis:

FIRs Registered (2010–12)

2010	2011	2012	Percentage increase
33	40	97	294% from 2010 to 2012
Charge Sheets Put Up in Court (2010–12)			
34	34	51	150% from 2010 to 2012

Thus, while in 2010, the number of FIRs lodged was 33, after completion of preliminary enquiries, highest as compared to the preceding years, the number of FIRs in 2011 increased to 40. Thereafter, the number of cases registered increased to more than two and half times from 40 to 97 cases in 2012. Similarly, EOW performed excellently in charge sheeting of cases in trial courts. While the number of charge sheets put up in the courts remained static at 34 in 2010 and 2011, the figure significantly rose to 51, a jump of one and a half time, that is, 150 per cent.

No doubt, while the EOW's strength and resources increased, the receipt of number of cases, simultaneously, too exceeded far more in relation to the augmentation of resources. For instance, data suggests that from mere 459 cases handled in 2000 (including cases carried over, registered in the year and cases transferred to the EOW), the number rose to 1,669 by 2012, a 360 per cent increase while the corresponding increase in number of investigating officers was around 175 per cent (from 40 to 70) over this period (Table 5.1).

Explanation of Data Compiled from EOW

The EOW data has been compiled into 4 Tables:
* Table 5.1 Total Number of Cases (RC + PE + Complaint) Registered and Disposed in the EOW: 2000–12, followed by an analysis of this data below the table.

This Table is broken up into its composite parts of RC, PE and Complaint data as shown below:

* Table 5.2 Number of Complaints Registered and Disposed in the EOW: 2000–12, followed by an analysis of this data below the table.
* Table 5.3 Number of PEs Registered and Disposed in the EOW: 2000–12, followed by an analysis of this data below the table.
* Table 5.4 Number of RCs registered and disposed in the EOW: 2000–12, followed by an analysis of this data below the table.

The above four tables may be seen below:

Table 5.1 Total Number of Cases (RC + PE + Comp.) Registered and Disposed in the EOW: 2000–12

Sl. No.	Year	A	B	C	D	E	F	G	H	I	J	K
1	2000	229	109	-	338	94	244	27.81%	40	8	2.35	5.11
2	2001	244	71	-	315	67	248	21.27%	35	9	1.91	6.27
3	2002	248	97	-	345	133	212	38.55%	22	16	6.05	1.98
4	2003	212	121	-	333	102	231	30.63%	33	10	3.09	3.88
5	2004	231	126	1	358	124	234	34.64%	39	9	3.18	3.77
6	2005	234	240	2	476	176	300	36.97%	36	13	4.89	2.45
7	2006	300	137	0	437	113	324	25.86%	32	14	3.53	3.40
8	2007	324	180	0	504	104	400	20.63%	33	15	3.15	3.81

Sl. No.	Year	A	B	C	D	E	F	G	H	I	J	K
9	2008	400	418	-	822	215	607	26.16%	37	22	5.81	2.07
10	2009	607	524	-	1,131	244	887	21.57%	35	32.	6.97	1.72
11	2010	887	542	4	1,433	325	1,108	22.68%	37	39	8.78	1.37
12	2011	1,109	352	-	1,461	326	1,135	22.31%	70	21	4.66	2.58
13	2012	1,135	475	-	1,610	404	1,206	25.09%	70	23	5.77	2.08
Total		6,160	3,392	11	9,563	2,427	7,136	25.38% or 25%	40 (Avg.)	18 (Avg.)	5 (Avg.)	3 (Avg.)

Calculations and Analysis

A. Number of cases carried forward since previous year (from 2000 to 2012) = 6160

B. Number of cases registered = 3,392

C. Number of cases received by transfer or under re-investigation, etc. = 11

D. Number of cases for disposal (A + B + C) = 6,160 + 3,392 + 11 = 9,563

E. Number of disposal of cases per year = 2,427

F. Number of cases pending at the end of the year (D - E) = 9,563 - 2,427 = 7,136

G. Percentage of disposal of cases (E ÷ D x 100) = 2,427 ÷ 9,563 x 100 = 25.38 = 25%. Hence percentage of cases pending = 75

H. Average no. of IOs per year = 519 ÷ 13 = 39.9 = 40 [No. of IOs in EOW ranged from min. of 22 to max. 70 between 2000 and 2012]

I. Average. no. of cases per IO per year (D ÷ 13) = 9,563 ÷ 13 = 736 ÷ 40 (Avg. no. of IOs) = 18

J. Average disposal of cases by each IO per year (E ÷ 13) = 187 ÷ 40 (Avg. no. of IOs) = 4.67 = 5

K. Average No. of Months taken in disposal of one case (12 ÷ j) = 40.49 ÷ 13 = 3.11 = 3 (in months) [Disposal time ranged from min. of 1.37 months to max. of 6.27 months]

Table 5.2 Number of Complaints Registered and Disposed in the EOW: 2000–12

Sr. No.	Year	A	B	C	D_1	D_2	D_3	D	E	F	G	H	I	J
1	2000	59	60	119	1	2	41	44	75	36.97%	40	2.98	1.1	10.9
2	2001	75	39	114	7	1	26	34	80	29.82%	35	3.26	0.97	12.4
3	2002	80	69	149	8	1	79	88	61	59.06%	22	6.77	4.00	3.0

Sr. No.	Year	A	B	C	D_1	D_2	D_3	D	E	F	G	H	I	J
4	2003	61	65	126	4	6	41	51	75	40.48%	33	3.82	1.55	7.8
5	2004	75	49	124	4	4	67	75	49	60.48%	39	3.18	1.92	6.2
6	2005	49	123	172	6	13	86	105	67	61.05%	36	4.78	2.92	4.1
7	2006	67	108	175	3	2	41	46	129	26.29%	32	5.47	1.44	8.3
8	2007	129	156	285	1	7	59	67	218	23.51%	33	8.64	2.03	5.9
9	2008	218	342	560	16	8	114	138	422	24.64%	37	15.14	3.73	3.2
10	2009	422	446	868	16	3	168	187	681	21.54%	35	24.80	5.34	2.2
11	2010	681	491	1172	22	9	214	245	927	20.90%	37	31.68	6.62	1.8
12	2011	927	298	1225	23	2	242	267	958	21.80%	70	17.50	3.81	3.1
13	2012	958	357	1315	61	11	247	319	996	24.26%	70	18.79	4.56	2.6
Total		3,801	2,603	6,404	172	69	1,425	1,666	4,738	26%	40 (Avg.)	12 (Avg.)	3 (Avg.)	5.5 (Avg.)

Calculations

A. Complaints carried forward since previous year (from 2000 to 2012) = 3,801

B. Complaints registered in the year = 2,603

C. Total Complaints (A + B) = 6,404

D. Total disposal of Complaints (D1 + D2 + D3) = 172 + 69 + 1,425 = 1,666

    D_1. F.I.R = 172

    D_2. P.E. = 69

    D_3. Complaints = 1425

E. Pending at the end of the year (C - D) = 6404 – 1666 = 4738

F. % of disposal with respect to total (D ÷ C x 100) = 1,666 ÷ 6,404 x 100 = 26%

G. Average no. of IOs in EOW = 519 ÷ 13 = 39.9 = 40

H. Average no. of Complaints per IO per year (C ÷ G) = 146.81 ÷ 13 = 12

I. Average disposal of Complaints by IO per year (D ÷ G) = 40.02 ÷ 13 = 3

J. Average no. of months taken in disposal of one Complaint (12 ÷ J) = 71.1 ÷ 13 = 5.5 (in months)

Table 5.3 Number of PEs Registered and Disposed
in the EOW: 2000–12

Sr. No.	Year	A	B	C	D_1	D_2	D_3	D	E	F	G	H	I	J
1	2000	39	20	59	4	6	14	24	35	40.68%	40	1.48	0.6	20
2	2001	35	13	48	3	11	-	14	34	29.17%	35	1.37	0.4	30
3	2002	34	11	45	4	15	-	19	26	42.22%	22	2.05	0.86	14
4	2003	26	27	53	11	8	-	19	34	35.84%	33	1.61	0.57	21.1
5	2004	34	42	76	11	15	1	27	49	35.53%	39	1.95	0.69	17.4
6	2005	49	95	144	7	30	3	40	104	27.78%	36	4	1.11	10.8
7	2006	104	11	115	10	23	-	33	82	28.70%	32	3.6	1.03	11.7
8	2007	82	17	99	4	16	-	20	79	20.20%	33	3	0.6	20
9	2008	79	44	123	7	22	-	29	94	23.58%	37	3.32	0.78	15.4
10	2009	94	45	139	8	27	-	35	104	25.18%	35	3.97	1	12
11	2010	104	18	122	7	32	7	46	76	37.70%	37	3.29	1.24	9.7
12	2011	77	14	91	6	18	1	25	66	27.47%	70	1.3	0.35	34.3
13	2012	66	21	87	20	11	3	34	53	39.08%	70	1.24	0.49	24.5
Total		823	378	1,201	102	234	29	365	836	30%	40 (Avg.)	2 (Avg.)	1 (Avg.)	18 (Avg.)

Calculations

A. PE carried on since previous year (from 2000 to 2012) = 823
B. PE registered in the year = 378
C. Total PEs (A + B) = 1,201
D. Total disposal of PE (D1 + D2 + D3) = 102 + 234 + 29 = 365
D_1. F.I.R = 102
D_2. Filed = 234
D_3. Transferred = 29
E. Pending at the end of the year (C - D) = 1,201 – 365 = 836
F. % of disposal with respect to total (D ÷ C x 100) = 365 ÷ 1,201 x 100 = 30%
G. Average no. of IOs in EOW = 519 ÷ 13 = 39.92 = 40
H. Average no. of PE per IO per year (C ÷ G) = 32.18 ÷ 13 = 2
I. Average disposal of PE by IO per year (D ÷ G) = 9.72 ÷ 13 = 1
J. Average no. of months taken in disposal of one P.E. (12 ÷ J) = 240.9 ÷ 13 = 18 (in months)

Table 5.4 Number of RCs Registered and Disposed in the EOW: 2000–12

Sr. No.	Year	A	B	C	D	E_1	E_2	E_3	E	F	G	H	I	J	K
1	2000	131	29	-	160	10	16	-	26	134	16.25%	40	4	0.65	18.5
2	2001	134	19	-	153	15	4	-	19	134	12.42%	35	4.37	0.54	22.2
3	2002	134	17	-	151	7	19	-	26	125	17.22%	22	6.86	1.18	10.2
4	2003	125	29	-	154	16	16	-	32	122	20.78%	33	4.67	0.97	12.4
5	2004	122	35	1	158	12	10	-	22	136	13.92%	39	4.05	0.56	21.4
6	2005	136	22	2	160	17	14	-	31	129	19.38%	36	4.44	0.86	14
7	2006	129	18	-	147	19	15	-	34	113	23.13%	32	4.59	1.06	11.3
8	2007	113	7	-	120	8	9	-	17	103	14.17%	33	3.64	0.51	23.5
9	2008	103	32	4	139	37	11	-	48	91	34.53%	37	3.76	1.29	9.3
10	2009	91	33	-	124	17	5	-	22	102	17.74%	35	3.54	0.63	19
11	2010	102	33	4	139	25	8	1	34	105	24.46%	37	3.76	0.92	13
12	2011	105	40	-	145	27	7	-	34	111	23.45%	70	2.07	0.49	24.5
13	2012	111	97		208	44	7		51	157	24.52%	70	2.97	0.73	16.4
	YEAR	1,536	411	11	1,958	254	141	1	396	1,562	20%	40 (Avg.)	4 (Avg.)	1 (Avg.)	17 (Avg.)

Calculations

A. Cases carried forward since previous year (from 2000 to 2012) = 1,536

B. Cases registered in the year = 411

C. Cases received by transfer or under re-investigation = 11

D. Total cases (A + B + C) = 1,536 + 411 + 11 = 1,958

E. Total disposal of cases $(E_1 + E_2 + E_3)$ = 254 + 141 + 01 = 396

E_1. Charge Sheet = 254

E_2. Filed = 141

E_3. Transfer = 01

F. Pending at the end of the year (D - E) = 1,958 - 396 = 1,562

G. % of disposal with respect to total investigated (E ÷ D x 100) = 396 ÷ 1,958 x 100 = 20%

H. Average no. of IOs = 519 ÷ 13 = 39.92 = 40

I. Average no. of cases per IO per year (D ÷ H) = 52.72 ÷ 13 = 4

J. Average disposal of cases by IO per year (E ÷ H) = 10.39 ÷ 13 = 1

K. Average no. of months taken in disposal of one RC (12 ÷ J) = 215.7 ÷ 13 = 17 (in months)

As explained, inquiry into corruption can begin in three ways: through a Complaint (C); Preliminary Inquiry (PE) based on intelligence or otherwise and Registered Complaint (RC). However, since Registered Complaint (RC) plus Preliminary Enquiry (PE) plus Complaint present the complete picture of total number of cases to be investigated, only this Table, that is, Table 5.1, has been described and analyzed in great detail here. The columns, inter alia, consist of a serial number, year, cases carried over from previous year (A), registered in the year (B), cases received on transfer (C) and total cases to be investigated (D=A+B+C). Disposal of cases (E), pending at the end of the year (F), percentage of disposal with respect to the total under investigation (G=E*100÷D), number of Investigating Officers/IOs (H), number of cases per IO (I = D÷H), average disposal of cases by IOs per year (J=E÷H) and average time taken in disposal of one case in months (K=12÷J). This examination essentially displays the growing efficiency of the EOW in terms of cases received for investigation, disposed after investigation and the rate of performance in terms of cases handled per investigating officer and time taken thereof.

Inferences from EOW Data of 2000–12 (Table 5.1)

Despite the continued mismatch in cases received and pending enquiry/investigation with respect to IOs available, the investigators did well to enhance their output by handling an average of 8 cases per year in 2000 to 23 by 2012. The average number of cases disposed off by the investigating officers rose from 2.35 in 2000 to 5.77 in 2012. The investigators managed to also reduce the time taken to complete the investigation from an average of 5.1 months in 2000 to 2.1 months by 2012. Yet, despite more than doubling the disposal of cases by the IOs, the pendency of complaints increased much more than the disposals.

The major reason for growing pendency of cases was that during the period 2000–12, every year on an average only 25 per cent of the cases (Registered Complaints, PEs and FIRs) were disposed while 75 per cent remained pending. Thus, despite the best efforts of EOW, more than three fourths of the cases remained pending at the end of each year. In terms of average numbers, out of an average of total cases of 737 for disposal, only an average of 187 cases could be disposed, while 549 remained pending. It is significant that from 2000 to 2012, pendency rose almost six times; from 244 to 1206. This growth in number of complaints is also explainable from a common observation. Whenever, a public unit begins to perform efficiently and effectively it promotes faith amongst the people and thereby encourages more citizens to come and report to it. Clearly, the undeniable inference is that such large pendencies and consequently such low disposals cannot combat corruption effectively, despite EOW's determined performance and constant empowerment by successive governments.

Another significant conclusion is that the shortage of IOs vis-à-vis the number of cases to be investigated has been one of the primary reasons for such huge pendencies. Thus, during the 13-year period from 2000–12, while the average number of cases to be inquired/investigated in a year in the EOW worked out to be 736 (9,563 ÷ 13), the average number of IOs during the same period was 40. Thus, the number of cases per IO was 18 (736 ÷ 40) cases per annum. However, the average number of disposals per year by a single IO was only 5 (187 ÷ 40 = 4.67 or 5). Hence the pendency per IO per year alone stood at 13 cases. This empirical analysis irrevocable makes a case for a substantial increase in the number of IOs for quicker disposal of cases for the role of deterrence to come into play. Enormous delays during investigations and trials of a case, as discussed earlier in this chapter, has a dampening effect on deterrence. This has given rise to the belief that the criminal justice system can be 'managed' and worse of all the 'chalta hai' attitude (It's ok to break rules as others do so as well) towards corrupt practices.

In this regard, it is pertinent to point here that the All India Bi-Annual Conference of Chiefs of ACBs and EOWs of all the states which was organized by CBI in 2011 examined the workload of an IO in dealing with corruption cases. The conference adopted a resolution to develop standard norms for professional working of the Anti-Corruption Bureaus. These norms took account of the requisite needs of personnel and technical equipment required by an ACB/EOW of a state. The Committee, after due deliberations, recommended the standard of 4.5 cases per IO per year to ensure timely and efficient investigation and disposal of cases.[1]

Going by this norm set by a professional body of anti-corruption officials, EOW appears to have performed extremely well in achieving disposal of an

---

1   One of the authors was a member of this committee.

average of 5 cases per year by an IO. Yet the end result was that more than 75 per cent of the cases still remained pending. Another empirical inference is that taking into account the committee's disposal norm of 5 cases per year per IO, the number of IOs required to dispose all cases and bring about zero pendency for cases pending at the end of 2012 would be 1206 ÷ 5 = 241. Compared with the presence of an average of 40 IOs in the EOW, the empirical inference is loud and clear: The Wing would require a large increase in the number of IOs in order to restrict pendencies to acceptable levels and to make some dent in corruption by bringing out speedy disposal of cases.

At the same time, even such a theoretical mathematical calculation of increase in the number of IOs to 241 can never be viable as this does not take into account the ever-burgeoning fresh complaints that would continue to be received in the subsequent years. Based upon this data, the average number of inquiries being registered fresh every year was 261 (3392 ÷ 13). This would imply that the number of IOs to be added each year to the existing personnel would be 52 (261 ÷ 5).

This, as would be apparent, does not appear to be neither a practical nor a comprehensive solution, as every year the number of complaints received as per the trend will go on increasing. This would necessitate regular increase in the number of IOs each year to keep pace with the annual increase in the number of complaints. In such a scenario, no government would be able to make such heavy investments financially in terms of sanctioning this theoretical massive increase of IOs. Furthermore, vigilance within the EOW, would assume significant dimensions. A separate apparatus may have to be created to 'police the police', given the enormous powers exercised by the IOs under different statutes vis-à-vis senior administrative and political formations. Clearly, the increase in number of IOs commensurate with the cases to be investigated to provide the requisite deterrent effect is not a solution as it leads to only an absurd situation. The answer to combating corruption effectively, therefore, lies elsewhere as we shall examine later in this book.

Yet, in terms of a short-term solution and to bring down pendency to reasonable levels, this need to substantially increase the number of IOs is being reiterated here even at the cost of repetition. It is pertinent to acknowledge the government's support to bolster anti-corruption efforts of the EOW. In 2013 sanction for the creation of two more field units at Sagar and Ujjain was granted, thereby lightening the burden of the Jabalpur and Indore units and making the units more effective. Nevertheless, the additional number of IOs remained much smaller than the required number based upon the recommended disposal rate.

It would be relevant to mention here that the EOW relies almost entirely for its personnel resources, including IOs, upon the MP police, which itself was then carrying more than 20 per cent vacancies. Often for bureaucratic reasons the natural priority for filling vacancies is accorded to the general police. EOW does not recruit its personnel directly, or rather they are deputed for a limited period from the general police ranks. It is worthwhile to note that few IO's are able to put in two to three years' tenure in the EOW. Consequently, a particular corruption case would generally involve investigation by three to four IOs. This situation prevails in all anti-corruption agencies and adversely affects both the quality and time taken for investigation and prosecution of sensitive cases. It might not be irrelevant to point out here that in a large number of cases referred by the EOW to various departments for their comments or inquiries require protracted and extensive correspondence to elicit a response. More often than not, it is the reluctance and sometimes deliberate attempts of the departments concerned to impede the progress of investigation and eventually scuttle investigations for documentary evidence that contribute to the tardy pace of investigations. The simple and inevitable conclusion from the above analysis is that the solution to combat corruption effectively has to be looked for beyond the enforcement agencies, such as the EOW, however efficient it may be in its functioning.

Analysis of Other Compiled Data 2000–12

We also provide other tables that display data of corruption in various public offices handled by EOW and the lag that occurs at the trial stage starting from the lower courts all the way up to the Supreme Court. This suggests that the efficiency of the police agency alone is not the sufficient condition to combat corruption effectively. The legal requirement to prove a criminal charge of corruption beyond reasonable doubt is a time consuming and slow process. In other words, the entire criminal justice system has to be empowered in terms of manpower, infrastructural facilities and other technological and electronic resources to provide the credible deterrence that is the primary objective of such a system. The rights of the citizens need to be honored and the police agencies cannot act without checks and balances in a democratic society. However, this invariably implies that combating corruption through the empowerment of police agencies alone is not the panacea that is proclaimed by the proponents of Lokpal and other voices.

The following describes the additional data that we have compiled to provide further analysis to examine the efficacy of EOW and the response of the administrative and criminal justice system to combat corruption effectively:

Table 5.5　Statistics of Complaints Received from Various Government Departments.

Table 5.6　Complaints Registered against Major Government Departments: 2000–12.

Table 5.7　Average Time Taken by Trial courts in Disposal of Cases: 2000–12.

Table 5.8　Average Time Taken by High Courts in Disposal of Cases: 2000–12.

Table 5.9　Average Time Taken by Supreme Court in Disposal of Cases: 2000–12.

Table 5.10　Statistics of Prosecution Sanction Sought by EOW: 2000–12.

Complaints Received from Government Departments

As per the circular of the state government, the EOW was essentially established to investigate corruption and economic cases pertaining to public servants of various government departments. Therefore, the EOW, with its expertise, was conceived as an agency of the government that would assist the departments to enquire into and investigate corruption and financial crimes, thereby saving the departments themselves from spending time in such inquiries and instead focus on their core functions. It was, therefore, natural to expect that a large number of cases would be referred to the EOW by various ministries and government agencies.

However, analysis of statistics from 2000–12 shows a dismal picture of an average of only 14 cases having been referred by various departments of the government in a year to the EOW. The logical and inevitable inference was that the departments themselves exercised no vigilance in detecting corruption and financial irregularities either due to indifference or turning a

Table 5.5 Statistics of Complaints Received from Various Government
Departments: 2000–12

Sl. no.	Year	No. of complaints received
1	2000	29
2	2001	20
3	2002	18
4	2003	22
5	2004	11
6	2005	7
7	2006	13
8	2007	9
9	2008	10
10	2009	7
11	2010	12
12	2011	9
13	2012	13
	Total	180
	Average	180 ÷ 13 = 14

blind eye to the on goings in their own 'homes'. The small number of referrals also suggest the apathy of public officials towards corruption in their unit and their indifference in seeking specialized assistance to combat economic crimes. In principle, the practice is for the departmental heads to keep a close eye, exercise vigilance on irregularities under their charge and to hold a preliminary inquiry if something is suspected and also take suitable action wherever warranted. This could, thereafter, be forwarded to the EOW for further investigation and prosecution of the accused for wrongdoing. If the departments themselves could take up these preventive and deterrent roles, considerable leakage of funds could be checked at the initial stage. The maxim 'prevention is better than the cure' is clearly necessary for public departments in the country. In fact, anti-corruption agencies like the EOW step in only when the damage has been done and the crime has already taken place.

In Table 5.6, we provide some data about the shenanigans of various public departments in MP. It needs to be remembered that such departments all over the country in other states too are known for their corruption. In order to give a better and clearer idea of the level of corruption in top 10 government departments, the above Table 5.6 has been summarized below.

Table 5.6 Complaints Registered against Major Government Departments: 2000–12

Sl. no.	Department name	No. of complaints registered in the year													Total
		2000	2001	2002	2003	2004	2005	2006	2007	2008	2009	2010	2011	2012	
1	Urban Administration and Development	3	2	4	3	3	10	7	15	25	65	34	198	270	639
2	Water Resources	5	3	8	6	2	4	13	9	25	54	47	116	146	438
3	Cooperative	1	1	0	3	3	18	6	3	13	51	50	94	184	427
4	Revenue	1	1	0	1	8	6	5	12	41	31	41	173	196	516
5	Panchayat and Rural Development	3	2	8	5	3	3	6	10	22	47	31	191	252	583
6	Public Works Department (PWD)	0	7	6	10	7	3	7	14	31	22	25	88	95	315
7	Housing and Environment	10	8	5	6	2	2	4	10	23	15	15	35	64	199
8	Higher Education	3	0	1	2	3	4	2	9	20	8	14	71	64	201
9	Public Health Engineering (PHE)	1	2	0	5	3	1	4	5	13	13	11	47	38	143
10	Forest	3	8	10	7	5	2	4	2	4	14	16	49	48	172
11	Public Health and Family Welfare	2	1	2	0	4	4	3	4	16	10	6	35	67	154

contd.

contd.

Sl. no.	Department name	2000	2001	2002	2003	2004	2005	2006	2007	2008	2009	2010	2011	2012	Total
		No. of complaints registered in the year													
12	Agriculture	2	2	3	4	3	3	5	9	8	0	19	76	129	263
13	School Education	0	1	2	2	5	5	6	2	7	7	11	95	160	303
14	Energy	1	0	1	2	2	2	2	2	6	14	16	22	72	142
15	Tribal Welfare	3	4	2	0	0	3	5	4	7	8	12	54	77	179
16	Transport	1	0	1	1	3	4	1	3	6	13	9	39	38	119
17	Commercial Tax	0	1	0	2	3	0	2	0	10	2	21	33	60	134
18	Food and Civil Supplies	2	1	1	0	0	4	6	0	0	7	19	20	30	90
19	Commerce and Industry	1	1	2	3	0	4	4	3	15	1	8	0	17	59
20	Medical Education	1	0	0	1	0	0	0	7	13	5	5	25	10	67
21	Home	0	1	1	0	4	0	2	1	4	7	7	85	118	230
22	General Administration Department (GAD)	2	1	1	2	0	0	1	0	0	1	22	26	41	97
23	Animal Husbandry	1	2	0	1	0	3	4	2	6	2	6	15	9	51
24	Finance	0	1	2	1	0	0	0	2	11	4	2	5	9	37
25	Rural Industry	0	1	1	1	0	4	0	0	2	5	2	28	46	90

contd.

contd.

Sl. no.	Department name	No. of complaints registered in the year													Total
		2000	2001	2002	2003	2004	2005	2006	2007	2008	2009	2010	2011	2012	
26	Mineral Resources	1	0	1	1	0	0	2	0	0	3	6	15	24	53
27	Narmada Valley Development	2	0	1	2	0	7	0	1	1	0	2	6	18	40
28	Women and Child Development	1	2	1	1	1	0	1	2	1	2	2	18	25	57
29	Technical Education	0	0	1	1	0	3	0	1	0	1	4	8	14	33
30	Ayush	1	0	0	1	0	2	5	0	0	1	0	3	5	18
31	Relgious Affair (_Dharmasva_)	0	0	0	0	0	0	0	0	4	1	0	0	0	5
32	Labor	1	1	2	1	0	0	0	0	0	0	4	3	5	17
33	Horticulture (_Udyaniki_)	1	2	1	3	0	0	0	0	2	1	1	13	5	29
34	Public Relations	1	0	0	1	0	1	1	0	1	1	1	2	9	18
35	Culture	1	1	0	1	0	0	0	0	1	0	1	1	5	11
36	Law	2	2	1	1	0	0	0	0	0	0	1	4	0	11
37	Science and Technology	0	0	0	1	0	0	0	0	0	1	0	2	3	7

Complaints Registered against Government Departments

The top 10 government departments against whom the largest number of complaints received during the period 2000 to 2012, that is, 13 years, were:

Sr. No.	Department	No. of complaints
1.	Urban Administration and Development	639
2.	Panchayat and Rural Development	583
3.	Revenue	516
4.	Water Resources	438
5.	Cooperative	427
6.	Public Works Department	315
7.	School Education	303
8.	Agriculture	263
9.	Home	230
10.	Higher Education	201

While the above statistics do not provide conclusive data about the levels of corruption in order of the most corrupt or lesser corrupt, they certainly do provide information about the extent of corruption and financial irregularities existing in these ministries/departments. They are also indicative of the level of disaffection in the people with respect to the functioning and services provided by the government agencies as most of the complaints, more than 95 per cent, emanate from these departments. It would also be seen that the malaise of corruption seriously afflicts the departments responsible for growth and development in key and core sector areas. Yet no effective alternate mechanism has been put in place to check and prevent such corruption and economic crimes.

Statistics Relating to Delay in Disposal of Cases by the Trial Courts, High Court and Supreme Court

The following data in Tables 5.7 to 5.9 has been collected from the information available with the EOW only and reflects corruption cases prosecuted by the agency. There are also some gaps in the data since registered cases reach the trial stage after a lag of time. The figures are indicative of delays in the judicial system in the disposal of cases.

Table 5.7 Average Time Taken by Trial Courts in Disposal of Cases: 2000–12

Sl. no.	Year	Average time taken by the trial courts in disposal of cases in various units (in months) in the year.					Total (in months)	Average of the year (in months)	Total no. of cases under trial in the year	Cases disposed by the court in the current year	Cases pending at the end of the year
		Bhopal	Indore	Jabalpur	Gwalior	Rewa					
		A	B	C	D	E	F = A + B + C + D + E	G = F ÷ 5			
1	2000	44	78	191	134	-	447	89.4	320	33	287
2	2001	48	97	160	117	205	627	125.4	302	28	274
3	2002	101	27	117	91	-	336	67.2	288	18	270
4	2003	244	249	97	17	-	607	121.4	284	31	253
5	2004	-	155	173	39	98	465	93	266	29	237
6	2005	194	102	165	-	174	635	127	259	55	204
7	2006	137	262	162	77	111	749	149.8	225	51	174
8	2007	50	215	135	148	18	566	113.2	195	21	174
9	2008	196	240	119	23	36	614	122.8	205	26	179
10	2009	-	240	-	-	-	240	48	205	9	196

contd.

155

contd.

Sl. no.	Year	Average time taken by the trial courts in disposal of cases in various units (in months) in the year.					Total (in months)	Average of the year (in months)	Total no. of cases under trial in the year	Cases disposed by the court in the current year	Cases pending at the end of the year
		Bhopal	Indore	Jabalpur	Gwalior	Rewa					
		A	B	C	D	E	$F = A+B+C+D+E$	$G = F \div 5$			
11	2010	99	177	112	-	164	552	110.4	218	26	192
12	2011	59	108	166	-	-	333	66.6	214	25	189
13	2012	35	156	20	-	227	438	87.6	239	26	213
Total		1,207	2,106	1,617	646	1,033	6,609	1,321.8 Avg. time = $G \div 13$ = 101.68 Months (8.5 YR)	3,220	378 % of Disposals = 12%	2,842 % of Pendency = 88%

Table 5.8 Average Time Taken by the High Court of MP in Disposable of Cases of EOW: 2000–12

Year	Average time taken in the year in disposal of cases of the units (in months) Bhopal (A)	Average time taken in the year in disposal of cases of the units (in months) Indore (B)	Average time taken in the year in disposal of cases of the units (in months) Jabalpur (C)	Average time taken in the year in disposal of cases of the units (in months) Gwalior (D)	Average time taken in the year in disposal of cases of the units (in months) Rewa (E)	Total F = (A + B + C + D + E)	Average of the year (in months) G = F ÷ (No. of entries in the year)
2000	–	–	22.67	–	–	22.67	22.67
2001	–	–	–	–	–	–	–
2002	–	–	11	–	–	11	11
2003	–	–	–	–	–	–	–
2004	–	–	6	–	–	6	6
2005	–	3	37.27	–	–	40.27	20.1
2006	–	–	–	–	–	–	–
2007	–	–	–	–	–	–	–
2008	–	22	–	–	206	228	114
2009	–	–	–	120	–	120	60

contd.

157

contd.

Year	Average time taken in the year in disposal of cases of the units (in months) Bhopal (A)	Indore (B)	Jabalpur (C)	Gwalior (D)	Rewa (E)	Total F = (A + B + C + D + E)	Average of the year (in months) G = F ÷ (No. of entries in the year)
2010	–	–	–	–	–	–	–
2011	–	130	20	–	–	150	75
2012	–	93.38	–	22	–	115.38	57.7
Total		248.4	96.9	142	206	693.3	366.47 months Average = 366.5 ÷ 8 = 45.8 months (3.8 years)

Table 5.9 Average Time Taken by the Supreme Court of India in Disposable of Cases of EOW: 2000–12

Year	Average time taken in the year in disposal of cases of the units (in days) Bhopal (A)	Average time taken in the year in disposal of cases of the units (in days) Indore (B)	Average time taken in the year in disposal of cases of the units (in days) Jabalpur (C)	Average time taken in the year in disposal of cases of the units (in days) Gwalior (D)	Average time taken in the year in disposal of cases of the units (in days) Rewa (E)	Total (in days) F = (A + B + C + D + E)	Average of the year (in days) G = F ÷ (No. of entries in the year)
2000	–	–	–	–	–	–	–
2001	–	–	–	–	–	–	–
2002	–	–	–	–	–	–	–
2003	–	–	–	–	–	–	–
2004	–	–	–	–	–	–	–
2005	–	–	–	–	–	–	–
2006	174	–	–	–	–	174	174
2007	–	–	–	–	–	–	–

contd.

159

contd.

Year	Average time taken in the year in disposal of cases of the units (in days) Bhopal (A)	Average time taken in the year in disposal of cases of the units (in days) Indore (B)	Average time taken in the year in disposal of cases of the units (in days) Jabalpur (C)	Average time taken in the year in disposal of cases of the units (in days) Gwalior (D)	Average time taken in the year in disposal of cases of the units (in days) Rewa (E)	Total (in days) F = (A + B + C + D + E)	Average of the year (in days) G = F ÷ (No. of entries in the year)
2008	–	–	–	–	–	–	–
2009	–	–	–	–	–	–	–
2010	–	–	–	–	–	–	–
2011	1,955	1,700	205	–	–	3,860	1,287
2012	–	56	5,930	–	–	5,986	2,993
Total	**2,129**	**1,756**	**6,135**			**1,0020**	**4,454** Average = 4,454 ÷ 3 = 1,485 days = 4 years

Inferences regarding pendency of cases in various courts

This compilation and analysis of available data over 13 years from 2000–12 shows that the average time taken by Trial Courts to decide corruption cases is 102 months, that is, eight years and six months. Similarly, the time taken for High Courts to dispose of cases work out to be 45.8 months, that is, 3 years and 8 months. Average time taken by the Supreme Court in disposal of appeals and petitions is about 4 years. Thus, from the stage of registration, investigation and charge sheeting of cases (three years five months) to disposals by Trial Courts, High Courts and the Supreme Court, takes an average of 20 years and 4 months! No wonder corruption is everywhere in the country.

The picture regarding the disposal of cases by Trial Courts in a year is even more dismal and alarming as it works out to be 12 per cent disposal of the total number of cases under trial per annum, which is nearly half of the disposals by the EOW (around 25 per cent) in inquiry and investigations. Either way, it signifies the virtual failure of the criminal judicial system, comprising the enforcement agency and prosecution and courts, to exercise its deterrent effect by ensuring speedy and timely action against the corrupt officers and white-collar criminals. The aforementioned statistics clearly reflect the perilously tardy administration of justice following which the deterrent effect of the law stands greatly diminished. In absence of a credible deterrence, other officials too feel emboldened to indulge in corruption.

Causes of Delay of Cases in Courts

Some of the main factors responsible for the pendency of cases in courts are the increasing number of state and central legislations, accumulation of first appeals, continuation of ordinary civil jurisdiction in some of the High Courts, vacancies of judges, appeals against orders of quasi-judicial forums going to High Courts, number of revisions/appeals, frequent adjournments, indiscriminate use of writ jurisdiction, lack of adequate arrangement to monitor, track and bunch cases for hearing, frequent change in IOs, summons not served on witnesses, overburdening of cases on prosecution and poor pleading. We examine below some of these factors to suggest the challenges of prosecuting those charged with corruption:

Table 5.10 Pending Cases as on March 31, 2016

Sl. No.	Court	No. of criminal cases
1.	Supreme Court	11,063 cases
2.	High Courts	10,47,804 cases
3	District and subordinate courts	1,91,33,992 cases
4.	Total	2,01,92,859 cases
5.	No. of cases pending in district/ subordinate courts of MP	9,36,261 Cases

Source: *Supreme Court News*, XI, no.1 (January–March 2016).

Number of judges and vacancy (as on March 31, 2016)

In India, there are 13 judges per 10,00,000 people. The total number of sanctioned posts of judges in the Supreme Court is 31 with a current vacancy of 6 judges. In the High Courts, the sanctioned strength is 1,041 with a vacancy of 442 judges. In the district and subordinate courts, the sanctioned strength is 21,017 and the vacancy is 4,882. Thus, while the combined strength of the judges in the country is 22,089, the total vacancy is 5,330. The overall vacancies in all the courts put together works out to be 24 per cent as on March 31, 2016 (*Supreme Court News*, 2016).

Number of criminal cases per judge

In MP, the total number of cases pending under trial in the district and subordinate courts was 9,36,261. The total working strength of judicial officers was reported to be 1,250. Therefore, the average number of cases pending per judge was 749 (*Supreme Court News*, 2016).

These statistics speak for themselves. With such large vacancies and huge number of cases to be disposed off by each judge, it can be safely inferred that the judiciary, like the enforcement agencies, is also terribly handicapped to provide 'speedy' justice. The credible deterrence is thus lacking in the criminal justice system to curb corruption crimes as well as other criminal cases effectively in India.

Current Tussle between Judiciary and Executive Over Appointment of Judges

It is pertinent to point out that lack of personnel resources affects all organs of the criminal justice system. Currently, a bitter tussle between the judiciary and the government over appointment of judges is playing out. The Supreme Court has opined that all such appointments will be made by the collegium of judges while the government obviously wishes to have some say and transparency in these appointments. This battle needs a quick resolution for it is adversely affecting the judicial system in the country. In the famous Three Judges Cases (*SP Gupta v. Union of India* 1981; *Supreme Court Advocates-on Record Association vs Union of India 1993*; *Special Reference 1 of 1998*) the Supreme Court established the primacy of the judiciary in judges' appointments.

The current tug of war between the central government (executive) and the Supreme Court (judiciary) has its roots in the National Judicial Appointments Commission (NJAC) Act, 2014 that was established by amending the Constitution (99th Amendment) passed by the Lok Sabha on August 13, 2014 and by the Rajya Sabha on August 14, 2014. Alongside, the Parliament also passed the NJAC Act, 2014, to regulate the NJAC's functions. Both Bills were ratified by 16 of the state legislatures and the President gave his assent on December 31, 2014. The NJAC Act and the Constitutional Amendment Act came into force from April 13, 2015. It is significant to note that the passing of these legislations received the support of the majority of the political parties irrespective of their ideologies and priorities. The elected representatives were sending the message that Parliament is supreme in determining the law of the country.

The NJAC was supposed to be a constitutional body and it was put in place to make the appointments of High Court and Supreme Court judges and Chief Justices more transparent. The NJAC would consist of six members— the Chief Justice of India, the two most senior judges of the Supreme Court, the Law Minister and two 'eminent persons'. These eminent persons were to be nominated for a three-year term by a committee consisting of the Chief Justice, the Prime Minister and the Leader of the Opposition in the Lok Sabha and were not eligible for re-nomination.

However, in this battle between the executive and the judiciary, the

Supreme Court declared unconstitutional the amendment to validate the NJAC Act, 2014 which sought to provide a significant role for the executive in appointing judges in the higher judiciary. Effectively sealing the fate of the proposed system, a five-judge Constitution Bench ruled with a 4:1 majority that judges' appointments shall continue to be made by the collegium system in which the Chief Justice of India will have 'the last word'.

The 20-year-old collegium system prescribes appointment of judges by a panel comprising of five senior-most judges of the Supreme Court and High Courts, with the power to confirm appointments. The Supreme Court judgment of October 2015 also recommended 'appropriate measures' to improve the working of the collegium system. A separate order, passed by a five-judge bench in December 2015, listed factors—these included eligibility criteria, transparency in the appointment process, secretariat and complaints —for preparing the Memorandum of Procedure (MoP). The judiciary made clear that it will not let the elected members determine their power over appointment of judges!

At the root of the current ongoing tussle over rejection of some of the judges recommended for appointment by the government on grounds of complaints against them, also lies in the fact that the MoP of appointment of judges has still not been framed on grounds of disagreement on some of its clauses between the center and the Supreme Court. The worst sufferers in this tug of war is the judicial system itself and of course the people looking for speedy justice. This development is also denting the efforts of the anti-corruption agencies like the EOW to provide the requisite deterrence to the perpetrators of corruption and thereby curbing this menace due to the huge length of time consumed in deciding the cases.

Causes of Delay in the Trial Courts

Case trials also get delayed due to one or several reasons listed below:
1. non-appearance or delayed appearance of public prosecutors during the trials;
2. the public prosecutors not studying the cases before appearing in court;
3. the failure of public prosecutors to produce a case diary and other documents during the appearance of a witness;

4. the non-appearance of witnesses on the specified dates;
5. non-servicing of summons to the witnesses;
6. the failure to submit original documents along with the charge sheets;
7. the apathy of judges towards timely disposal of cases;
8. delays in trials due to stays by the higher courts;
9. delays in submission of FSL reports;
10. deliberate lingering on of cases by the defense by seeking adjournments after adjournments on some pretext or the other.

Prosecution Sanction (Table 5.11)

An analysis of statistics for the period 2000–12 over 13 years reveals that while prosecution sanctions have been accorded in 51 per cent of the cases as many 49 per cent remain pending for want of prosecution sanction. This too, substantially, contributed to the pendency of cases and delay in their disposals by the EOW.

EOW Case Study: Important Inferences

From the above empirical study of the EOW of 13 years from 2000–13, following inferences can be safely drawn:

1. More than 75 per cent of complaints/cases remain pending at the end of each year.
2. In spite of best efforts of the EOW, even after optimum performance during the author's tenure (2011–13), the pendency could be reduced only marginally.
3. The average number of cases/complaints per year handled by an investigating officer was seen to be 18 for EOW that far exceeded the CBI norm of 5 per IO per annum. This implied that the number of corruption cases pending investigation annually will be 13 and would grow exponentially.
4. Corresponding increase in the number of IOs is not a sustainable option as the increase in the receipt of complaints in the EOW also rises drastically every year. However, given the current state of affairs, there are enough justifications, as of now, to increase the sanctioned strength of IOs to bring down the pendency to acceptable levels at least.

Table 5.11 Statistics of Prosecution Sanctions Sought: 2000–12

Sl. no	Year	Pending prosecution sanctions carried over from the previous year	Proposal of prosecution sanctions sent in the year	Total	Prosecution sanctions received in the year					Pending at the end of the year
					Prosecution sanctions received within a period of 6 months	Prosecution sanctions received in the period of 6–12 months	Prosecution sanctions received in the period of 1 to 2 years	Prosecution sanctions received in a period of more than 2 years	Total	
		A	B	C = A+B	D	E	F	G	H = D+E+F+G	I = C-H
1	2000	0	0	0	0	0	0	0	0	0
2	2001	0	1	1	0	0	0	0	0	1
3	2002	1	3	4	1	0	1	1	3	1
4	2003	1	4	5	1	1	2	1	5	0
5	2004	2	2	4	1	0	0	0	1	3
6	2005	3	5	8	2	3	0	0	5	3
7	2006	3	10	13	3	2	5	0	10	3
8	2007	5	4	9	0	3	1	0	4	5

contd.

contd.

Sl. no	Year	Pending prosecution sanctions carried over from the previous year	Proposal of prosecution sanctions sent in the year	Total	Prosecution sanctions received in the year					Pending at the end of the year
					Prosecution sanctions received within a period of 6 months	Prosecution sanctions received in the period of 6–12 months	Prosecution sanctions received in the period of 1 to 2 years	Prosecution sanctions received in a period of more than 2 years	Total	
		A	B	C = A+B	D	E	F	G	H= D+E+F +G	I = C - H
9	2008	5	9	14	1	4	3	1	9	5
10	2009	5	7	12	3	2	1	1	7	5
11	2010	5	9	14	7	1	0	1	9	5
12	2011	5	9	14	4	2	0	0	6	8
13	2012	8	19	27	4	1	0	0	5	22
	Total	43	82	125	27	19	13	5	64 64 x 100 ÷ 125 =51%	61 x 100 ÷ 125 = 49 %

* P.E.: Preliminary Case
** IPC: Indian Penal Code
*** PCA: Prevention of Corruption Act, 1988
**** R.C.: Regular Criminal Case
***** I.O.: Investigating Officers
***** F.I.R.: First Information Report

5. It was seen that the principal reasons for delay in investigation was the indifference of unit managers and in the procurement of documents from the concerned departments and their allied bodies and organizations. It is pertinent to note here that virtually all cases in the EOW, as with other such anti-corruption bodies, including the CBI, relating to both the corruption crimes and economic offences are based on documentary evidence in the custody of the concerned departments. Accordingly, non-cooperation from public officials and units is a serious cause of delay.

6. Along with the above two main causes of tardy investigation, the delay in granting/denying prosecution sanction against the public servant involved also contributes to the delay in putting up the charge sheets before the trial courts.

7. Frequent transfers and postings of IOs is also a destabilizing factor and contribute to the pendency as well as adversely affect the quality of investigation and prosecution. One of the biggest problems of the EOW, as with the CBI and other anti-corruption investigating agencies, is that they do not have their own cadres of investigating officers. Hence, they have to rely mostly on officers on deputation from the state police forces, which unfortunately, also carry large vacancies. Naturally, the state forces are reluctant to let officers go on deputation. At the same time, the cutting-edge level of IOs are also unwilling to come on deputation because they do not want to give up the 'attractive' field postings and at the same time not enough motivated to take up these arduous investigations.

8. The time taken by the Trial Courts (8 years and 5 months), High Courts (3 years and 8 months) and Supreme Court (4 years), based on data available with the EOW from 2000–12, to decide a case is concerned, presents a dismal picture of deterrence. When added up the entire judicial process takes as many as 16 years and 1 month.

9. It is also noteworthy that while the EOW was created primarily to look into complaints received from government departments, just 180 cases in 13 years were submitted by all the public units for investigation. This constituted only 1.9 per cent of the total number of complaints received by the EOW in these 13 years. The fact that the bulk of the cases,

that is, 98.1 per cent were based on complaints by the citizens against public officials, points to the apathy of the departments themselves to unearth and prevent corruption crimes and economic offences.

Discussion

The data analysis described above suggests some interesting, though uncomfortable perspectives. First, adding resources and administrative support to the police agency certainly helps in improving its performance. The numbers of cases inquired, investigated and prosecuted shows an upward trend. For any government seeking to combat corruption, it is clearly necessary that the police agencies are provided adequate resources and given legal support to function properly. Amongst these resources the number of personnel is a crucial factor but infrastructural support in terms of tools and technology are also needed. The corrupt are forever looking for loopholes and cleavages in the system and the government must address these limitations by strengthening the legal and administrative measures to equip the police agencies. Yet there is clearly a limit to the number of personnel that can be provided. The police investigating and prosecuting agencies cannot continue to grow in strength. Some other recourse is needed as well to combat corruption effectively.

However, more important than any of these methods is the firm determination and 'political will' that makes a difference. The support by the top most echelons of the government and faith in the professionalism of the police officers is a crucial factor in empowering the agency to function efficiently and effectively. This also sends a strong message throughout the bureaucracy that helps bring about some semblance of deterrence. Not sparing even senior officers and pursuing the crimes to their logical end serves good examples and help build an environment of integrity in public affairs. As discussed in Chapter 2, most of these corrupt practices become possible due to opportunities that offenders weigh and act accordingly in a rational manner. The offender weighs the risks in seeking rewards. As such, political support to police investigators increases the risks of offending and thereby helps in keeping the fence sitters from jumping into the pit of corruption.

Nevertheless, these measures are still inadequate in dealing with corruption as is amply clear from the EOW case study. Despite a manifested increase in efficiency and improved performance, the EOW could only make a marginal difference in combating corruption within the state of MP. Notwithstanding increase in resources, both in terms of personnel and material, the number of corrupt brought to justice was only a fraction better than previous years. Although the number of corrupt public officials exposed, investigated and prosecuted did show an upward appreciable trend, it failed to act as a credible deterrence to significantly reduce the corruption in the state. The departments and undertakings where corruption was rampant continued to maintain their reputation of sleaze and extortion. In fact, year to year the cases show a remarkable upward trend. Even when senior officers were caught and incarcerated the junior functionaries continued to operate with dishonesty and impunity. At no time could the public and the media perceive that corruption has been curtailed in the state.

The inescapable conclusion is that policing enforcement efforts in a weak criminal justice system devoid of appropriate resources are hardly able to deal the 'deterrence blow' so essential to curb crimes such as corruption and economic offences. Thus, the role of such agencies as the EOW MP gets limited to dealing with crimes in general and corruption in particular. Political will, strong police leaders and resources make a difference but only to a marginal extent. Even targeting senior public officials and confiscating the ill-gotten gains of corrupt practices did not prove to be a sufficient deterrence. While one official is caught and punished, many others, working in the same unit, continue to indulge in bribery and extortion. Even when a dedicated and empowered unit is created to deal exclusively with this vice in public affairs, the impact is peripheral. The opportunities to commit fraud and sleaze in the government are immense. The extent of dishonesty has spread far and wide. Political and police leadership by themselves cannot prevent corrupt practices. Some other method and path have to be adopted to bring integrity in public affairs of the country. We examine this in the subsequent chapters of this book.

The aforementioned conclusions have been further reinforced by the outbreak of the 'Vyapam Scam'. In the bargain, unfortunately, the excellent efforts of the EOW received a major blow when the 'Vyapam Case' came to light in 2013 when the Indore crime branch registered an FIR after arresting 20 people who had come to impersonate candidates for the Pre Medical Test (PMT) in 2009. This scandal greatly dented the image of the BJP government, which had the vision and political will of backing the EOW during an earlier phase. The scam was all about the manipulation in the selection process for the government colleges and jobs conducted by the Madhya Pradesh Professional Examination Board (MPPEB) or Madhya Pradesh Vyavsayik Pariksha Mandal (Vyapam). It involved the impersonation of candidates, rampant copying, blank answer sheets and fake marks. The state government established a Special Task Force (STF) on August 26, 2013 although the case could have been handed over to the EOW. Later, in July 2015, the state government under public pressure, pressure from the media and political leaders, transferred the probe to the CBI. The case continues to be under investigation.

The above empirical analysis further suggests that senior public officials are neither proactive nor concerned about checking corruption within their own organizations. Perhaps, reporting or checking corruption runs the risk of drawing attention to their administrative failures. Moreover, the political-bureaucratic nexus survives or rather thrives on mutually beneficial symbiotic relationship and few top officials are willing to stand up to these vested interests. Ultimately, the anti-corruption agencies, the EOW, the ACB or even the Lokayuktas are left to combat corruption in which every other public functionary as it would seem, is an unwilling partner.

An additional issue based upon our experience also merits attention. While the vast proportion of complaints are brought to the EOW by aggrieved parties, sometimes the motivation is driven by enmity to settle scores or worse still for political considerations. The opposition in its crusade of labeling the ruling regime as corrupt often lodge complaints or have them sponsored through members of the public. This game is played irrespective of the political party in power. The RTI Act has, no doubt, given a boost to anti-corruption efforts by the conscientious social activists. However, it has been often observed that social activism gets embroiled with political opportunism and worse, take to blackmailing public officials.

A disturbing but unavoidable conclusion is that there is no concerted or targeted effort to curb corruption. Sporadic complaints, maybe genuine, maybe motivated, is what anti-corruption agencies handle and find themselves overwhelmed by the load of cases. The state is happy that these agencies provide the safety valve to assuage the people or media when some corruption is exposed. As we have stated this model of 'structures of irresolution' enables the façade of a state combating corruption when in reality it is subverting genuine efforts and partnering the corrupt in their loot of public funds. Furthermore, these agencies are no holy cow either. The stock of the enforcement officers is no different. They are drawn from the same bureaucracy which, more often than not, seem eager to be 'his masters' voice' or 'the caged parrot' in the eloquent words of the Supreme Court.

Obviously, to tackle corruption seriously other alternate solutions need to be explored!

6

Lokpal and Lokayukta
A Critical Examination

An ombudsperson by the nomenclatures of 'Lokpal' at the central government level and 'Lokayukta' at the state level, to address the inadequacies of the current anti-corruption systems, have been major issues of agitation by Anna Hazare and many citizen groups in the past few years. These Indian 'ombudsperson' armed with the power and independence to investigate and prosecute cases of corruption are purported by these agitators to be the best mechanism for handling growing corruption in the country. The Lokpal and Lokayuktas Act, 2013 (No. 1 of 2014) has come into existence. While it will take time to assess the operations, impact and the efficacy of Lokpal, its possible role in combating corruption can still be examined on the basis of its provisions, structure and from comparative perspectives. The current discourse questions the perspective that an independent Lokpal alone is capable of combating corruption in the country. We pay special attention to the composition, selection and powers of the Lokpal to judge its powers and functioning. Specific examples from different Lokayuktas, already operational in different states, further provide the context to make this assessment. A comparative evaluation of the powers and performance of several international systems of ombudsperson are also analyzed to determine how far this design of Lokpal will be successful in its mission of combating corruption effectively in the country. We argue that such ombudsperson needs to go beyond the limited objective of prosecuting the corrupt officials. Prevention of corruption must be an integral part of its functions and it must also serve to educate and engage the citizens to deal with corruption. We provide evidence that Lokayuktas that have been in operation for many years have failed to evolve as institutions that can reform the 'rotten barrel' which spoils the apples.

Introduction

The need to have an institution independent of the government that can examine the complaints against public servants, including ministers serving the government, was felt as early as the eighteenth century when parliaments in Europe asserted their independence from the monarch ruling the country. Sweden was the first country that established the office of ombudsperson, an officer appointed by the legislative body to receive and investigate complaints against unjust administrative action. Since the king appointed the ministers and public servants, the objective clearly was to give the Parliament a means of balancing the wide powers exercised by the King. This institution has globally attracted considerable attention and public approval. 40 or so years ago, the ombudsperson institution was confined to a handful of countries and the word 'ombudsperson' meant nothing to most people outside Scandinavia. 'In the late 1990s, the office of Ombudsman became a worldwide phenomenon, estimated to be operative in something like 90 countries'. (Gregory and Giddings, 2000, 1)

> By May 2007 the institutional membership of the IOI [International Ombudsman Institute] stood at 146 classical and human rights Ombudsman offices, illustrative of the popularity of the institution both at national and sub-national levels of government with a consequential increase in the interest in research and scholarship on the Ombudsman concept. (Reif, 2008, 1)

In the course of this transplantation, the 'Ombudsman has shown remarkable adaptability. It has been adapted by small and large countries, by central, state [provincial] and local governments by both developed and developing countries' (Rowat, 1984, 207), by international, continental and regional organizations, by democratic and non-democratic political systems, and also by both public and private sectors. It has also been adopted 'for general or specific areas of administration and in the form of a single or plural [commission of] Ombudsman' (Rowat, 1984, 207).

Ombudsperson has taken many shapes and is also called the parliamentary commissioner, public defender, people's advocate and the likes in some countries. The job titles assigned to those performing the ombudsperson function illustrate this new role. In Spain, the constitution foresees a 'Defensor del Pueblo', a Defender of the People. In Ukraine, there is a 'Commissioner for Human Rights'. In Bulgaria, the annual report of the ombudsperson must contain information on the status of human rights. In Bosnia–Herzegovina and Albania, there is a 'Human Rights Ombudsman' (Roosbroek and Walle, 2008, 289). Historically, the public-sector ombudsperson investigates citizens' complaints about virtually every part of public administration. But over time, some countries have introduced ombudsperson that is responsible for specific topics (for example, gender equality, children) or specific parts of the public sector (for example, transport, pensions). Thus, the International Bar Association (IBA) defined the ombudsperson in 1974 as:

> an office provided for by the constitution or by action of the legislature or parliament and headed by an independent high-level public official, who is responsible to the legislature or parliament, who receives complaints from aggrieved persons against government agencies, officials and employees or who acts on his own motion, and who has the power to investigate, recommend corrective action, and issue report. (Cited in Goetherer, 1974)

· Based on this definition the International Ombudsman Institute (IOI) constitution set the criteria for institutional membership as: a public institution whether titled ombudsperson, mediator, parliamentary commissioner, people's defender, human rights commission, public complaints commission, inspector general of government, public protector or like designation, shall be eligible to become an institutional member provided it exercises fully the following functions and meets the following criteria:

1. It is created by enactment of a legislative body whether or not it is also provided for in the Constitution.

2. Its role is to protect any person or body of persons against maladministration violation of rights, unfairness, abuse, corruption or any injustice caused by a public authority.

3. It does not receive any direction from any public authority which would compromise its independence and performs its functions independently of any public authority over which jurisdiction is held.

4. It has the necessary powers to investigate complaints by any person or body of persons who considers that an act done or omitted, or any decision, advice or recommendation made by any public authority within its jurisdiction, has resulted in actions of the kind specified in sub-paragraph (2) above.

5. It has the power to make recommendations in order to remedy or to prevent any of the conduct described in sub-paragraph (2) and, where appropriate, to propose administrative or legislative reforms for better governance.

6. It is held accountable by reporting publicly to the legislature or other appropriate authority.

7. Its jurisdiction is national, regional or local.

8. Its jurisdiction applies to public authorities generally or is limited to one or several public authorities or to one or several public sectors.

9. Its incumbent or incumbents are appointed or elected, according to the relevant legislative enactment, for a defined period and can only be dismissed, for cause, by the legitimate and competent authorities (cited in Gottherer, 1974, 3).

The characteristics described by the IOI resolution are significant. While acknowledging the statutory nature of the body and the role of legislative process in its creation the IOI stipulates independence of operations for such an ombudsperson and power to investigate public authorities and contribute towards good governance. The over-riding requirement for such a body is the ability to act on behalf of the citizens and to hold public officials accountable to them.

The concept of an ombudsperson itself is rather simple. A citizen aggrieved by some public official should be able to state his complaint to a functionary empowered to investigate and resolve the complaint (Gellhorn, 1965). The functionary should also be empowered to initiate punitive action against the delinquent official and assist in developing better rules so that such complaints do not occur in the first place. Clearly, an institution of this nature and power is likely to promote good governance and hold public officials accountable on behalf of the citizens. In any democracy, such a mechanism is desirable and particularly so where the bureaucracies are indifferent, inefficient and corrupt.

The reasons for the spread of ombudsperson institution around the world comes from the growing powers and impact of bureaucracy over citizens. The decisions and actions of large and complex bureaucratic organizations increasingly affect the life and livelihood of the individual while the problem of effective control over public officials becomes complex, distant and more intractable. For citizens, the ombudsperson is an alternative to expensive and complicated judicial procedures. Individual problems are often solved in a quick and flexible way. The ombudsperson represents a system wherein a citizen can take his grievance against a public official to a functionary who is independent and empowered to investigate the complaint.

The primary responsibility of the ombudsperson is to 'redress grievances of citizens against the administration' (Rowat, 1984, 1) and by doing that he/she protects or defends human rights, resolves conflicts between people and the bureaucracy and ensures transparency and good governance. *Time* (1966) magazine, while paying tribute to the ombudsperson, called it the 'People's Watchdog'. Other terms that have been used include, 'mediator' and 'citizens' defender' (Hill, 1974, 1076). The ombudsperson is indeed a facilitator in the process of grievance management and conflict resolution. The Annual Report of Ombudsman of Barbados (2006, 9) states:

> Although the Ombudsman does not have the power to reverse a government decision or action, the power which he/she has is the power of enquiry, the power of reporting ... the power of persuasion, [and the power] of exposing any act of government which may [not] amount to ... a constitutional or legal infringement of the rights of the individual citizen, but what might amount to, in some ways, an injustice, or an act ... which can be considered unfair although not necessarily illegal.

Rowat (1968, xxiv) suggests that the ombudsman represents the 'unique combination of [three] characteristics': first, 'the Ombudsman is an independent and non-partisan officer of the legislature, usually provided for in the constitution [or by an Act of Parliament], who supervises administration'. Second, he/she 'deals with the specific complaints from the public against administrative injustice and maladministration' and third, he/she 'has the power to investigate, criticize and publicize, but not to reverse, administrative action' (cited in Abedin, 2010, 224). This is the *individual* role of an ombudsperson. Based on its experience with citizens' complaints, the ombudsperson can also give recommendations that seek to alter laws, regulations and/or organizational structures. This is the *collective* dimension of the ombudsperson function. The ombudsperson does not have the power to make binding decisions but does have the right to reveal problems within organizations and persuade those organizations to follow his or her recommendations (Reif, 2008; Roosbroek and Walle, 2008).

Scandinavian Ombudsperson

The *Swedish* ombudsperson has gained wide popularity and is worth examining. The jurisdiction of the Swedish ombudsperson is to supervise the observance of laws and statutes. The ombudsperson may prosecute those who, while exercising their official duties, have through partiality, favoritism or other causes committed any unlawful act or neglected to perform official duties properly. However, in its functions, the ombudsperson bears the same responsibility and obligations as are prescribed for public prosecutors by general civil and criminal laws and the laws of procedure. The Swedish ombudsperson has been empowered with many strong and interesting rules that enable it to discharge its functions and responsibilities effectively. Thus, the ombudsperson may sit in on the deliberations of any Swedish court or administrative board and observe its processes. This power enables it to ensure that the process of justice is not negated or hindered by even judicial bodies and maintains faith of the citizen in its functions. However, the ombudsperson may not express their opinions during this observation.

Furthermore, the ombudsperson has access to records of all the courts, administrative boards and public offices. This is a powerful mechanism to monitor the activities and functions of all public officials. The knowledge that records are subject to external scrutiny promotes greater transparency in public dealings and hence helps keep the officials honest and maintains integrity in the system. The ombudsperson also has the authority to inspect prisons, hospitals and other public offices and essentially examine anything that affects the lives of citizens. Such an ombudsperson also has had a substantial impact on criminal procedure by seeing that the maximum time during which an accused may be kept under arrest is not exceeded, that abusive force is not used, that sentencing is correct and that the execution of penalties follows proper form. This institution has sought to expedite judicial process and even given much attention to personal behavior of judges by enforcing the prohibition against their engagement in other activities. The ombudsperson has been vigilant in ensuring that judges do not sit in cases in which they may be biased and that they promote proper and courteous behavior to the public. Significantly, in these functions and in holding all public institutions accountable, there has been no complaint in Sweden that the ombudsperson has impaired the independence of the courts or other offices.

The Swedish ombudsperson has also pioneered in the field of civil rights. Proactive functions of the ombudsperson have made it possible that an illegal arrest is likely to lead to prosecution of the police officer. The ombudsperson has served to check the exercise of discretion by the police and led to improvements in prison conditions. Furthermore, the ombudsperson has also served as a protector of freedom of speech and freedom of the press. In earlier times, the ombudsperson almost always ordered prosecutions for negligence even if no appreciable harm was done to private citizens. But eventually it became the practice in minor cases to replace prosecution by a letter from the ombudsperson admonishing the officer at fault. Since 1956, the practice is to write a letter explaining why the ombudsperson refuses to act on a complaint (Orfield, 1966, 15).

The ombudsperson makes an annual report to the Riksdag, which is often more than 500 pages in length.

> That is the Ombudsman's real weapon, nobody wants to have his name in that book. It is a kind of *Who's Who in reverse* of public officials and civil servants. There you see an important thing—perhaps the important thing —about the Ombudsman's office—its very existence prevents any number of faults and abuses of power. (Bainbridge, 1965)

Under the Swedish law, every citizen has access to most official documents; it follows that with very few exceptions, all letters of complaint, explanations given by officials and the ombudsperson's own minutes and decisions are public and are open to the press (Gellhorn, 1965). Inevitably, some files are deemed secret, such as those on security matters, trade secrets and the treatment of alcoholics and the insane (Orfield, 1966, 19). Professor Hans Blix of the University of Stockholm Law School has pointed out that much protection against bureaucracy is obtained from the press and from public opinion, discussion in Parliament, public access to relevant documents and the existence of a professionally well-trained civil service and judiciary (Blix, 1965). Yet the ombudsperson presents an alternative mechanism open to the citizens to seek redressal of their grievances. It also serves as a watchdog that deters officials from transgression into illegal and unwanted behavior.

In 1919, Finland adopted the office of ombudsperson as it had been in Sweden, since this country had been a part of Sweden for many centuries before 1809. No field of public activity is outside the jurisdiction of the ombudsperson. He may deal with the whole body of officials, the courts, local government officials and the self-governing organs of the church. The boundary line between his work and that of the Chancellor of Justice is pragmatic in character. Each refrains from interfering in the work of the other. Under the law of November 10, 1933, the Chancellor of Justice was relieved of (1) cases concerning military courts, the Defense Ministry, defense institutions and the National Guard and (2) prisons and prisoners. These matters were the sole authority of the ombudsperson (Orfield, 1966, 25).

Denmark established its ombudsperson in 1953 to accomplish two ends: (1) to control the exercise of delegated legislative power by administrative agencies and (2) to be a safeguard of law and order for the individual. In practice, the second objective has been the more important one (Christensen, 1961). Ministers are under the supervision of the Danish ombudsperson when they exercise their functions as heads of government departments. After investigation, if the Danish ombudsperson finds that a minister or a former minister should be called to account under civil or criminal law, he submits a recommendation to that effect to the Parliament (Orfield, 1966, 34). Interestingly, the Danish ombudsperson can question discretionary judgments of the ministers too. However, these can be criticized only when there is expert knowledge and reliable documentary evidence to contend that the decision was arbitrary or unreasonable (Christensen, 1961). He/she has access to departmental files and empowered to see the inward and outward correspondence such as police reports. However, the ombudsperson's access to internal minutes and documents recording discussions within the department remain a grey area, as the law is silent on this issue. But the ombudsperson is often given access to such minutes and will not decline to investigate cases even where there is some official demand for secrecy. But no confidential information is given to the complainants (Orfield, 1966, 36).

Norway's ombudsperson took office in 1963 and was structured more on the lines of the ombudsperson of Denmark than of Sweden. The ombudsperson has been given the authority to scrutinize each member of the cabinet in his capacity as head of a ministry. Under Section 7 of the Act the ombudsperson has a wide authority to demand information and production of documents from all officials. Unlike Denmark, the ombudsperson in this country does not have access to the internal working papers of the administrative bodies. The ombudsperson has the same right as the courts to demand information hedged by rules of professional secrecy. In judicial proceedings, the official must have permission from superior authority in order to testify about certain matters (Orfield, 1966). Thus, a grey area persists that clouds the powers of the ombudsperson to hold public officials accountable but generally the system has worked smoothly with mutual respect and cooperation.

New Zealand is another country which has followed the Scandinavian model and created the office of a powerful ombudsperson. While there were no scandals affecting the politicians and hardly any demand from the citizens, the Parliament created the ombudsperson 'not to clean up a mess, but rather, simply to provide insurance against future messes' (Gellhorn, 1965, 1166). The New Zealand ombudsperson structure is similar to its counterpart in Sweden but some shield has been provided to public officials and their ministers. For example, comments made by a bureaucrat in a document regarding informing the minister about an issue have been opened to the ombudsperson but the final decision of the minister is shielded from external scrutiny (Gellhorn, 1965, 1168). Another novelty is to educate the bureaucrats and civil servants to express more trust in the citizens and not put official rules above citizen convenience. Thus, an IRS commissioner discourages 'his subordinates from insisting that every debatable issue be tested out in formal appellate proceedings' (1965, 1174). An internal memo by the commissioner makes this point poetically: 'Taxpayers are people; we want you handle cases with speed; with reasonableness and with every possible courtesy and consideration. You must not strain the law purely in order to protect the revenue' (Gellhorn, 1965, 1174).

The European ombudsperson was first established in the Maastricht Treaty of 1992. While the ombudsperson has been empowered to receive complaints about instances of maladministration, the power does not extend to inquire into the functions of the Court of Justice. If the ombudsperson finds examples of maladministration, these must be first brought to notice of the institution concerned and subsequently a three months period is to be provided for the institution to provide an explanation. Upon receipt of the opinion, the ombudsperson must prepare a report to the Parliament and must inform the person lodging the complaint about the outcome of the inquiry (Cadeddu, 2004). Interestingly, the ombudsperson has started performing a dual role —investigating citizen complaints against public officials and developing preventive mechanisms against maladministration.

Inquiry proceedings generally begin upon the receipt of a written complaint by the ombudsperson, but these may also be initiated sue motu. The ombudsperson first determines the admissibility of the complaint and if the decision is to go ahead with the inquiry, a copy of the complaint must be provided to the public office concerned and to request that an opinion be submitted within three months. If, on the other hand, the ombudsperson finds that there has been an instance of minor maladministration, the first attempt is to reconcile the parties. If the parties decide to settle, the case is closed and archived as a friendly solution. This often occurs when the institution acknowledges its wrongdoing, provides an apology to the complainant and offers compensation for any damages. If, on the other hand, this does not occur, the ombudsperson may close the file by providing a critical remark against the institution. However, the observations and recommendations of the ombudsperson, as well as its periodic reports, are not binding on the institutions that they address. These actions by the ombudsperson do not impose legally binding restrictions, but rather serve to express opinions, to expose problematic areas and to suggest potential solutions. Therefore, the outcome is that they cannot be challenged in court (Cadeddu, 2004) and hence limits the effectiveness of the ombudsperson.

Strength of the Ombudsperson

This institution has been successful in the above mentioned and some other countries because of its ability to provide a free system of seeking redressal of public grievances. The ombudsperson has functioned as a facilitator in managing complaints and resolving conflicts between the citizens and public officials. Its independence from the legislatures and power to inquire into the domains of the elected and senior public officials has been its major strength. The 'key to understanding the Ombudsman's popularity is its relative simplicity' (Hill, 1974, 1076). 'The investigation conducted by the ombudsperson is usually characterized by speedy, inexpensive and informal procedures. No attorney is required and tellingly, the aggrieved citizen does not have to pay fees for filing a complaint' (Abedin, 2010, 223). Once a complaint is made 'the Ombudsman becomes the moving party' (Frank, 1975, 57) initiating an investigation and taking all necessary steps to address grievance of the petitioner. The ombudsperson can investigate a complaint quickly, impartially and 'informally yet thoroughly; and he can give a well-balanced report on the pros and cons' (Holmgren, 1968, 229).

A notable feature has been its distinction from judicial courts. The courts of law have traditionally played a very important role in addressing abuses by public officials. However, a judicial process is slow, cumbersome and costly. Unlike the ombudsperson office, regular courts cannot conduct informal investigations. Litigation is an expensive, time consuming, protracted, slow and very complicated and cumbersome process that often frustrates the complainant. In many cases, the citizen bears with injustice because he cannot afford to follow up the litigation. Moreover, 'the courts are limited to basically adverse party proceedings' (Frank, 1975, 56). The judicial process is also highly impersonal and formal, which it should be in view of special position and responsibility of the judiciary in society. On the contrary, as noted above, the process of an ombudsperson's investigation is very informal and flexible and there is an element of personal touch and concern. Furthermore, as the complainant pays a nominal or no fee, the ombudsperson provides 'much cheaper justice than the regular legal system can offer' (Sawer, 1968, 72). It supplements, at least partially, the role and functions of the regular judiciary (Abedin, 2010, 227).

Most nations have also created administrative tribunals and courts to address some of the problems of judicial inquiry into citizen grievances against public officials. While these do provide quicker access and cheaper alternatives but 'relatively speaking, [while] these tribunals operated much more informally', they 'still follow court like adversary procedure' (Frank, 1975, 56) and suffered most of the disadvantages of regular courts of law. Abedin (2010, 228) points that 'parallel existence of an ombudsperson and a Supreme Administrative

Court in Sweden has not resulted in unnecessary overlapping or duplication of functions'. Even France, which has a strong and well-regarded administrative court/law system in the world, has introduced the ombudsperson system in the early 1970s 'to complement the work of the Counseil d' é tat' (Stacey, 1978, 92), that is, the Council of State which acts as the highest administrative court in that country.

The strength of the ombudsperson system of justice comes from its ability to deliver the most effective level of individual and public benefit (Abraham, 2012). Such an institution, reputed for its integrity and functioning as a bridge for resolving issues between the citizens and public officials, generally commands respect and hence has the power to evolve amicable solutions to the grievances of the people. Furthermore, since it occupies a defined position within the constitutional arrangements of the country, it is able to grow and promote public policies that serve the people efficiently and satisfactorily. However, the major strength comes from 'the relationship between Ombudsman and other integrity institutions, including inspection and regulatory functions; of the balance between the fire-fighting, fire-watching and fire prevention aspirations of Ombudsman; and of the arrangements for inaugurating future Ombudsman schemes'(Abraham, 2012, 101).

In India, an ombudsperson like institution has been in demand to solely combat corruption in public offices. Hitherto, the mantle of protecting human rights rested on the judiciary, a major subject for the ombudsperson in many countries. In particular, the PIL system evolved by the Supreme Court (Verma, 2001) has been effective in this regard. Furthermore, the establishment of the NHRC has also provided a strong institution to check for violation of human rights in the country. These mechanisms have limited the need for an ombudsperson to venture into this subject. Additionally, the inability of the courts to vigorously pursue corruption cases and the growing delay in completing trials has fueled the demand for an exclusive independent agency to pursue high-level corruption.

Lokpal—the Indian Ombudsperson

The term 'Lokpal' (caretaker of the people) was coined for the first time in 1963 by Dr L. M. Singhvi. The then Law Minister, Ashoke Kumar Sen, first proposed the concept of a constitutional ombudsperson in the Indian Parliament in the early 1960s. The term 'Lokpal' is the Indian version of a Swedish ombudsperson. It was in 1966, that a Lokpal was proposed at the center and a Lokayukta in the states. For the first time in 1968, this bill was referred to the joint committee of the two Houses and was passed by the Lok Sabha. While the Bill was pending before the Rajya Sabha, the Lok Sabha was dissolved and the Bill could not be passed. The House passed it in 1969, but while it was pending, the Lok Sabha was again dissolved and the Bill lapsed. This Bill was further reintroduced in 1971, 1977, 1985, 1989, 1996, 1998 and 2001 but was never passed. In the year 1977, during the fifth Lok Sabha, Indira Gandhi introduced the Bill but it again lapsed after waiting for six long years in a queue to be considered; the reason being that the Lok Sabha was dissolved. In the same year, Morarji Desai's government again introduced the Bill after the joint committee vetted it in the year 1978. While the Bill was under consideration with the Lok Sabha, the latter got prorogued and dissolved and therefore the Bill again lapsed. In 1985, the then Prime Minister, Rajiv Gandhi presented the Lokpal Bill and this was referred to the joint committee, which again led nowhere. Despite such failures this Bill was again introduced in the year 1989, 1996, 1998, 2001, 2005 and more recently in 2008. Each time the Bill was introduced in one House, it was referred to other committees for recommendations such as the joint committee and before the government could take a final decision the House was dissolved. Each time a failure and the road to its success seemed tough. Successive failures of governments after independence to pass the Lokpal Bill is an unambiguous reflection of the lack of political will to enact such a law.

Meanwhile, the issue of corruption in public offices reached a crescendo in 2011 when the Anna Hazare led movement staged spectacular protests in Delhi and other parts of the country. The series of scams emerging since 2010 exposed high level corruption within the UPA II government of Manmohan Singh. Irrespective of the fact that the PM continued to be viewed as honest, corruption cases engulfing his ministers in scams relating to Commonwealth Games, purchase of helicopter from Italy and the allotment of coalmines cast a dark shadow over his government. He was deemed incapable of controlling his cabinet ministers and pursuing the criminal charges to their logical end.

The shenanigans of the Law Minister to dictate to the CBI and dilute its investigations further enraged the country. In this background, the demand to have an independent Lokpal to ensure integrity in public office caught the imagination of the citizens who came out in large numbers to support Hazare and his demand for combating corruption.

Fifty-two years after its first introduction, the Lokpal Bill was finally enacted in India on December 18, 2013. The reasons for the enactment of this Act was perhaps catalyzed by the stunning victory of Aam Admi political party that won a large number of seats in the assembly elections of Delhi in 2013. The rise of the Aam Admi Party itself was rooted in the struggle for Lokpal with which Arvind Kejriwal was associated. While Anna Hazare started the agitation as a civil and apolitical movement against corruption and demand for Lokpal, Arvind Kejriwal moved away to create a political party with the avowed purpose of fighting corruption. He parted ways with Anna Hazare group on the issue of entry in political arena of the 'India against Corruption' movement. Perhaps, in view of the fact that national elections were due in April 2014, all the political parties quickly resolved their differences and legislated this new Act. Anna Hazare also expressed his approval to this version of the law, bringing closure to the chapter of struggle by India against Corruption to get a strong anti-corruption law passed.

The Lokpal and Lokayuktas Act, 2013 (No. 1 of 2014)

This is an Act that provides for the establishment of a body of Lokpal for the unions and Lokayuktas for the states to inquire into allegations of corruption against public functionaries. The Act provides for the Lokpal chairperson to be selected by a panel comprising the Prime Minister, Lok Sabha Speaker, Leader of the Opposition in Lok Sabha, Chief Justice of India or his nominee (another Supreme Court judge) and an eminent jurist nominated by the President of India. Interestingly, amongst the remaining eight members of the Lokpal, 50 per cent of the seats are reserved for SCs, STs, OBCs, minorities and women. Furthermore, 50 per cent of the eight members are also stipulated to have a judicial background with the reservation clause to apply to them as well. The Act enables inquiry against all categories of public officials including the Prime Minister. However, the Lokpal has been restricted into examining matters related to international relations, external and internal security and maintenance of public order, atomic energy and under the charge of the Prime Minister. The Lokpal and the Lokayuktas both have been empowered to receive complaints against elected representatives, the MPs, MLAs and other public officials and serve as final appellate authority for all grievances related to public service functions. In another novel move, the Lokpal has the power to inquire against NGOs receiving more than ten lakh rupees or more of foreign funds.

In an attempt to further empower the Lokpal, the Act provides for a new prosecution wing within the CBI. The Lokpal will have supervisory control over the CBI or any other investigative agency into corruption cases referred by it to the agency. This has created confusion, for the CVC has simultaneously been permitted to supervise the cases referred to the CBI. An attempt has been made to shield investigating officers by ensuring that their transfer will take place only upon approval of the Lokpal. The bill also incorporates provisions for attachment and confiscation of property acquired by corrupt means, even while prosecution is pending.

Can Lokpal be Effective against Public Corruption in India?

Effectiveness of an ombudsperson and anti-corruption agencies is a subject of major research.

> The effectiveness of the Ombudsman office is largely measured by how well it is able to deal with individual complaints, the discretion it uses when determining which problems to address and to a more limited extent, its ability to influence broader administrative reforms. Office effectiveness and efficiency are often influenced by the legal authority granted to the Ombudsperson and the realities of operating such an office. (National Democratic Institute for International Affairs, 2005, 23)

Ingredients of a sound ombudsperson are many and the institution needs to function independently to address concerns of the citizens and keep the public officials accountable.

Gottehrer (2009) argues that the irreducible minimum characteristics for an effective ombudsperson must be independence, impartiality and fairness, credible review process and confidentiality. Independence is best guaranteed when an ombudsperson is created by an act of Parliament rather than through executive decree or regulation. Furthermore, the selection of members to serve on the ombudsperson would ensure independence when they are not seen as political appointments. A fixed long term appointment and an adequate budget, sufficient to support the office's functions, the ombudsperson having the sole power to appoint and remove staff, immunity for the ombudsperson and staff from liability and criminal prosecution for acts performed under the law, removing the ombudsperson actions from court review except to determine the ombudsperson's jurisdiction, and authorizing the ombudsperson to appeal to courts to enforce the office's powers, are other factors that help establish the independence of the body.

Appointing prominent citizens known for their integrity to the post and removing the institution from political considerations best establishes the impartiality and fairness of the ombudsperson. Further, allowing anyone to bring a complaint to the ombudsperson without paying a fee and giving the right to be heard to the accused officials helps earn respect and cooperation from the citizens and the government alike. The inquiry process of the ombudsperson is seen to be credible when it has a broad defined general jurisdiction. The ombudsperson must be authorized to investigate anyone's grievances concerning any decision, recommendation or any act done or omitted relating to matters specified by law, by any organization or person over whom jurisdiction exists, including government or semi-government departments and agencies (Gottehrer, 2009, 7). Moreover, giving the ombudsperson subpoena power or a similar power to compel production of records and people to speak without restrictions is a basic necessity for an effective institution. It is of course expected that the ombudsperson will publish and publicize its findings and recommendations periodically to keep citizens informed about its functions. Finally, maintaining the confidentially of complainants and its sources is equally important. People who complain to the ombudsperson and government officials and employees who respond to the ombudsperson investigations may fear reprisals. The ombudsperson needs to keep those communications confidential. In nearly all circumstances, the ombudsperson may not be forced to testify or produce records to reveal whistleblowers and others, exposing corrupt practices.

Reif (cited in Gottehrer, 2009, 16) has identified some important indicators for evaluating the effectiveness of a classical or hybrid ombudsperson. These are democratic governance of the state, independence of the institution from government, expanded jurisdiction to cover all public institutions, extent and adequacy of powers, accessibility of the office to members of the public, level of cooperation with other bodies, operational efficiency (level of financial and human resources), accountability and transparency, personal character and expertise of the person(s) appointed to the head of the institution, behavior of government in not politicizing the institution and having a receptive attitude toward its activities, and above all, the credibility of the office in the eyes of the populace.

Mary Rowe who served as an MIT ombudsperson from 1973 to 2014 states (2001) that the ombudsperson exists to further principles of fairness and equity, legal and honorable organizational practices, and humane and just administration. Moreover, the ombudsperson seeks to attain these objectives as an independent, neutral, confidential and informal practitioner. While it seeks to curb corruption and other malpractices in public administration, it does so by offering options for dealing with citizen concerns, fostering appropriate, efficient redressal of grievances and even working for appropriate systems change. It is also important to note that ombudsperson is part of a system; the entire edifice of the government exists to provide a large number of services and basic rights of the citizens. The ombudsperson cannot take responsibility for all the functions of the state. It can only work as a bridge between the citizen and the agents of the state to emphasize the issues of fairness, safety, equity, justice and welfare. The ombudsperson is deemed to be a neutral institution that mainly seeks to foster a fair *process* rather than delivering a specific *outcome* (ibid., 2001, 2). It is therefore conceivable that an ombudsperson may work competently and honorably without satisfying all stakeholders in a given complaint. An effective ombudsperson would perhaps offer informal dispute resolution options rather than seeking to punish someone. Thus, the ombudsperson will be effective if it focuses upon listening, coaching, intervening, mediating and facilitating generic approaches to a problem. Such an ombudsperson will support changes to the system, prevent needless disputes and maintain confidence of whistle-blowers (ibid., 2001, 3).

The above discussion makes it clear that the effectiveness of the constituted Lokpal in India can only be assessed after it begins functioning and establishes its credentials over a period of time. However, we can begin to assess the potential of such an ombudsperson based upon its proposed structure, powers and functions as stipulated in the Act. We propose to evaluate this in several ways. Firstly, we examine its structure to assess the inherent powers and means made available to it for effective functioning. Secondly, we examine and assess the existing Lokayuktas in various states, and based upon their experience, predict the effectiveness of this newly created Lokpal.

Critique of Lokpal and Lokayuktas Act, 2013

The major problem in effective functioning of the newly established Lokpal is the process of appointment of the Lokpal itself. While the overall provisions of this law appear to be in consonance with Anna Hazare's Jan Lokpal Bill, an in-depth reading suggests that enough leeway has been left for the government in the Act to 'pack' the Lokpal with favorable members. Section 3 (2) (a) of Chapter II of the Lokpal and Lokayuktas Act, 2013 states, 'The Lokpal shall consist of (a) Chairperson, who is or has been a Judge of the Supreme Court or an *eminent person who fulfills the eligibility specified in clause (b) of sub section 3: ...'* (italics is our emphasis).

Furthermore, the eligibility clause (b) of sub-section 3 describes an *eminent person* as 'a person of impeccable integrity and outstanding ability having special knowledge and expertise of not less than 25 years in the matters relating to anti-corruption policy, public administration, vigilance, finance, including insurance and banking, law and management'. The parameters outlined for qualifying as an eminent person appear to indicate that these are tailored for administrators, serving or retired bureaucrats, legal luminaries and solicitors, who have been under obligation of the government at some time or the other. There is little attempt to bring outsiders, not connected with the government, with impeccable record of selfless public service and moral uprightness into the organization.

An important provision of the Act is the constitution of the selection committee that selects the members to serve in the Lokpal. The selection committee is defined and given the powers in Section 4 (1) (a), (b), (c), (d) and (e). The selection committee has five members comprising the Prime Minister as the Chairperson and members consisting of the Leader of Opposition, The Lok Sabha Speaker and the Chief Justice of India or a Judge of the Supreme Court nominated by him and one eminent jurist, to be nominated as the fifth member by the President. As may be seen here, the fifth member is crucial to tilt the balance in favor of the establishment.

Not surprisingly, a controversy erupted over the recommendation of PP Rao, a Supreme Court lawyer, as the fifth member as an eminent jurist of the Selection Committee. The then Leader of Opposition, one of the members of the selection committee, alleged that Rao was a 'Congress loyalist' and took the controversy to the doorsteps of the President, seeking his support for its demand for a consensus on the issue. It was alleged that only one name was suggested and subsequently approved by the President. At the official party briefing, the then BJP's deputy leader in Rajya Sabha, Ravi Shankar Prasad, blamed the former Prime Minister for the row and accused him of having 'failed' in his duty on the Lokpal appointment issue as it went against the spirit of Parliamentary approval. He further charged that Prime Minister Manmohan Singh, by insisting upon this one particular name and forcing its approval was seeking to negate the entire spirit of the selection committee recommendations and Parliamentary approval.

The rules guiding the appointment of members are two pronged and equally subject to manipulation. Once the selection committee is constituted, it then appoints a search committee that identifies suitable members for the Lokpal. The provisions guiding the function of the search committee are similarly loaded in favor of the establishment. According to Section 4(3):

> The Selection Committee shall for the purposes of selecting the Chairperson and Members of the Lokpal and for *preparing a panel of persons* to be considered for appointment as such, constitute a Search Committee consisting of at least *seven persons* of standing and having special knowledge and expertise in the matters relating to anti-corruption policy, public administration, vigilance, policy making, finance including insurance and banking, law and management or in any other matter which, in the opinion of the Selection Committee, may be useful in making the selection of the Chairperson and Members of the Lokpal. Provided that not less than 50 per cent of the members of the Search Committee shall be from amongst the persons belonging to the Scheduled Castes,

the Scheduled Tribes, Other Backward Classes, Minorities and women. (Italics is our emphasis)

Furthermore, the Act stipulates that the Selection Committee may also consider any person other than the persons recommended by the Search Committee.

It is pertinent to note that two eminent jurists refused to join the Lokpal search committee on account of the fact that, being eminent jurists themselves, they examined the law and the rules framed therein and found fundamental flaws. Senior advocate Fali Nariman declined to serve on the search committee, voicing the fear that in the two-stage selection process, the most competent, the most independent and the most courageous will get overlooked (*India Express*, 2014). A retired Supreme Court judge, Justice K. T. Thomas, who went through the rules framed under the Lokpal and Lokayuktas Act, also objected that the search committee's recommendations were not binding on the selection committee, headed by the Prime Minister.

The processes involving the functions of the search committee are further constrained. The rules stipulate that the search panel will scrutinize only those applications forwarded to it by the Department of Personnel and Training. The rule circumscribes the search committee's role in choosing names outside the list submitted by the government and blocks any independent nomination from the people at large. Furthermore, there the selection committee retains the discretion *not* to accept the panel of names recommended by the search committee. In fact, the selection committee is free to consider names from outside the panel too. All this makes the process of choosing members to serve on the Lokpal extremely complex, open to manipulation and casts doubts on the integrity of the institution and the sincerity of the government in actually setting up an autonomous and courageous Lokpal.

The functioning of the Lokpal is also inhibited by unavoidable delays, inbuilt in the law and the system. This is evident from the constitution of benches of the Lokpal. There will be eight members and a chairperson in the Lokpal body according to Section 3 (2) that stipulates (a) a Chairperson, who is or has been a Chief Justice of India or is or has been a Judge of the Supreme Court or an eminent person who fulfills the eligibility specified in clause (b) of sub-section (3) and (b) such number of members, not exceeding eight out of whom 50 per cent shall be judicial members. However, according to Section

16 (b) of the Act, a bench to examine a complaint may be constituted by the chairperson with two or more members as the chairperson may deem fit. This, in practice, would mean that at any given point of time there would be a maximum of four benches only if the lowest number of two members is taken into account. Considering the volume of complaints that would be generated, these four benches would be overloaded and therefore cause delay in disposals of cases, as is the current state of the investigating agencies in India.

The Lokpal also has a rather curious provision wherein the chairperson has extraordinary power to transfer a case to another bench. Section 18 of the Act states that on an application made by the complainant or the public servant for transfer, the chairperson, after giving an opportunity of being heard by the complainant or the public servant, as the case may be, may transfer any case pending before one bench for disposal to any other bench. This provision is going to be widely used or rather misused to delay proceedings at various stages, particularly by the public servant. It also signals that the integrity of the members constituting a bench could be called into question at any stage and hence compromises the sanctity of the Lokpal per se.

The Act has been designed with little consideration for deliberate acts by the accused to delay or vitiate the inquiry. The process to be followed by the Lokpal has inbuilt delay in inquiry and investigation procedures. Following are some of the provisions of law which show that the legal process appears to be rather defensive and slow in investigating and inquiring into the allegations against public servants.

Section 20(b), paragraph 3 stipulates that before ordering an investigation under clause (b), the Lokpal shall call for comments of the public servant so as to determine whether there exists a prima facie case for investigation. As can be seen, no time limit has been prescribed and hence such a call for comments will only delay the inquiry. Similarly, Section 20(2) provides a complex process for investigation into complaints against public officials. For instance, during the preliminary inquiry referred to in sub-section (1), the Inquiry Wing or any agency (including the DSPE) shall conduct a preliminary inquiry and on the basis of material, information and documents collected as also after seeking the comments on the allegations from the public servant and the competent authority submit, within 60 days from the date of receipt of the reference, a report to the Lokpal. Interestingly, a time limit of 60 days has been provided for this inquiry while the entire time for completion of enquiry is set at a maximum of 180 days. Given the past experience, it is doubtful that this limit would be respected or maintained.

Similarly, Section 20(3) provides for a bench consisting of not less than three members of the Lokpal who *shall* consider every report received under sub-section (2) from the Inquiry Wing or any agency (including the DSPE), *and after giving an opportunity of being heard to the public servant,* decide whether there exists a prima facie case, and proceed with one or more of the [following] actions. Thus, there will be two stages where the investigative agency and then the bench will determine if the allegations are prima facie true. Moreover, the official will be able to contest the complaint at both these stages. Again, no time frame has been prescribed and it is clear that such procedures will cause inordinate delays in the functioning of the Lokpal and thereby defeat the very purpose of speedy investigation and charge sheeting of the accused public official.

The Lokpal has several other provisions that are likely to be exploited and cause deferment in the inquiries. Thus, section 20(7) states that a bench consisting of not less than three members of the Lokpal shall consider *every* report received by it under sub-section (6) from any agency (including the DSPE) and *after* obtaining the comments of the competent authority and the public servant may proceed with the inquiry. Similarly, section 21(b) has provisions wherein the Lokpal shall provide that person a *reasonable opportunity* of being heard in the preliminary inquiry and to produce evidence in his defense, consistent with the *principles of natural justice.* The inference is obvious! Time frame of 6 months provided for the completion of the preliminary enquiry and 12 months for investigation of cases would be practically impossible to be adhered to given the long rope that would be given to the accused public servant before deciding the next course of action, that is, prosecution in the case.

Apart from the inordinate delay that is inbuilt into the law governing the Lokpal, the Act does not provide for expanding the scope of inquiry. We have described before that corruption becomes possible due to the opportunities and lack of transparency provided by the system. Unless these are exposed and departmental rules and procedures are amended, similar corrupt practices will continue. The Lokpal needs to be empowered in ways similar to the Swedish ombudsperson to have the power to expand its inquiry and examine the institutional processes and culture where corruption has been exposed. It is only when the Lokpal acts to reform the processes and forces public officials to move towards a culture of integrity and transparency that corruption can be effectively curbed. A limited Lokpal, lacking powers to examine the performance, functions and culture of affected institutions will barely make a dent in the wide-spread corruption harming the country.

Current Status of the Lokpal and Lokayuktas Act, 2013

Though this Act received the Presidential assent on January 1, 2014, and came into force from January 16, 2014, as per the Gazette Notification, the appointment of a Lokpal and the implementation of the Act still remains pending. It is noteworthy to mention here that the anti-corruption crusader, Anna Hazare, broke his fast in December 2013 on the assurance of the enactment of the Lokpal law. The Act was passed by the previous UPA II government. The current NDA government, led by the Prime Minister, Narendra Modi, was sworn in, May 2014. However, even after the Lokpal and Lokayuktas Act, 2013 received the Presidential assent on January 1, 2014, the current NDA government, in power since May 2014, has neither been able to appoint a Lokpal nor implement the Act so far (till April 2018).

These provisions of the Principal Act, enshrined in Section 44, Sub Sections 2 (a) and (b), were substituted through Section 2 of the Lokpal and Lokayuktas (Amendment) Act, 2016 as such: '44. On and from the date of commencement of this Act, every public servant shall make a declaration of his assets and liabilities in such form and manner as may be prescribed.'

The Amendment, thus, does away with the responsibility hitherto cast upon the public servant to declare assets of the spouse and dependent children also. The inference is obvious and there for all to see.

In fact, contrary to the spirit of the Hazare anti-corruption movement, the current government has, through the Lokpal and Lokayuktas Act (Amendment) Act, 2016, diluted the provisions relating to the declaration of assets by a public official by substituting the provisions of Sub Section 2 (a) and (b) under Section 44 of the original Act of 2013 in which the public official was required to furnish information to the competent authority about the assets of which he, his spouse and his dependent children are, jointly or severally, owners or beneficiaries; as also his liabilities and that of his spouse and his dependent children.

These provisions of the Principal Act, enshrined in Section 44, Sub Sections 2 (a) and (b), were substituted through Section 2 of the Lokpal and Lokayuktas (Amendment) Act, 2016 as such: '44. On and from the date of commencement of this Act, every public servant shall make a declaration of his assets and liabilities in such form and manner as may be prescribed'.

The Amendment, thus, does away with the responsibility hitherto cast upon the public servant to declare assets of the spouse and dependent children also. The inference is obvious and there for all to see.

It is an open secret, as borne out by investigation of a large number of corruption cases, that the modus operandi of a corrupt public official has been to 'invest' and launder the ill-gotten wealth in the name of the spouse and or dependent children by buying properties and jewelry, purchase of 'benami' land, and flats/houses, setting up of businesses in wives' and/or children's names, payment of high value premium on insurance policies in the name of the spouse and the dependent children, setting up of shell companies in the name of spouse and children, etc.

The major hurdle in the selection of the Lokpal and implementation of the Act is the that the Lokpal and Lokayuktas Act, 2013 is yet to be amended by the Parliament to substitute the term 'Leader of the Opposition' by the term 'Leader of the Majority Party'. It is pertinent to point out here that the single largest Congress party has not been accorded the status of the principal opposition party and hence there is no Leader of Opposition in the Lok Sabha (House of the People). Under Section 4 of the Act, the chairperson (Lokpal) and members shall be appointed by the President after obtaining the recommendations of a selection committee consisting of the Prime Minister (chairperson) and four other members comprising the Speaker of the House of People (Lok Sabha), the leader of the opposition in the House of People (Lok Sabha), the Chief Justice of India or a Judge of the Supreme Court nominated by him and one eminent jurist as recommended by the chairperson and the four members to be nominated by the President.

Already, we are witnessing impediments in the establishment of the Lokpal even before it has been operationalized and tested in practice. The new BJP government, elected to office with full majority in May 2014, in the name of removing certain difficulties and in making the Lokpal functional, has adopted dilatory practices. The Lokpal Act refers to the nomenclature of the Leader of Opposition (LOP) in the selection committee. However, as no LOP is in existence in the current Lok Sabha, the government, after considerable delay introduced a modification simultaneously both in the Lok Sabha and the Rajya Sabha on December 7, 2015. Thereafter, the Lokpal and Lokayuktas and other Related Law (Amendment Bill), 2014 was referred to a 31-member Parliamentary committee headed by Congress MP, EM Sudarsana Natchiappan. The committee has now considered this amendment and recommended integrating CVC and anti-corruption wing of the CBI to work directly under the command and control of the Lokpal to deal with corruption cases. As suggested by the government, the leader of the single largest opposition party in the Lok Sabha will be included in the panel in case there is no recognized LOP. This is significant since the panel will be choosing the chairperson and members of the Lokpal. However, this recommendation must now be accepted by the Parliament where it is languishing.

The amendments recommended will no doubt further water down the original Act in other ways too. Besides substituting the term LOP with the Leader of the largest Opposition Party, the Bill has strayed into certain areas which can be construed as dilution of the earlier Act. The government succumbed to the pressure exerted by the bureaucracy that did not wish to have any provision regarding annual declaration of property (both immovable and movable) to the competent authority within 30 days of the Act coming into force. The government has agreed that the public servant would need to declare only the movable assets owned/acquired/inherited by him/her. In other words, movable assets in the name of wife and children need not be disclosed. The above mentioned Parliamentary Standing Committee has also reiterated that public disclosure of assets and liabilities of public servants, including employees and politicians may not be necessary. Siding with the public officials, the committee commented that the colonial mindset of suspecting the officials needs to be discarded! It added that any inquiry into the assets of the official must be done in a professional manner so as not to give rise to a feeling that every government servant is suspect and under surveillance. Furthermore, it should be ensured that the government servants are not subjected to unnecessary clarifications or queries as a result of such a scrutiny. The original demand by the protesters and citizen groups to keep checks upon the public officials has been surreptitiously watered down.

Similarly, to give teeth to the secretary of the Lokpal, and enable him/her to carry out his/her task fearlessly, the Act had provided that the rank be that of Secretary to the Government of India. The selection committee has downgraded the rank of the Lokpal Secretary to the status of Additional Secretary. Under this dispensation, the Lokpal Secretary would be one rank below the rank of all the secretaries of the Government of India and after his/her tenure with the Lokpal, would still be looking forward to another promotion to the rank of a secretary before retirement. The Lokpal secretary would thus continue to be beholden to the elite bureaucracy. In the same vein, the Act had laid down that the Director of Inquiry and the Director of Prosecution of Lokpal were to be of the rank of Additional Secretary. The Committee has now recommended downgrading this rank to the level of joint secretary. Such a move obviously seems to be aimed at diluting the strength of the officers, who would play a major role in the investigation of charges against those in senior positions.[1]

Lokpal and Ombudsperson: Comparative Perspectives

It is also useful to compare the Lokpal with the ombudsperson of nations known for their virtually corruption-free environment and high integrity of their officials. In this context, we examine two schools of thought that consider utility and appropriateness of the ombudsperson institution in dealing with corruption in public institutions. Sir Ronald Algie, former Speaker of the New Zealand House of Representatives, argues that the 'Ombudsman system probably would not work well everywhere' and that it works in New Zealand because 'corruption is so rare as to be deemed virtually non-existent' (cited in Gellhorn, 1965, 1211). The implication is that it is an institution for more developed countries. But some scholars argue that suitable reforms and a positive environment can usher change and that in due course of time, this

---

1 See Chairman of the Department-related Parliamentary Standing Committee on Personnel, Public Grievances, Law and Justice, Rajya Sabha's 77th Report on the Lokpal and Lokayuktas and Other Related Law (Amendment) Bill, 2014 dated December 3, 2015.

institution can become effective in combating corruption (Caiden, 1984; Ombudsman of Jamaica, 1981; Rowat, 1984).

We argue that the ombudsperson functions effectively and with high reputation in developed nations because the public officials themselves maintain high standards of probity, service and accountability to the citizens. In these nations, the citizens expect and receive services of high quality and their grievances are quickly and professionally addressed. Accordingly, the number of complaints against such public officials is small and the ombudsperson handles these quickly and in a fair manner. This further reinforces the perception of a good quality service and general satisfaction from public officials. We test this by an examination of the workload of an ombudsperson in many developed nations.

The workload of reputed ombudsperson

Largely, the workload of most ombudsperson in developed nations is comparatively light. According to the 2011–12 annual report of Denmark's ombudsman, 4,922 cases were brought to its notice of which 1,001 (20.3 per cent) were substantively investigated and 3,921 (79.7 per cent) were rejected. Substantive cases are those where the ombudsperson carries out an investigation and submits the case to the relevant authority or authorities for consultation and concludes the case with a statement. These cases may be complaint cases, inspections or cases initiated on the ombudsperson's own initiative. Interestingly, only 153 of the substantively investigated cases led to criticism and recommendation to the concerned authority; the highest proportion being that of ministry of justice where 36 out of 256 led to some criticism or recommendation (Danish Parliamentary Ombudsman, 2011, 91). Furthermore, 1,898 cases were rejected because the citizens could complain about the matter or appeal the decision within the administrative appeal system. However, the ombudsperson does inform the complainant of the possibility of returning after his or her complaint/appeal options have been exhausted and a final decision has been made.

The workload of the ombudsman in Finland, another Scandinavian nation known for its corruption-free image, is similarly light. In 2012, there were 6,695 new cases and 1,693 cases pending from previous years taken up by the ombudsperson. Of these 5, 002 could be resolved through various mechanisms in which significantly only 834 led to some action such as reprimands (39); rebuke (379) recommendations (27) and none for prosecution (Parliamentary Ombudsman of Finland, 2013, 131). Equally significantly, in 2, 460 cases, no action was taken for variety of reasons and in 1,340 cases no investigation was launched as the complainant had other recourses.

The Norwegian ombudsman inquired into 3,046 cases in 2012 and it could dispose of 3,167 cases (some pending from previous years). Of these 1,489 were simply dismissed and only 11 per cent of the cases led to some form of criticism or recommendation to the concerned public agency (Norway Ombudsman, 2012, 31). The Norwegian ombudsperson interestingly also provides a chart informing the time it has taken to hold its inquires.

Average case-processing time

	2012	2011	2010
Cases dismissed	16 days	17 days	15 days
Cases closed without raising with the public Administration	46 days	47 days	39 days
Cases closed after being raised with the public Administration	210 days	183 days	170 days

The ombudsperson acknowledges that while its productivity has increased but working on individual cases is both time and resource consuming. Further, it assures that in order to be fair and just, it will continue to handle the cases in an objective and thorough manner.

The office of Nova Scotia (Canada) ombudsman combines an effective early resolution process, called administrative reviews, with formal or in-depth investigations and detailed examinations of systemic policy issues. Another key strategy is proactive problem solving used extensively by the youth services unit involving onsite identification and informal resolution of potential problems. In 2012–13, the number of matters addressed by the office of the ombudsman was 2,435 comprising 1,226 administrative review cases, 558 meetings with youth in care and custody, 598 inquiries referred to other jurisdictions and 53 youth evaluation surveys. Significantly, 957 out of the total 1226 administrative reviews were resolved by mediation between the complainant and the respondent (Nova Scotia Ombudsman, 2013, 6).

The Corrupt Practices Investigation Bureau (CPIB) of Singapore is the premier agency to inquire into charges of corruption against public officials. In 2012, CPIB received a total of 906 complaints of which 64 per cent were corruption related and the rest were concerned with misappropriate of funds, cheating and such cases that were referred to the concerned departments for inquiry (CPIB, 2013, 4).

The above brief summary of workload of the ombudsperson and anti-corruption agencies in countries with high degree of reputation for probity is meaningful. These ombudspersons are well regarded, for they are effective in meeting citizen complaints fully. In general, the public officials in these countries enjoy good reputation and complaint against their actions is relatively small. Since citizen satisfaction about public offices is high, the small fraction of complaints lodged by the citizens is easy to resolve. As seen in all these countries, very few of the complaints result in prosecution or punishment for the guilty. Most are mediated and citizens are satisfied with the outcome. The percentage of cases in which the ombudsperson ends up criticizing the public agency and making recommendations for changes is small. All these suggest that the role and close supervision of the ombudsperson is not the major reason that brings transparency and probity in public life. The ombudsperson ends up correcting a very small percentage of aberrations that color public functions in these nations.

Caribbean countries

On the other hand, in developing nations where public services are of poor quality, where officials are generally perceived to be corrupt and citizens carry many grievances, the functioning of a well-structured ombudsperson leaves much to desire. For instance, the ombudsperson in Caribbean nations are perceived to be ineffective in discharging their responsibilities. Abedin (2007, 231) states: 'In the developing countries (including developing democracies such as Caribbean countries and the like) it [Ombudsman] has run into a wide variety of difficulties and inadequacies that, relatively speaking, making it much less effective and its operation problematic in varying degrees'.

The Law Commission of Trinidad and Tobago (1998, 8) observed, 'It is clear that the effectiveness of the office is undermined by many factors'. The principal three factors are the following: First, 'a general lack of respect for the office by members of the public [i.e., civil] service and public authorities resulting in an apparent disregard for the requests and recommendations of the Ombudsman'. Second, 'unwarranted delay on the part of public servants and authorities in responding to requests [for information and documents] from the Ombudsman coupled with a seemingly unwillingness to conciliate matters'. And third, 'the non-implementation of the recommendations of the Ombudsman owing to the infrequency of voluntary compliance; the lack of Parliamentary attention to Annual Reports and Special Reports [of the Ombudsman] and the questionable impact of the publicity'.

The government agencies that fall under the scrutiny of the ombudsperson adopt a variety of tactics to hamper and delay the inquiry against them. For example, Justice Rees (ombudsman of Trinidad and Tobago, 1981, 13–14) stated, he is 'totally dependent on the government printer for stationery and printing and it is entirely at the discretion on the government printer to determine when I should be supplied with my requirements or whether I should be supplied at all'. The Parliamentary Commissioner of St Lucia similarly laments that his office cannot investigate the departments that control the resources for his office. Lack of proper budget and personnel resources seriously affect and undermine the functions of the ombudsperson in many countries.

Another problem is one of non-cooperation and lack of attention to the requests made by the ombudsperson. Since all complaints are about procedures and individual lapses, it is pertinent that the concerned office expeditiously provides the ombudsperson with all the reports and information to aid the inquiry. However, the officials adopt various bureaucratic obstacles to thwart and interrupt the proceedings. The Ombudsman of Jamaica (1993, 2) states aptly, 'The Ombudsman institution can work efficiently only to the extent that there is response and cooperation from those upon whom it operates', [but] 'the successful implementation of the stated objectives have on occasions been thwarted by dilatoriness and cavalier response on the part of the public bodies'.

In most Caribbean countries, the ombudsperson have not been provided with adequate staff. For example, in Antigua and Barbuda, Barbados and Belize the ombudsperson offices have only one investigator. The Parliamentary Commissioner (PC) of St Lucia does not have any investigator.

Moreover, public bureaucracies or agencies, often ignore or turn a blind eye to the findings and recommendations of the ombudsperson in these countries. Most ombudsperson does not have the power to impose sanctions or to reverse or quash an administrative decision and lacking support from the politicians, their recommendations are simply ignored. Furthermore, the Parliament itself remains indifferent to the reports and recommendations of the ombudsperson. During the five-year period from 1999 to 2004, 84 questions on the ombudsperson were tabled. But only 26, that is, less than 30 per cent were answered (Munroe, 2004, 5). A Trinidad and Tobago newspaper column entitled 'Retrieving the Ombudsman from the shadows' reported that on a television program, ombudsman Rees 'made the point that Parliament had never bothered to debate a single one of the five Annual Reports, and one Special Report, he has issued so far' (*Sunday Express*, 1984). Abedin (2007, 235) also makes a pertinent observation that 'most Caribbean societies are small and most persons in high positions know one another well. As a result, such an action may create a rather delicate and embarrassing situation'. This situation exists in most developing countries where elites tend to associate through common schools, caste-based marriage alliances and interactions at many levels.

After examining the workload of the ombudsperson in developed and developing countries, it is now appropriate to examine the functioning of the Indian ombudsperson, Lokayukta, functioning in various states of this country. The Lokayukta in many states of India face similar problems. There are Lokayukta institutions in 20 states, the latest state entrant being Goa (2013), out of the 29 states in India. We focus in some detail on the situation of MP Lokayukta since it provides comparative perspectives with the functioning of the EOW that we have discussed in the previous chapter.

Madhya Pradesh Lokayukta

This institution came into existence in February 1982 after the Madhya Pradesh Lokayukta and Up-Lokayukta Act, 1981 (hereinafter called the Act) was enacted by the state legislature. An attempt to establish an independent organization similar to the ombudsperson started in mid 1970s after the State Administrative Reforms Commission (State ARC) recommended that the State Vigilance Commission, which was then functioning as an instrument to prevent/check corruption, should be replaced by an organization with statutory base and powers. Examining the role and limitations of the State Vigilance Commission, the State ARC had observed that in the absence of a constitutional or even statutory recognition of its position, the Vigilance Commission might act at best as a department of the government to check corruption.

In view of the above observations and on the basis of various recommendations received from the Government of India, the Madhya Pradesh Lokayukta and Up-Lokayukta Bill was moved in the MP Legislative Assembly in the year 1975, which received the Presidential assent in September 1981. The Lokayukta replaced the Vigilance Commission and surprisingly was made independent from the executive influence. Indeed, the institution is designed to function as an instrument of control over the executive by the legislature. The Lokayukta has to be either a Judge of the Supreme Court, Chief Justice of a High Court or Judge of any High Court in India. The tenure is for six years and reappointment is barred.

The Lokayukta and Up-Lokayukta are vested with powers under the Evidence Act 1872 and Criminal Procedure Code, 1973 for conducting enquiries. All proceedings before them are deemed to be judicial proceedings and they exercise the power of the Contempt of Court Act 1971. Madhya Pradesh Special Police Establishment provides the investigation agency for the Lokayukta. The officers have been given the same powers of investigation as the station house officer of a police station under the Criminal Procedure Code. In principle, the investigative arm is deemed to be free from executive control and influence and has also been empowered by posting a senior rank officer who can be of the rank of an Additional Director General of Police or Director General of Police. It may, thus, be seen that the Act has been very well conceived with all the relevant provisions in it to act in an independent manner, free from executive influence.

However, we are unable to assess its functions and impact since Lokayukta does not provide sufficient and meaningful data for analysis. Some bare tables are described on its website that list numbers under some restricted categories for the period 1982–2014 only (MP Lokayukta, 2017). The limited information suggests that during this period 542 complaints against the Chief Ministers and other ministers of the state were received by the

Lokayukta. Based on some kind of processing, 355 of these complaints were finally registered for inquiry. Yet in only 21 cases a report was sent. According to a report (*Times of India*, 2015), it seems these 21 were those cases where investigation was completed. Since an essential column is the processing of the completed investigations by the court, Lokayukta should have provided this information. However, there is no information about the situation at the judicial stage. Furthermore, the Lokayukta sent 189 requests to the government to grant sanction for prosecution against bureaucrats involved in corruption, but these are still pending. We also know that this Lokayukta is plagued with large vacancies of investigative and supervisory officers as they have to be taken on deputation from MP police. For an important independent institution such as Lokayukta, transparency and keeping citizens informed should be its basic characteristics. But this does not seem to be the case with the Lokayukta in MP.

Problem of workload

A significant problem with Lokayukta institutions in India is the heavy workload that they are asked to bear. Despite all the limitations in staffing, non-cooperation from the government and limited powers, the Lokayukta remains the best option for citizens to seek redressal against corrupt practices of public officials. The criminal justice system has been failing to address citizen concerns on this and other issues and consequently, citizens rush to clutch the straw provided by the Lokayukta. According to the annual report of Karnataka Lokayukta (2012) a total of 14,984 cases were pending inquiry at the beginning of the year 2012; 4,819 cases were received for inquiry but it could dispose of only 5,555 cases in the year. This means that at the end of the year 14,348 cases remained pending (14,984 + 4,819 = 19,803 − 5,555 = 14,348). It can thus be seen that, at the end of the year, as many as 14,348 cases were pending against a total of 19,803 at the beginning of the year. In other words, the Lokayukta Karnataka is just able to maintain the status quo with the situation no different in the neighboring state of Andhra Pradesh (AP). The annual report from AP informs that in the year 2011, a total of 3,060 complaints were received, in addition to the 2,286 complaints that were pending at the beginning of the year. Out of 5,346 complaints available for disposal, 1,769 complaints were disposed of during 2011 leaving a balance of 3,577 complaints.

Similarly, in 2012, the Maharashtra Lokayukta (2013) received over 6,500 complaints but it was able to dispose only around 250 complaints per month, leading to large arrears. Furthermore, due lack of powers and investigators, it is able to handle complaints largely pertaining to service issues, pay arrears, post-retirement claims and pensions. Godbole report (2001) on good governance observed that despite completing 25 years in existence, the Lokayukta's impact on the public life in Maharashtra has been minimal. It has largely remained preoccupied with grievances of the staff and has not made any significant contribution to the cleansing of public life in the state. This will be possible only if the Act is amended extensively (cited in Kulkarni, 2013). The newly created Lokayukta of Jharkhand state too could dispose off 455 complaints out of the 811 received in 2012. Thus, every Lokayukta, plagued by a growing number of complaints and increasing expectations, is unable to handle the workload. It is largely a toothless caged tiger in every sense of the word. Moreover, Verma and Shetty (2013) argue that the Lokayukta simply tends to disproportionately select personnel from the lower echelons of the governmental system for anti-corruption action. The profile of complainants is also skewed: the study indicates that people from lower social classes are *less* likely to use the Lokayukta's services.

Problem of appointment and resources

The Gujarat Lokayukta, for example, could not operate for almost 10 years due to the conflict between the Chief Minister and the Governor over the appointment of the chairperson of the Lokayukta. The Chief Minister refused to accept the nomination of Justice Mehta that was recommended by the governor. The Karnataka Lokayukta, touted as the best institution of its kind in the country, has also been dogged by controversies. First, the Lokayukta's post remained vacant for several months after the incumbent Shivaraj Patil quit amidst charges of securing allotment of a site in his wife's name from a private housing cooperative society violating rules. Thereafter, the post could not be filled as the Governor refused to accept the nomination of Justice Bannurmath, who too was facing allegations of securing allotment of a residential site in violation of rules (*Zee News*, 2011). The Uttar Pradesh Information Commission in an ironical twist issued notice to the Lokayukta office for not providing information under the Right to Information (RTI)

Act on the plea that that it was not in the ambit of the Act (*The Hindu*, 2013). For strange reasons the UP Lokayukta was attempting to shield its functions by arguing that as an investigating agency it was not covered by the RTI Act!

The Jharkhand Lokayukta in its annual 2011 report pleaded for several changes in the Act and its functions to be more effective. It requested to tag one investigation agency totally under its jurisdiction so that independent and fair enquiry can be made without any unnecessary delay. The Lokayukta also asked for powers to conduct raid, search and seizure, to attach the property acquired illegally by the corrupt public servants in order to make a dent in prevailing corruption amongst public officials (Jharkhand Lokayukta, 2011, ii). In a tone familiar across many such ombudsperson, the Jharkhand Lokayukta also states:

> Besides all these efforts, we are facing paucity of adequate office space and infrastructure. In the absence of independent building the office of the Lokayukta is presently running in an old building in the campus of Audrey House in which several other offices, e.g., Vigilance Bureau, Hajj Committee, Commercial Taxes Tribunal etc., are functioning. Even no separate courtroom for hearing of cases, visitors' rooms, Library Hall, have been provided. The litigants and the office staff are suffering for want of proper accommodation and lavatory. Further, the Lokayukta has 'to depend on the other agency like State Police, Vigilance Bureau, and CID who are themselves overburdened with their own work causing unnecessary delay in the disposal of the cases'. (Ibid, 2011, 4)

Aji (2012) details a large number of problems with the Lokayukta in various states of India. He states that these ombudspersons are being 'ground to dust by the politicians' and the 19 states institutions are in 'moribund state'. Most are 'hobbled by lack of prosecution powers, basic infrastructure and staff'. There is a deliberate attempt to undermine these institutions and in many states positions are not filled for years. Moreover, the posts of investigators attached to the Lokayukta are similarly left vacant, seriously hampering the functions of the Lokayukta. In Kerala, while the Lokayukta has been given power to operate all over the state and can investigate corruption complaints, but has been denied the power to hold suo motu proceedings. It does not have its own staff and has to function from the state legislative complex. The same story is repeated in UP where the Lokayukta is denied powers of prosecution and has inadequate staff. The Maharashtra Lokayukta has power to investigate but cannot hold inquiry and has no separate investigation agency under its command. The state government has also not formed the vigilance commission that is meant to assist the Lokayukta. The Rajasthan Lokayukta is restricted to inquiring only the public officials in service; it has no investigative agency of its own and it lacks any punitive or compelling powers over the government. The AP Lokayukta has a skeleton police staff for investigation and has no power for search or seizure as part of the investigation. Aji (2012) states forcefully, 'it seems the political class is happiest without an Ombudsman at the center and Ombudsman at the state looking over their shoulders'. Chandrashekaran (2014) further complains that in general the Lokpal Act is unreadable, poorly written and vague on important issues.

Conclusion

As we mentioned above, the demand for Jan Lokpal by Anna Hazare spread like wild fire particularly among the urban middle classes and the urban youth. Unlike previous years when corruption became a major issue from the Bofor's case or periodic scandals seen at the highest political levels, this agitation proved decisive. For the first time, hitherto unknown and uncharted power of the social media, an alternate life of virtual world for the young and the restless, was unleashed in mobilization of the youth and middle classes for the Lokpal movement. Sites like Twitter, Facebook, YouTube, blogs and above all the more convenient SMSs through mobile phones were readily available tools, particularly for the youth. All these modern communication systems enabled them to give vent to their intense anger and frustration against corruption in the country that was choking their growth and development. Anna Hazare's movement caught people's imagination, as it was just a manifestation of the underlying seething rage against rampant corruption and helplessness in face of widespread mis-governance and criminalization of politics. The movement, therefore, acted merely as the proverbial light to the already existing keg of explosive.

Yet the movement lost its steam and once again it appeared as if the political class would override the demands for structural changes. However, if the government had to give in to most of the provisions of the Jan Lokpal proposed by Hazare in 2013, one wonders what prevented it from doing so in 2011! Connecting the dots of the recent past, the passage of the Bill was perhaps due to the historic necessity of a political movement that sought to eradicate corruption and transform the political class and bureaucracy from being rulers to servants of the people.

The most important argument that has been advanced in this book is that a couple of anti-corruption agencies including Lokpal/Lokayukta, whether constitutional or governmental, at the center and in the states, cannot combat the wide-spread corruption effectively and efficiently in India. Broadly speaking the entire criminal justice system in India, comprising the police, prosecution, judiciary and jails are overworked and overloaded and under-staffed and under-resourced. Consequently, enormous numbers of cases are pending investigation, pending prosecution, pending trials/appeals, while the jails are packed beyond capacity.

The problem will further be confounded as according to the provisions of the Lokpal and Lokayukta Act, 2013, the bulk of the enquiries and investigation of complaints referred to the Lokpal would fall in the lap of the already over-worked and over-loaded CBI (Section 20), as would be evident from our analysis based on authentic data in Chapter 4. And the fact that such a preliminary inquiry would have to be completed within a maximum period of 180 days, that is, six months and the investigation within a year (Section 20 sub-sections 4 and 5) would certainly lead the CBI to prioritize the Lokpal complaints vis-à-vis the equally important and time bound cases referred to it by the Supreme Court, High Courts of India, various states and central government ministries, apart from the regular ones that the CBI takes up on its own. Hence, while on paper the time frame provided appears laudable, in practice it does not appear to be implementable for reasons discussed above.

Again, the Act laudably proclaims in Chapter III Section 11, 'provided that till such time the Inquiry wing is constituted by the Lokpal, the Central Government shall make available such number of officers and other staff from its Ministries and Departments as may be required by the Lokpal to conduct preliminary inquiries under this Act'. Similarly, Section 11 (2) confers the power of conducting a preliminary inquiry to the officers of the Inquiry Wing not below the rank of an Under Secretary. This too appears to be ambitious in terms of making available investigating officers of the rank of Deputy

Superintendent of Police (Under Secretary) for the Inquiry Wing since their numbers are small, even within the police departments.

Let us examine this formulation. The government can make available to the Lokpal staff and inquiry/investigation officers in two ways:

1. Direct recruitment: This process would take more than three years to recruit, train and position the officers who, at the end of the day, would be bereft of practical experience of handling complicated corruption crimes.

2. Deputation: Most of the state police forces are already under-staffed and heavily committed and thus reluctant to send officers on deputation.

Similar is the case with IPS officers who would be required to supervise investigations. In a written reply to the Rajya Sabha on August 22, 2013, Narayanasamy, Minister, Personnel and Training, Public Grievances and Pension stated that there is a shortage of 1,093 IPS officers (23 per cent) out of the total authorized strength of 4,730 IPS officers per the 2013 civil list. With respect to shortage of officers in the CBI, the Press Information Report of Ministry of Personnel of August 18, 2011 is relevant. The report states that as against a sanctioned strength of 6,565, the actual strength as on date in CBI is 5,389. Out of 1,176 vacancies, 720 are under deputation quota, which are filled by officers of state police forces/central police forces and other organizations of the central and the state governments.

The reasons for these vacancies in the CBI were given as provided below:

1. Some new posts have been created in 2010 and 2011, which are to be filled through UPSC/SSC.

2. Unwillingness of some state governments to spare officers for deputation.

3. Unwillingness of officers of some states and some other organizations to join CBI on account of higher pay scale/pay package in their own cadres/organizations.

4. Time taken in recruiting officers under deputation quota in the ranks of Deputy Superintendent of Police/Additional Superintendent of Police/ Public Prosecutor and Senior Public Prosecutor.

5. Non-availability of officers from the CPOs like BSF, CRPF, CISF, ITBP, etc., on deputation as these organizations are expanding and are unable to spare officials for CBI.

It is in the light of the foregoing, that the creation of the Lokpal would make little impact in substantial terms in combating corruption apart from perhaps raising a media storm in some high-profile cases now and then. The crux of the problem lies in the total inadequacy of the criminal justice system, the enforcement agencies, the prosecution as well as the judiciary, to deal with the exponential growth in the number of complaints and inadequate manpower, financial and technological resources to deal with them. Hence, the desirable deterrent effect that quick investigation, quick prosecution, quick trial and conviction can bring about and thus help in preventing and curbing corruption, is practically absent in India.

Furthermore, Lokayuktas that have been operational in many states have failed to address the dichotomy inherent in the conceptualization and functioning of the Indian state. Lokayuktas have failed to pursue preventive measures and grow beyond individual action, culpability and punishment. There was no attempt to examine the functioning of the organizations and change the culture of indifference to public service. If the emphasis was on individuals then the focus remained on the 'bad apples' and not on the 'rotten barrel' that spoilt the apples.

It is apparent from the above discussion that despite the best intentions of the Lokpal movement and perhaps of the political leadership, the Lokpal is not likely to live up to its expectations and effectively curb corruption no better or worse than the current dispensation of CBI, CVC, state Lokayukta, etc. This inference stands reinforced by threadbare discussions and analysis of EOW MP experience in Chapter 5. Furthermore, Lokpal and Lokayukta or for that matter any enforcement agency step in mostly when the damage has been done, when the corruption crime has been committed and unlawful gain or unlawful loss has taken place. The need is to focus on the preventive dimensions of anti-corruption strategy, which seeks to prevent corruption crimes from taking place in the first place. It is, historically, the right time to look for alternate and novel solutions that focus on checking corruption right at the doorstep rather than await a complaint to be made to bring the corruption offence to the operation table of investigation, prosecution, trial and conviction.

The ombudsperson (Lokpal/Lokayukta) can only strengthen trust in government and public administration to a limited extent. The indifference of other public offices and ministries, lack of support from the elected representatives and the Parliament as well suspicion about its scrutiny, all combine to weaken the ombudsperson. Furthermore, the heavy workload, denial of cooperation from other institutions and shortage of qualified investigators, all make the responsibility of the ombudsperson difficult to execute. The major problem is the absence of internal mechanisms amongst public bodies to address issues of corruption and indifference to provide service to the citizens. Largely, all the public institutions refuse to play their role in maintaining the integrity and legitimacy of their offices. These public bodies expect an external agency, such as the Vigilance department, the CBI, the Lokpal/Lokayukta and ACBx in the states to intercede and act against its delinquent officers rather than preventing the delinquency from taking place. The external agency can at best investigate few complaints and successfully act against a limited number of delinquent officers. The heads of public institutions have to play a proactive role in cleaning up their organizations of corrupt officials. They will have greater success in doing so themselves than waiting for an external agency to clean their house.

Moreover, in our view, the Lokpal and the Lokayukta should more consistently take the role of 'change agents' that propose organizational improvements from a citizen's perspective (Wagner, 2000). The Lokpal needs to reflect on the meaning of 'maladministration' and its relationship with illegality and to function more to correct than to prosecute. The Lokpal/ Lokayukta must look at other complaint-handling schemes, how they overlap, reinforce and at times undermine one another, how the access arrangements, the powers of investigating and reporting currently serve the interests of justice, and how they might be strengthened, for example, by the creation of an 'own initiative' investigation power (Abraham, 2012). Institutions are central in the combat against corruption. Institutions need to function effectively to enforce proper economic and social policies, enforce the laws, manage public finances and maintain legitimacy of the governing system. Corruption is a cause of institutional failure.

Part III
Way Forward
Alternate Solutions

7

Empowering and Professionalizing
Anti-Corruption Agencies

In this chapter, we will examine various proposals to augment the existing anti-corruption measures in the country. There are a variety of recommendations made by different committees and internal study groups to strengthen and professionalize the investigative agencies. The CBI Study Group Report provides many attractive suggestions that can assist the agency to be more effective and efficient. The same is true of state police agencies that handle the bulk of corruption cases. Evaluation of their training, resource mobilization and applications of technology suggest practical ways of enhancing the performance of these anti-corruption mechanisms. Additionally, many new legislative measures are needed to address the obstacles in effectively dealing with corruption.

Finally, participation of people at large as stakeholders need to be an essential factor in all functions of the officials. Furthermore, universal directives as per the UN Convention against Corruption, systems operational in Singapore, Hong Kong, Scandinavian countries and the RICCO provision in United States are also considered to develop a strong blue print of an anti-corruption strategy in the country.

Introduction

In 1962, the Santhanam Committee identified administrative delay, overburdened government, exercise of discretion in administrative judgments and cumbersome procedures as the four major causes of corruption in the country. The recommendations of the Committee led to the establishment of the CVC as an apex and independent body for prevention of corruption in central government units. In the *Vineet Narain and others versus Union of India*, the Supreme Court directed that statutory status be conferred upon the CVC. Following this judicial directive, the CVC Act of 2003 was promulgated for the constitution of a CVC to inquire into offenses alleged to have been committed under the PC Act, 1988. The Act also empowered the CVC to exercise superintendence over the CBI and to review the process of grant of sanction for prosecution against the guilty officers pending with competent authorities. An important process known as the *Whistle Blowers Resolution* was also adopted by the Commission to provide protection to whistle blowers from victimization and power to take action against complainants making vexatious complaints. A bill titled *The Whistleblowers' Protection Bill 2011* has been signed into law by the President on May 2014. The legislation aims to protect a person who exposes alleged wrongdoing in public offices, projects and functions. In particular, the law provides protection to those who expose corruption, cheating, fraud and even mismanagement in public bodies but its impact is yet to be tested.

The new Whistleblower Protection Law empowers the CVC to receive complaints, assess public disclosure requests and safeguard the complainants. The CVC has the power to restore the positions lost by whistleblowers who suffered retaliation by the employers or superiors. Moreover, the new law puts the burden of proof on the public official to show that any adverse action taken against a whistleblower was not retaliatory. The law balances the situation by also imposing penalties upon those who make frivolous and false charges. The punishment may range from a fine of ₹ 20,000 and even imprisonment of up to two years.

Various concerns have been raised about the limitations of this Act (Liu, 2014). The law lacks specific punishment against those carrying out physical attacks on whistleblowers—a phenomenon that is of serious concern in the country (Mukherji, 2013). There are also no civil penalties for workplace retaliation. Whereas other countries like the United States, the United Kingdom and Canada define 'disclosure' and 'victimization' broadly for purposes of their respective whistleblower protection laws, India's law does not define 'victimization' and has a relatively narrow definition for 'disclosure'

(Liu, 2014). This too limits the effectiveness of the Act in protecting the complainant. The major problem is the lack of trust that the citizens have in public institutions and apprehensions whether the government will enforce the provisions effectively and unbiasedly.

Inadequacies of Anti-Corruption Agencies

Today, the three major agencies, the CVC, the Central Information Commission (CIC) and the CBI are proving quite incapable of curbing corruption effectively. The CVC, thanks to the Supreme Court, has become a major institution for combating corruption in the country. The empirical data given in its annual report suggest that the citizens 'perceive' it to be an effective mechanism for dealing with corrupt practices amongst the central government public officials. However, the number of complaints submitted to the Commission shows a declining trend. In 2012, almost 37,000 complaints were received as compared to 17,407 in the year 2011. But in 2013, the Commission received only 35,332 complaints. While more than 20,000 penalties, both major and minor, were imposed on all categories of public servants, as a result of punitive action during the year 2012, the number for 2013 is a mere 17,672. Again, in 2012, major penalties were imposed against 5,825 officers and minor penalties were imposed against 14,984 officers. However, the numbers for 2013 are 5,106 and 11,749 respectively. The numbers may not reveal much, but the truth is that corruption continues to remain all pervasive and the biggest impediment in the growth and development of this country.

Moreover, the Commission, no doubt, has been advocating transparency, equity and competitiveness in public procurements and introducing the Integrity Pact (IP), a concept promoted by Transparency International (2016) as a useful tool in this direction. IPs are a tool for preventing corruption in public contracting. They are essentially an agreement between the government agency offering a contract and the companies bidding for it that they will abstain from bribery, collusion and other corrupt practices for the extent of the contract. To ensure accountability, IPs also include a monitoring system typically led by civil society groups. To facilitate implementation of the IP to quickly resolve disputes in procurement, the Commission has approved names for appointment of Independent External Monitors in more than

74 ministries/departments/organizations so far. The Commission has been continuously emphasizing on leveraging technology like e-procurement, e-payment and reverse auction for reducing scope for corruption and improving transparency. The CVC has also announced the introduction of 'perception index' (*Economic Times*, 2016) in 25 public institutions and ministries to determine public opinion about corruption. Yet effective implementation still remains a far cry. The serious intent of the government will be judged by how quickly and effectively this law and such mechanisms are implemented both in letter and spirit.

Similarly, the establishment of CIC at the center and in the states to enforce the RTI, 2005 is perhaps the most potent instrument in independent India to tackle corruption. It has enabled as well as empowered citizens of the country to be informed and be aware about the functioning of processes and procedures of governance, hitherto shrouded in a culture of secrecy. It has also heralded a new era of transparency and accountability in the functioning of the public authorities and thereby in the entire process of governance. The RTI 2005 grants every citizen the right to seek information, subject to provisions of the Act from every public authority about the various tasks and activities performed by them. The Act essentially focuses on maximum disclosure and minimum exceptions. It prescribes two approaches to achieve the twin objectives of (1) an appellate mechanism for adjudication and review of functioning of public authorities and (2) penal provisions to check and contain intentional and willful non-disclosure of information. This legislation also has an elaborate code of disclosure of information comprising streamlining of record maintenance including in digital mode of proactive disclosure and effective dissemination among the citizenry. The Act also empowers the CIC to obtain reports from every public authority on specific issues to enable it to analyze and discern the status and emerging patterns about the implementation of the Act. It is, therefore, not surprising that the number of citizen requests for information from public officials has been growing exponentially. While 7,05,976 requests were filed in the year 2011–12, the number rose to 11,65,217 in 2015–16 (CIC, 2017). The law also provides for the establishment of State Information Commissions and a nodal officer in every publicly funded department to be responsible for providing information to the citizen about its functions.

However, there seems to be a strong opposition amongst the public officials to effectively implement this Act. A study (Jha and Ahmed, 2007) about the performance of the State Information Commissions found that there was a general reluctance to penalize the erring public information officials. The State Commissions ignored complaints of harassment, threats and deliberate delay at the hands of these officers, responsible for providing information to the citizens. That this avant-garde law, as far as India is concerned, is making a serious impact on making public officials more accountable is borne out by the gruesome fact that an alarming number of RTI activists are being attacked and in some cases, even killed. The numbers of attacks on those seeking to expose corruption are growing steadily. Data gleaned by the Commonwealth Human Rights Initiative (CHRI), 2016 shows Maharashtra has seen 53 attacks on RTI activists, including 9 cases of murder, between 2005–12 period. Gujarat comes second with 34 attacks, including 3 murders. Delhi, Bihar, Uttar Pradesh, Haryana, Andhra Pradesh and Karnataka follow with over 10 reported attacks on RTI activists during these 8 years. The data points to around 251 cases across India where people were either attacked, murdered, physically or mentally harassed or had their property damaged because of the information they sought under the RTI. The data throws up 32 alleged murders and two suicides that were directly linked with filed RTI applications (Mukherji, 2013).

As a consequence, the Chief Information Commission has resolved that if it receives a complaint regarding assault or murder of an information seeker, it will examine the pending RTI applications of the victim and order the concerned department(s) to publish the requested information suo motu on their website as per the provisions of law. Such a provision is likely to deter offenders from seeking to harm people using the RTI to bring transparency in public functions. The Commission has also been active in meeting the demands of citizens. Around 70 per cent of the requests filed by the people are being disposed off annually by the Commission and with its strength going up, this is bound to improve. The Commission has also been using information technology in its working to facilitate filing of appeals and complaints on line. The citizenry has utilized this facility extensively but the requirement of the signed copy of the appeal/complaint filed on line, for identification and verification of appellant/complainant, has resulted in accumulation of a large number of provisionally registered appeals and complaints. These cases, though registered provisionally, can't be taken up for adjudication unless corresponding signed copies are received. While it may be too early to assess the impact of this Act in curbing corruption, it seems reasonable to state that the Act has enabled citizens to question public institutions on their performance and promote a new form of democracy in which the relationship between citizens and the state is direct and engaging. The people now finally have an instrument that empowers their right to know about what public officials are doing and to check their corrupt practices.

While the RTI Act has been well received and utilized by the citizens, there are still several management problems in the system that inhibits its full impact in making governance transparent. All units of the government need to set their own house in order and develop proper record management systems. Many public sector entities do not even bother to report their compliance with the Public Record Act of 1993. It is also a problem that this Public Record Act, 1993 does not apply to state governments where transparency and accountability is more urgently needed. It seems pertinent to question the reasons why the information commissions are plagued by a large number of citizen requests. Clearly, departments need to look inward to address this issue and overhaul the way they deal with proactive disclosure, processing of applications and disposing off first appeals.

A telling and suspect methodology of the government(s) to reduce the efficacy of such institutions is to 'pack' it with retired and beholden civil servants and maintain vacancies to rob important institutions to perform at its optimum level. Thus, according to a commendable study by the CHRI titled, 'Information Commissions and the Use of RTI Laws in India: Rapid Study 2.0' in July 2014, about 90 per cent of the information commissions at the central and state levels continue to be headed by retired civil servants as was the case in 2012. A little less than a half (49.46 per cent) of the state information commissioners are retired civil servants belonging to either the AIS or the State Civil Services, prompting the Supreme Court of India to issue a directive in September 2012, in the matter of *Namit Sharma vs Union of India*, while disposing a PIL to the governments to ensure that retired judges of the Supreme Court and Chief Justices of the High Courts be appointed as chief information commissioners. However, the central government and the state government of Rajasthan sought a review of this judgment resulting in the Supreme Court recalling in September 2013 its earlier judgment. The Court, diluting its earlier order, issued fresh directions that require the government to make the effort *to identify candidates other than retired civil servants* for appointment to the information commissions. The Court also directed that only such candidates be appointed who have expertise and experiences in the fields mentioned in Sections 12(5) and 15(5) of the RTI Act.

CIC ruling on bringing political parties under RTI Act

In a landmark ruling, the CIC on January 3, 2013 held that India's political parties are public authorities and answerable to citizens under the RTI Act. The order is with respect to specifically six national political parties since they were the ones mentioned in the petition before the Commission: the Indian National Congress (INC), the Bhartiya Janta Party (BJP), the Nationalist Congress Party (NCP), the Communist Party of India (Marxist) or CPM, the Communist Party of India (CPI) and the Bahujan Samaj Party (BSP). The ruling means that these parties, if queried, will have to disclose sources of funding as well as details of expenditure. The Commission based its ruling on parties being substantially funded indirectly by the union government and having the character of public authorities under the RTI Act as they perform public functions. The implication of the judgment is that these parties would be liable to maintain records for public scrutiny and shall have to provide information when sought under the RTI Act.

Not surprisingly, this has been met with stiff resistance by all the parties. The government, unusually receiving the opposition's support, is hoping to pass a legislation to insulate political parties from the RTI Act. These parties contend that they 'are not public authorities', and cannot function if they have to keep responding to RTI queries on 'confidential matters'. They also argue that the parties would be flooded with queries and be used as a potent weapon by rival parties. The Congress party, that passed the RTI Act, has been contesting the CIC's ruling asserting that CIC 'is neither a court nor a competent authority to exercise plenary jurisdiction and the order is arbitrary and illegal' (*Times of India*, 2016). However, this is in violation of the principle of 'same rules for king and subject' and eloquently reveals lack of political will to function in a transparent manner.

Parliamentary Standing Committee

A Departmental Standing Committee of Parliament on Personnel, Public Grievances, Law and Justice also examined the functioning of the CBI (Parliamentary Standing Committee, 2008). The Committee found that while the workload and expectations from the CBI have been increasing, resources, particularly trained investigators, are lacking. The Committee recommended strengthening the CBI in terms of legal mandate, infrastructure and resources. In particular, the Committee expressed concern about the shortage of human resources, limited infrastructural facilities, need for financial and administrative empowerment and a weak Directorate of Prosecution. The Committee recommended a separate statute under the title *Central Bureau of Intelligence and Investigation Act* to streamline and empower the agency.

It was noted that the jurisdiction of the CBI is confined only to union territories for investigation of offences notified under Section 3 of DSPE Act, 1946 and that it requires consent of the concerned state government under Section 6 and a corresponding notification from the central government under Section 5, before taking up the investigation of a case outside the union territories. It was further noted that under the existing DSPE Act, procedural nuances involved in obtaining the consent of the state government for investigation of cases within its jurisdiction cause inordinate delays. The Committee expressed alarm on the fact that

> Section 6 of the DSPE Act clips the wings of the CBI and due to this legal hurdle, the CBI cannot be the first responders in case of crimes, which even threaten the security of the nation, such as a terrorist attack. By the time the CBI is handed over the case, precious time is lost which not only results in loss of crucial evidence, but also provides ample time for criminals to escape who operate at electronic speed or move the ill-gotten wealth in safe havens across the globe. Moreover, the CBI does not get an opportunity to build the required database and collate intelligence absolutely essential for successfully investigating such type of cases, more so in the present era wherein the dangerous convergence of terrorism and traditional crimes presents obvious and acute dangers. (Parliamentary Standing Committee, 2008, Sec. 16.9.3)

The problem in setting up an empowered central agency has been that most of the states, see this as an infringement on the jurisdiction of states under the constitutional scheme.

There is a move to have an empowered committee, comprising the Union Home Secretary, Law Secretary, the Director General of Police or the Home Secretary of the concerned state and the Solicitor General to be constituted and that in event of any terrorist attack or such instances which threaten national security, this Committee would get activated. It could make a recommendation, which after approval by the competent authority defined in the statute itself, will decide if the case should be taken over by the CBI or some other agency. Interestingly, the

> Committee sought the views of the Department of Legal Affairs, Ministry of Law and Justice on the feasibility of granting powers to the CBI to take cognizance of crimes having inter-state, inter-organization and international dimensions. The opinion given by them was that the Parliament could, in light of provisions of Article 253 and Entry 14 of List I of the Constitution, enact a legislation which could contain list of offences created under various statutes to give effect to international treaties, convention or agreements and that a separate investigating agency could be established which would have a specific body with special experts to deal with such offences. It was also emphasized that in case the proposal to create a central investigating agency was carried through, the said agency for the purpose of investigation and prosecution of the specified offences would have a concurrent power along with the state police and would not have the effect of violating jurisdiction of the state government to deal with such offences. (Parliamentary Standing Committee, 2008, Sec 16.9.10.1)

Meanwhile, it is interesting to note that a National Investigation Agency has started functioning as the central counter-terrorism agency in a concurrent jurisdiction framework, with provisions for taking up specific cases under specific Acts for investigation. This agency, however, is seen exclusively to deal with terrorism-related cases. It remains uncertain if a similar agency or even the CBI will be empowered to deal with corruption that affects national economy. While the Constitutional provision seems clear, it remains to be seen if the Parliament will pass such a law and strengthen the investigators to pursue corruption cases with determination.

> [The] Committee also supported granting powers to the CBI to take up offences under the Prevention of Money Laundering Act (PMLA), 2002. Their view was that the powers to investigate and prosecute for offences

under the PMLA were conferred on the Enforcement Directorate (ED) since the workload of the ED in regard to investigation and adjudication of cases under Foreign Exchange Management Act (FEMA) was expected to decline and the available skilled manpower and infrastructure of the ED, with some additional inputs, could be gainfully utilized for investigation of cases under the PMLA. (Parliamentary Standing Committee, 2008, Sec 16.9.10.2)

The Committee also saw many similarities between the provisions of Foreign Exchange Regulation Act (FERA) and the PMLA in respect of investigation into matters under these two Acts, and hence sought to bring the two agencies together.

> The Committee strongly argued that regardless of whereabouts in any state in India, every Indian citizen, whether a native of that state or not, has, by virtue of citizenship, a right to protection by the Government of India of life, liberty and property, and that the Government of India has a corresponding obligation. Hence, the Committee felt that vesting the CBI with appropriate statutory backing to take suo motu cognizance of crimes would in no way affect the essentials of the federal structure. This would not only enable the CBI to deal with such investigation with due promptitude but also play a proactive role in the collection of intelligence, creating institutional memory and capacity building. (Parliamentary Standing Committee, 2008. Sec 16.9.15)

Furthermore, the Committee believed that

> a proactive and holistic approach is required to deal with threats thrown up by the linkages between organized crime and terrorists to the national security and localized and disjoint actions against such crimes cannot be successful. The Committee strongly felt that the central government should be given adequate powers to take prompt and effective action on the intelligence available to them. The Committee recommended that in order to ensure proper management and prevention of such incidents, which threaten the security of the nation, the CBI should be envisaged as an enforcement agency also which would mean that apart from investigation and prosecution, the CBI would be given mandate to ensure prevention of crimes. (Ibid., Sec 16.9.16.1)

However, since law and order is a state subject under the Constitution, any attempt by the CBI or any other agency to intervene suo motu in criminal matters, including corruption, is likely to be met with stiff resistance by the states as witnessed in the enactment of the Lokpal and Lokayukta Act in the parliament.

It is unfortunate that despite such a strong endorsement by the Standing Committee, the government accepted none of the recommendations. The CBI is a powerful agency that the ruling politicians wish to control. Despite the efforts of citizen activists, the media and even the directives of the Supreme Court, the Parliament has not accepted demands to keep it independent from political interference. The CBI also remains handicapped by a lack of resources, legal provisions and administrative support. Consequently, in combating corruption it has been ineffective and limited in pursuing cases, particularly those involving the political class.

However, the CBI leadership has also not functioned in a manner that could elicit faith in the agency. The recent 2G scam case publicly exposed the shenanigans of the then CBI Director, Ranjit Sinha, who was constrained by the Supreme Court in an unusual step to recuse himself from the supervision of the case. Indeed, while autonomy to the CBI and interference from the government of the day seems to be the common refrain and even desirable, some form of checks and balances would be imperative to avoid the embarrassment that the CBI could face due to a powerful but tainted Director with unfettered powers.

National anti-corruption strategy

Recently, the CVC made another attempt to deal with corruption by setting up a group of consultants to develop a national anti-corruption strategy (CVC, 2018). This aims at systematic and conscious reshaping of the country's national integrity system. The strategy recommends a set of actions to be taken by the government and a set of actions by the political entities, judiciary, media, citizens, private sector and civil society organizations. The strategy also set the mission to channelize and integrate the resources and build synergy into the efforts of all stakeholders to promote integrity in governance. Such a strategy could progressively eliminate corruption from India through effective prevention, detection and punishment of all corrupt activities. The vision draft suggests a series of legal and statutory provisions to combat corruption. Thus, it advocates changing the provision of seeking prior sanction from competent authorities before prosecution could be initiated against the offending official. The document suggests that no prior sanction should be required in cases where the officer is caught red handed and, in other cases, prescribe a clear timeframe within which the sanctioning authority must communicate its decision either granting sanction for prosecution or rejecting the same.

Furthermore, in view of the importance of protecting whistle blowers, the CVC suggests appropriate legislative provisions be introduced either through amendment to the PC Act or through a separate legislation. The Act should include whistle blowing against private corporations and business and protection to the whistle blowers till completion of investigations. Giving or taking of bribe is a cognizable offense in the country but this does not discriminate between those giving a bribe under extortion by the official or deliberately to influence the official. The draft hence seeks an appropriate law to make a distinction, one that was also suggested by an eminent economist (Basu, 2011). Since delay in prosecution is common and somewhat inevitable, the draft recommends confiscation of property gained illegally through corrupt practices. Moreover, the very possession of properties disproportionate to known legal sources of income of a public servant should be declared as an offence and such properties be confiscated by the state even pending prosecution.

The draft makes another interesting recommendation about confiscation of illegally acquired wealth. Few states, like MP have already enacted laws, the MP Special Courts Act 2013, wherein provision has been made to confiscate disproportionate assets during investigation and trial of a corruption case. The draft states,

> Most of the wealth in India is accumulated through corrupt means and invested under false names in immoveable property, gold and jewelry, high value consumer goods and, other conspicuous consumption. The unique identification project presents an opportunity to curb this menace effectively. Quoting the unique identity number or presenting other appropriate identity documents should be made compulsory for all immoveable property transactions, purchase of gems and jewelry and for any other major expenditure above a certain threshold, and clear records regarding the same should be maintained. This would ensure that

property is not sold to non-existent persons or in fictitious names and would provide information about any expenditure disproportionate to known sources of income. (CVC, 2018, 10–11)

Empowerment of Regulatory Bodies

Another set of meaningful guidelines concern the empowerment of regulators themselves. In particular, those regulators who are engaged with the functions of economy with wide discretionary and executive powers. An important consideration is to think of a two-tier structure that distributes the powers into several hands and hence avoids the risk of corruption, which is higher when few people get to make most of the decisions. It is also incumbent that there be a transparent process of selection for the heads of these regulatory bodies. For instance, the controversies surrounding the appointment of the chairperson CAG and CVC by the outgoing Congress ministry of UPAII naturally weakened the independent role of these regulators.

> Governance structures that rely on the independent appointment and authority of boards of directors or trustees enable putting in place adequate internal controls and oversight on those with discretionary authority or who handle public funds and hence there is a need for transparency in appointment of key personnel of the Regulatory authorities. (CVC, 2018, 12)

The strategy also suggests that there be a proactive mechanism to regularly demand and collect information about personal wealth and assets of employees of these regulatory bodies. Sharing this information publicly is likely to deter corruption amongst employees and repose faith of the citizens in the independence and integrity of these regulators. A number of self-regulations also seem necessary. Some, such as, acceptance of post-retirement benefits especially from the private or public sector that ushers conflict of interest must be curbed. There must be a ceiling on the remunerations to be received by the members of regulatory bodies and something as simple as rotation of auditors every two to three years will enhance the integrity of the system.

Furthermore, some other measures are urgently needed too and can be taken immediately. Almost every public department in India needs restructuring, reinforcement and strengthening of existing anti-corruption mechanisms in terms of personnel-power, training, technical and financial resources. For far too long, even important departments like the police, civil administration and revenue collection are functioning in the mould set by the British during their colonial rule. The police personnel are poorly trained, ill paid and function under extremely deplorable working conditions. They have no set of regular working hours, lack basic resources such as communication and transport and even paper to write case diaries! They are not paid overtime for working beyond eight hours (Kumar, 2014) and most police stations lack basic amenities such as space and furniture. Record keeping in every department is neglected and even common information such as number of personnel in specific offices sometimes is difficult to find. Land records have not been updated for decades in many states, such as Bihar, that result in violent clashes over ownership claims. Almost every government hospital and school shows signs of extreme decay and crumbling structures with shortage of staff and indifference to citizens seeking public services. Unless these are paid attention to and restructured, corrupt practices are unlikely to be controlled.

While politicization of the police services is often viewed as the main obstacle in combating corruption, the fact remains that the bureaucratic system itself is rotten and incapable of enforcing the laws and implementing policies of public interest. Almost all units are poorly managed, ill staffed, lack resources and are overburdened with work. However, it is not only the lack of sufficient personnel and material resources that hinder effective action against corruption but the functioning of the administrative machinery itself. In a developing economy if the bureaucratic machinery is broken and not completely accountable to the people, then it cannot fight corruption effectively. We turn now towards some of those nations where anti-corruption efforts have been successful and which have built a good reputation for their institutions and even the country. We will examine them with a view to see what lessons these can provide to India.

Learning from Experiences of Other Nations

Singapore and Hong Kong

A number of countries have created specialized agencies for curbing corruption in public offices. Singapore established the Corrupt Practices Investigation

Bureau (CPIB) in 1952. Malaysia followed the practice by its own Anti-Corruption Agency in 1967 and the Independent Commission Against Corruption (ICAC) was formed in Hong Kong in 1974. It is interesting to note that corruption was rampant and pervasive in Singapore for a major part of its past. The British made feeble and token attempts to curb such practices during its colonial administration but with little success. The unit set by the British lacked personnel resources, had multifarious responsibilities and the fact that the larger police organization from where the personnel were drawn was itself extremely corrupt and unaccountable. 'An important reason for Singapore's success in combating corruption is its rejection of the British colonial method of relying on the police to curb corruption and its reliance on the CPIB' (Quah, 2010, 26). As well known, the People's Action Party led by the legendary Lee KuanYew, took strong steps to clean the system after gaining power from the British in 1959. The PAP introduced the Prevention of Corruption Act (POCA) in June 1960 and strengthened the CPIB by giving special power to the Director to appoint special investigators. The Section 17 of the Act also empowered the public prosecutor to authorize CPIB to investigate any bank, share or purchase transaction of any suspect. Section 18 also enabled the CPIB to inspect the bank account of the suspect public servant, those of his wife, child or agent if necessary. Moreover, Section 31 protected the informers by keeping their identity confidential. To emphasize the importance of role to be played by the CPIB, it was also empowered to screen candidates selected for senior public offices and statutory boards in the country. An interesting dimension of this unit was to create a research branch that reviewed work procedures of corruption prone departments and to reduce opportunities by identifying the modus operandi of corrupt civil officials.

The island colony of Hong Kong under the British also acquired a name for corruption in South East Asia. The monopoly exercised by the government over many public functions and the significant discretion given to the officials provided many opportunities for corrupt practices. Further, like Singapore, the police of Hong Kong were also tainted and incapable of combating corruption. The lack of democracy that could enable the citizens to demand accountability from the British government was a major inhibiting factor. The riots in 1967 and citizen unrest, finally forced the colonial government to act. A new law also known as the Prevention of Bribery Ordinance (POBO) was enacted in 1971 that provided for seizure of unaccounted property and inspection of bank accounts, safe-deposit boxes, property documents and other details. The law also requires a suspect to provide full details of his financial situation to the investigators. POBO 'reversed the traditional presumption of innocence until proven guilty' (Skidmore, 1996, 121). However, it took several years before the British agreed to create a separate and independent agency—the ICAC in 1974 to handle corruption cases.

The ICAC is a unique body that is limited to enforcement in its functions. It 'devotes enormous resources to the changing of attitudes and practices' (Skidmore, 1996, 122). It has a department of 'Corruption Prevention' that works with various agencies to develop means to avoid corrupt practices. Another department, 'Community Relations' engages in advertising against corruption and produces TV serials, information material and even reaches out to schools to develop consensus against corruption and strengthen public morality.

Quah (2010, 40) states that the most important reason for the effectiveness of the CPIB and the ICAC is the political will or commitment of the two governments in curbing corruption. Political leaders provided the agencies with adequate powers, resources and gave them the independence to implement their mission. This enabled the agencies to function effectively and be perceived by the people to be credible in controlling corruption professionally and impartially. Thus, the CPIB even when functioning under the office of the PM did not hesitate to investigate allegations of corruption against political leaders of the ruling party and senior civil servants attached to the PM's office. Moreover, CPIB rules stipulated that officers of impeccable integrity must staff the agency itself and must be publicly recognized as such. When 'a senior CPIB officer was caught cheating a businessman in Singapore in 1997, the then CPIB director, Chua Cher Yak, ordered polygraph tests for all his staff, including himself, to demonstrate their integrity' (Quah, 2010, 48). Such an action strengthened the public image of the CPIB officers as incorruptible. Hong Kong too has been conscious of ensuring the integrity of its anti-corruption agency. The ICAC in Hong Kong has an independent ICAC Complaints Committee, which receives and considers reports on all investigations of non-criminal complaints against the ICAC staff. The ICAC's investigation of all complaints against its officers and publicizing the punishment of those guilty officers with appropriate disciplinary measures has enhanced its public image and credibility (ibid., 2010, 48).

Quah (2010) also makes an important observation. The nature and functioning of a country's national integrity system depends on its policy context and its level of governance. A country's policy context can promote or hinder its incumbent government's anti-corruption efforts depending on whether the contextual factors are conducive or hostile to the implementation of public policies. Singapore and Hong Kong are effective in implementing anti-corruption measures, as both are affluent city-states with smaller populations.

Ian Senior (cited in Quah, 2010, 49) remarks, 'The principal people who can change a culture of corruption if they wish to do so are politicians. This is because they make the laws and allocate the funds that enable the laws to be enforced'. Moreover, an anti-corruption agency can only be effective if a government that is sincerely committed to eradicating corruption in the country supports it. In their analysis of the prerequisites for an effective anti-fraud and anti-corruption strategy in an organization, Nigel Iyer and Martin Samociuk (cited in Quah, 2010, 50) have observed that the tone at the top must be both genuine and credible. Nobody expects instant sainthood from management, but they should be seen to be aspiring to reach the corporate values, which they themselves have described in the company code of conduct.

Chua Cher Yak (cited in Quah, 2010, 50), a former CPIB's Director, makes a pertinent observation:

> It is far easier to have a good, clean government administering a good, clean system than it is for a good anti-corruption agency to clean up a corrupt government and a crooked system. In the latter case, the result is almost predictable: the anti-corruption agency is likely to come off second best. Clearly most governments will possess enough firepower to overwhelm even the most intense, well-meaning anti-corruption agency.

EU experience

An in-depth study of corruption within the EU member states found that corruption varies in nature and extent from one country to another but it affects all member states (European Commission, 2014). The report states succinctly,

EU Member States have in place most of the necessary legal instruments and institutions to prevent and fight corruption. However, the results they deliver are not satisfactory across the EU. Anti-corruption rules are not always vigorously enforced, systemic problems are not tackled effectively enough, and the relevant institutions do not always have sufficient capacity to enforce the rules. Declared intentions are still too distant from concrete results, and genuine political will to eradicate corruption often appears to be missing. (EC, 2014, 2)

The report cites survey results that suggest that at European level, three quarters of respondents (76 per cent) think that corruption is widespread in their own country. The countries where respondents thought corruption is widespread were Greece (99 per cent), Italy (97 per cent), Lithuania, Spain and the Czech Republic (95 per cent in each). Moreover, this survey also found that around three quarters of Europeans (73 per cent) say that bribery and the use of connections is often the easiest way of obtaining certain public services in their country. This belief is most widespread in Greece (93 per cent), Cyprus (92 per cent), Slovakia and Croatia (89 per cent in each). Also, around two in three Europeans (67 per cent) thought the financing of political parties is not sufficiently transparent and supervised (information *abridged* from EC, 2014, 6–7). This survey also informs that 40 per cent of the companies doing business in Europe thought corruption affected their operations with smaller companies encountering more corruption and nepotism in their dealings. Generally, it was found that in all European countries there were serious problems of corruption emanating from deficient control regulations.

In a promising development, anti-corruption polices in a majority of European nations are now high on the political agenda. The economic crisis of 2008, in particular, drew attention to the probity of administrators and focused upon the system of accountability. It became clear that the economic crisis was invariably linked to the issues of corruption and required strong anti-corruption policies and procedures. The European Union found that most of the member states stung by the financial crisis introduced measures and institutional steps to combat corrupt practices. The report (EC, 2014) also found that lack of anti-corruption measures in many states required comprehensive intervention from the central government. But only a small number of countries introduced some policies to deal with corruption. Amongst these steps the ones involving monitoring by the civil society and independent institutions appeared more promising. Even where such processes had not been set, greater transparency appeared to reduce corruption.

Political accountability

This report makes interesting comments about the state of political accountability in member states of the union. It reports that, provoked by the crisis, social protests in Europe have targeted not only economic and social policies but also the integrity and accountability of political elites (EC, 2014, 8). The crisis led to public discontent and questioning of the political system. It was learned that even codes of conduct for political parties and elected officials were ineffective in monitoring their actions. The public perceived the political and administrative leaders to be immune from accountability adding to the growing mistrust in the existing system. Several scandals extensively covered by the media and unethical actions of politicians led to wide-spread discontent and diminishing trust in the political system. In many nations, the integrity of the political class also became questionable. There were hardly any political parties developing and following code of conduct and even where these were presented, mechanisms for enforcement were lacking or very weak. In several countries, political interference and nepotism in the recruitment for mid-management and lower positions in public administration, both at central or regional/local levels, was perceived to be serious problems. It was highlighted that politicization of the administrative offices exposed avenues for corruption, introducing conflicts with public interests and affecting the credibility of public administration.

Financing of political parties

The system of financing of political parties was seen to be a major source of corruption in the member nations. This study suggested that many large-scale corruption cases involving illegal party funding affected politicians serving in high positions. The European Commission found many malpractices, such as purchasing of votes or inducements to the electorates, prevalent in many member nations. Use of illegal activities, such as bribing the voters or influencing public opinion through malpractices, were also noted in a number of countries. Encouragingly, evaluations by GRECO (Group of States against Corruption) on party funding catalyzed some perceivable impact on the reform of legal and to some extent, institutional framework in combating corruption (see Chapter 8). The public outcry appeared to have an impact for most of the European countries have now enacted new laws and ushered transparency regarding donations to the political parties and leaders.

Despite serious attempts and commitments, financing of political activities is a subject that remains vulnerable to corrupt practices. The funding of political parties remains opaque and many of the new laws have yet to show results in curbing corrupt practices. The European Commission also notes that when one loophole is plugged others seem to open and illegal party funding seems to continue unabated in most countries. Strict supervision of illegal party funding has still not become regular practices across the EU and more efforts are needed to ensure compliance by the political class.

However, in some nations steps have been taken that seem promising in controlling corruption. Promotion of public sector integrity, transparency and accountability has been actively promoted in the Netherlands. An Office for the Promotion of Public Sector Integrity has been created as an independent institution that encourages and supports the public sector in the design and implementation of integrity policies. Additionally, many communities are proactively engaged in developing specific policies to address corrupt practices and make them integral to their system of local governance.

In most European nations combating corruption through the criminal justice system is also now a high priority. Generally, anti-corruption agencies play a significant role in the prevention, investigation and prosecution of corrupt practices. However, it was apparent that systematic organizational corruption cannot be curbed without efforts to involve the central and local governments in developing effective mechanisms. European Commission (2014) found that forcing officials to reveal their assets enhances accountability of the system. Moreover, the provision of verifying these disclosures was another strong mechanism that brought greater transparency. The study found that unfortunately in nations affected by corruption it was seen that the agencies have limited powers in forcing these disclosures. Only a handful of countries, particularly the Scandinavian nations, provided examples of thorough verification and where specialized independent anti-corruption agencies were able to carry out their investigations. Furthermore, these agencies were equipped with necessary powers and tools to cross check the assets against a wide range of databases (such as Tax Administration and Trade Register) to identify potential incorrect declarations.

Another issue of concern in combating corruption was seen in the conflicts of interest wherein public officials used their contacts and experience to seek employment with private sector companies that they were monitoring. This was reflected in situations where public officials acted or created the appearance of benefiting private interests. Now, in many nations the issue of conflicts of interest are scrutinized through a range of anti-corruption tools and review mechanisms, including those related to the UN Convention against Corruption (UNCAC), GRECO and OECD.

EU has also set standards regarding criminal laws and procedures against corruption. Several member states have central anti-corruption agencies that combine prevention and investigation functions. Some have dedicated anti-corruption agencies empowered to deal with verification of assets, conflicts of interest and even funding of political parties. Yet it is also apparent that the setting up of such specialized anti-corruption agencies has not been sufficient to combat corruption. The functioning of these agencies also varied from one country to the other. However, the country analyses by the EU report show that some of these agencies have been effective in reforming the malaise and have achieved more sustainable results. The reasons for their success came from 'guarantees of independence and absence of political interference; merit-based selection and promotion of officials; multidisciplinary collaboration among operational teams and with other institutions, swift access to databases and intelligence, and focus upon developing necessary resources and skills' (EU, 2014, 13).

Good practices

A variety of good practices concerning anti-corruption agencies have been noticed amongst EU nations.

> The Slovenian Commission for Prevention of Corruption (CPC) has consolidated its role in seeking to 'uphold the rule of law through anti-corruption efforts', as recognized also by the Slovenian Constitutional Court. In spite of limited resources, CPC has a solid track record of

implementation, with over one thousand reviews and investigations per year. It has verified the assets and interests of leaders from all main political parties, revealing breaches of asset disclosure legislation and allegedly unexplained wealth of important political figures. (EC, 2014, 14)

The Romanian National Anti-Corruption Directorate (DNA) also has an impressive track record of pursuing corruption at the highest levels of politics and even the judiciary. In seven years, 'DNA has indicted over 4700 defendants and 90.25 per cent of its indictments were confirmed through final court decisions. Nearly 1500 defendants were convicted through final court decisions, almost half of them holding very high-level positions' (EU, 2014, 14). Similarly, the Latvian Bureau for Prevention and Combating of Corruption (KNAB) has garnered a strong reputation by focusing upon prevention, investigation and education, including the control of party financing. KNAB is endowed with traditional police powers and has access to bank and tax databases. The central Spanish specialized anti-corruption prosecution office similarly achieved a record of investigations and prosecutions, including high-level cases of illegal party funding.

But just as seen in India, even in EU some member states continue to be plagued by the shenanigans of political leaders. Several anti-corruption agencies that investigate politicians subsequently face direct or indirect pressure from their political masters. 'Such pressure includes public statements or other challenges to the legitimacy of the agencies' leadership or institutional powers and competences' (EC, 2014, 14). The conclusion seems clear: it is important to ensure independence for these anti-corruption agencies to enable them in carrying out their tasks without undue pressure.

Strong prosecution system

The European Commission (2014) report also suggests that repressive measures by anti-corruption agencies are insufficient to tackle corruption. Prosecuting the guilty is important and imposing strict sanctions by the judicial system adds to the deterrent efforts and sends the message of zero toleration to corruption. In many countries, law enforcement presents the most visible anti-corruption effort but better results are seen where prosecution is also effective. The report argues that independence of the judiciary is a key element of anti-corruption policies to effectively handle corruption cases. Independence of action and high ethical standards within the judiciary are significant mechanisms to control corruption in an objective and impartial manner.

Despite clear understanding and recognition of these factors not all EU states have been able to create such mechanisms. Public concerns have been raised on many occasions regarding political interference in corruption cases dealt by prosecution and courts. These concerns include partisan procedures to appoint, promote or dismiss leading prosecutors as well as dismissals or even attempts to discredit anti-corruption officers. There have been instances where anti-corruption law enforcement agencies have been subjected to political interference in their management and functioning. The legal powers entrusted to the anti-corruption institutions have been vitiated by poor accountability leading to perceptions that they are subject to external pressures.

The demand to develop a robust mechanism to select the top police leadership without political considerations has been an old demand in India and considered necessary to curb corruption. However, the EU experience suggests that there is no uniform standard that can be considered a model for appointment and dismissal procedures for heads of law enforcement or prosecution services. Such decisions are in the hands of governments in most countries and face threat from political masters. The EU report suggests that 'regardless of the procedure followed, the process needs to be credible and merit-based to avoid any impression of political bias and to allow police and prosecutors to investigate corruption wherever they discover it' (EC, 2014, 15).

Similarly, just as in India, long delays in court trials are a serious problem in Europe too. In several countries, judicial determination to enforce the procedures and capacity to handle sensitive corruption cases seems to be limited. In some European states, long and cumbersome judicial processes affected corruption cases by making them time barred. There were procedural rules that seemed to avoid finalization of court proceedings. The EU report points out that procedural shortcomings such as statutes of limitations or access to financial information often obstruct the investigation of corruption cases.

Addressing vulnerable factors

An important contribution made by the EU experience has been the identification of vulnerable sectors that are prone to corrupt practices. The study found that in several member states, some sectors seem particularly vulnerable to corruption. Urban development and construction were the sectors where corrupt practices seemed common. In the procurement of medicines and other medical supplies and the influence of pharmaceutical industry the healthcare sector seemed most vulnerable to corruption. Similarly, tax administration was another susceptible sector and prone to corrupt influences. Furthermore, EU member states did not have adequate risk assessment mechanisms or particular mechanisms to tackle corruption in vulnerable sectors. Furthermore, the integrity and transparency of financial sector was yet another crucial sector demanding attention of anti-corruption strategies. An investigation, not surprisingly, linked 'grand corruption cases with tax evasion through offshore companies and tax havens' (EC, 2014, 17). The study also pointed out to the menace of bribing foreign officials by businesses to gain lucrative contracts.

Some legislative efforts to deal with corruption in European nations are worth noting. A sound legislative framework to tackle domestic and foreign bribery is the UK Bribery Act 2010, which came into force on July 1, 2011. This not only criminalizes the payment and receipt of bribes and the bribing of a foreign official but also extends criminal liability to businesses that fail to prevent bribery committed on their behalf. This Act also makes it clear that enabling payments will be considered bribes and it further demands businesses to differentiate hospitality from disguised forms of bribery. The Act provides wide powers to investigate and prosecute serious and complex fraud, including corruption.

Finally, EU has pointed to the pernicious links between corruption and organized crime syndicates. In some member states, numerous cases of alleged illegal party funding at central and regional levels were found linked to organized crime syndicates. Contacts between organized crime groups, businesses and politicians remain a concern in public procurement, construction, maintenance services, waste management and other sectors. The Commission also reports that in member nations organized crime even influenced political activities. Political corruption was often seen as a tool for gaining direct or indirect access to power and not surprisingly, such nations were considered to have the highest level of shadow economy among EU nations. Corruption was a means for organized crime groups to infiltrate public and private sectors.

The European Commission (2014) study argues that effective policies in specific areas can reduce the opportunities for corruption. Some of these have relevance to India too. Thus, policies promoting transparency and freedom of information play a major role in combating corruption. Openness acts as a strong disincentive to corruption and can help to reveal illegal transactions when they occur. One European state has developed an online application that offers an overview of all public-sector expenditure on goods and services, a practice that needs to be adopted in India. Furthermore, move towards transparency of decision-making in public administration is another good practice that needs serious consideration by Indian anti-corruption crusaders. For instance, Greece adopted a law in 2010 that makes it compulsory for all public institutions to publish online their decisions, including in relation to public procurement. Only decisions that contain sensitive personal data and or information on national security are exempted from this obligation. Each document is digitally signed and automatically assigned a unique number. If there is a discrepancy between the text published in the Government Gazette and that on online site, the latter prevails. The public contracts finalized by various public organizations are also published.

Protecting the whistle blowers has been deemed important from the beginning and several steps have been taken in this regard. The EU experience is educative for it suggests that whistleblowing mechanisms allow pathways for reporting irregularities and can hence help uncover corruption. However, whistleblowing faces difficulties even in EU nations for there is similar reluctance to report corrupt acts within one's own organization and fear of retaliation by the powerful officials. 'In this regard, building an integrity culture within each organization, raising awareness, and creating effective protection mechanisms that would give confidence to potential whistleblowers are key [to curb corruption]' (EU, 2014, 20).

Another factor is the transparency of lobbying for policy changes. This is a common practice and all private sector companies maintain major lobbyists to seek political influence. Since public policymaking plays a major role in promotion business and economic activity, it is desirable for administrations to engage in a continuous dialogue with interested parties. European

Commission (2014, 20) study suggests that 'all interested parties should be able to have their say, but this should be done in a transparent way'.

The European nations have also made efforts to assist developing countries develop better mechanisms to combat corruption. Thus, OECD (2011) conducted an Integrity Review for Brazil with the objectives of making the government more cost-effective, improving accountability and preventing corruption. This assessment focused upon the Brazilian government's action in four key areas: promoting transparency and citizen engagement, implementing risk-based internal control systems, embedding high standards of conduct among public officials and enhancing integrity in public procurement. The review came up with some significant policy recommendations that we will consider for India too. The review recommended that departmental managers should be empowered to identify and manage the risk of waste, fraud and corruption in their respective operations, rather than leave the task to anti-corruption agencies. And for this to happen, the managers must be provided resources, training and continuing evaluations to ensure that they meet the expectations. Finally, the managers and anti-corruption agencies must integrate and coordinate their efforts for effective steps against corruption in public sector units.

The US experience

The United States combats corruption in public institutions professionally and comprehensively. One of the early challenges with corruption occurred when organized crime syndicates assumed threatening postures, particularly through the spread of drug culture in the country. Drug warlords operating from Columbia and other countries were able to spread their tentacles in the country by building extensive networks of distributors and, bribing the enforcement agencies. Corruption within the police and other criminal justice agencies grew in proportion to the growth in drug markets. Police forces of many cities such as Miami became so infected with drug money that almost every personnel had to be fired to reform the department. Money from drugs spread in legitimate businesses and fuelled the growth of Mafia in the country. Furthermore, it was difficult to successfully prosecute Mafia leadership, due to lack of evidence and legal loopholes that they could exploit adroitly. The prosecutors could only try mob-related crimes individually instead of shutting down an entire criminal organization. In 1970, the Congress passed the Organized Crime Control Act of 1970 and Title IX of the Act called the Racketeer Influenced and Corrupt Organizations Statute [RICO] (18 U.S.C. §§ 1961–68), commonly referred to as the 'RICO' statute, focused upon the elimination of organized crime and racketeering into legitimate commercial activities. This law is so broad that both governmental and civil parties use it against all sorts of enterprises, both legal and illegal. RICO helps target the entire membership of the criminal enterprise and mere association with a criminal syndicate could result in long sentences. John L. Smith described the impact of RICO in an article for the Las Vegas Review-Journal (*cited* in Justia 2014):

> After RICO, mob families began to crack under the very real threat that members and associates could be indicted en masse for a wide range of criminal activity ... [E]ven the strongest stand-up guy would have trouble facing the 20-year (and more) sentences that began accompanying RICO convictions.

While RICO was originally aimed at the Mafia, over the past 37 years prosecutors have used it against organized crime, street gangs, cartels, corrupt police departments and even politicians.

The statute targets a person engaging in a pattern of racketeering activity connected to an enterprise. The law defines 35 offences as constituting racketeering, including gambling, murder, kidnapping, arson, drug dealing and bribery, which are known as *predicate* offences. Moreover, the enterprise could be a crime family, a street gang or a drug cartel. But it may also be a corporation, a political party, or a managed care company. This brings organized pervasive corruption seen in police departments, political units, lobbying firms and private corporations seeking benefits by bribing the public officials into the ambit of the law. Interestingly, RICO enables prosecutors to seek long prison sentences and also the seizure of assets to deter benefiting from ill-gotten gains.

The US has also been proactive in the fight against international bribery. Aware of the practice in the private sector to bribe foreign government officials to gain favorable contracts, the government passed the Foreign Corrupt Practices Act that prohibits American companies from bribing foreign officials to seek undue business favors. The US government also browbeat the OECD nations into criminalizing bribery. The Anti-Corruption Convention by all the OECD nations was signed in 1997, that even the Transparency International described as a gold standard in combating corruption. The OECD council has also released 'good practice guidelines' to enhance the prevention and detection of foreign bribery and ensure strict compliance by the private sector to deal honestly in foreign lands. Significantly, the Anti-Bribery Convention is the first and only anti-bribery instrument that focuses only on the 'supply side' of the bribery equation. Member nations are obligated to enact laws, criminalizing foreign bribery and participate in a rigorous peer review process. Consequently, all member countries have passed foreign bribery laws and have established corporate liability under their legal systems. Regular publications of peer-reviewed reports inform about the countries which are doing and the countries which still need to do what it requires to combat corrupt practices especially in developing countries or where private sector corporations operate. These have further been strengthened by the OECD guidelines for multinational enterprises which are a comprehensive set of recommendations for responsible business practices. These incorporate standards that need to be complied to deal with allegations of bribery and enhance integrity in business practices. A recent addition is the OECD Global Forum on Transparency and Exchange of Information for Tax purposes that works to eliminate safe havens for corrupt money. National laws are being enacted to combat tax evasion, bribery, money laundering and terrorist financing. These efforts have helped in prohibiting companies headquartered in industrialized world from bribing officials in emerging markets. The US has also launched a number of bureaucratic initiatives, all with an anti-corruption centerpiece. In September 2011, the Obama administration launched an Open Government Partnership to support national efforts that promote transparency, fight corruption and empower citizens (Heineman, 2012).

Other efforts

Furthermore, a regular international feature is the hosting of the International Anti-Corruption Conference held in association with Transparency International. These conferences are conducted in partnership with some specific national government as the host and local civil society partners, which are usually a Transparency International National Chapter or National Contact Point. The host government has to make a commitment to curb corruption or boost transparency in the country in order to have opportunity to host a conference on its soil. This marks a major effort to bring attention to anti-corruption measures, develop transparent procedures to enhance integrity in governance and enable the government to make such a commitment.

A large number of independent and non-governmental organizations too have sprung up to raise awareness and combat corruption. The United Nations Convention against Corruption (UNCAC-Article 13) encourages NGOs in combating corruption. The UNODC assists in building the capacity and engagement of these non-governmental groups, especially from developing countries, through training and sharing information about evaluation procedures. The UNODC also supports their engagement in intergovernmental meetings and assists in working constructively with the governments and the private sector on bringing transparency and working together to combat corruption.

The number of non-governmental organizations crusading against corruption runs into thousands. The UNODC (2014) lists a large number of NGOs involved in crime prevention (including anti-human trafficking and anti-corruption activities) and criminal justice reforms. This database includes information provided by NGOs and input from UNODC's field offices where NGOs actively participate in operational projects. ONE is a grassroots advocacy and campaigning organization that fights extreme poverty and preventable disease, particularly in Africa, by raising public awareness and pressuring political leaders to support smart and effective policies and programs that are saving lives, helping to put kids in school and improving futures. ONE organized campaigns to prevent multinationals from bribing African leaders in exchange of lucrative contracts for natural resources. Sustained campaign finally forced European leaders to commit to a policy that requires oil, gas, mining, and logging companies to publish the payments they make to the governments. Previously, these payments were made in secret fueling corruption and now this policy will help promote a degree of accountability.

A number of nations have also set up independent bodies to monitor and combat corruption in public offices. The Anti-Corruption Commissions in Liberia, Zambia, Namibia, Cayman Islands, Bhutan, Jordan, Bangladesh,

Malaysia, Sierra Leone, Zimbabwe; the Anti-Corruption Commission of Swaziland, the Federal Ethics and Anti-Corruption Commission of Ethiopia, the Ethics and Anti-Corruption Commission of Kenya, the Anti- Corruption Commission and Civil Rights Commission of Korea and the Anti-Corruption Commission of the Organization of American state are some such independent units spearheading anti-corruption efforts in their respective regions. While most are mired in similar problems of interference by the government and not being able to function independently, still there are lessons for India from these varied international bodies and their experiences.

Assessment of Anti-Corruption Bodies

'Anti-corruption agencies (ACAs) are public [funded] bodies of a durable nature, with a specific mission to fight corruption and reducing the opportunity structures propitious for its occurrence in society through preventive and/or repressive measures' (Sousa, 2010, 5). The growth and expansion of EOWs, CVC, CIC, SEBI and several other regulatory bodies in India follows a pattern seen in other nations too. Most of such agencies, Singapore's Corrupt Practices Investigation Bureau (CPIB) and Hong Kong's Independent Commission Against Corruption (ICAC) becoming the role-models emerged from the attempts of newly independent nations to evolve governance free from the old exploitative culture and corrupt practices of the colonial powers. The transition from colonial administration to one answerable to the people through elected leaders, many of whom had fought against the colonial administrators brought corruption to the fore. No longer was public administration a means to exploit the citizens and remain unanswerable for its functions. The expansion in global trade and rise of multi-national corporations further exacerbated the process where bribery became a norm to peddle influence and exploit natural resources of developing economies. Several scandals led to the creation of special units such as the Australian New South Wales Independent Commission Against Corruption in 1988 and the French Service Central de Prévention de la Corruption (SCPC) in 1993. Repeated pressure by the European Union to adopt uniform standards in governance, led to the creation of Lithuanian Special Investigation Service (STT) in 1997, the Croatian Office for the Prevention of Corruption and

Organized Crime (USKOK) in 2001, the Latvian Corruption Prevention and Combating Bureau (KNAB) in 2002 and the Romanian National Anticorruption Directorate (DNA) in 2002. Indeed, 'Corruption became global, and so did anti-corruption efforts' (Sousa, 2010, 6).

Invariably, all anti-corruption special units form in response to the perception of the failures of regular police investigation units in dealing with corruption. Forced by public opinion to 'do something' about the scandals and growing incidents of corruption, particularly as collusion between the business, political leaders and senior bureaucrats, the governments respond in a knee-jerk manner to establish a specialized agency to handle such complaints. Ad hoc and ill-conceived plans introduce systematic design fault lines in their operational methods as well as misunderstanding the environment that facilitates corruption in the first place. Accordingly, most fall short of the public expectations. Patchwork attempts to strengthen them through greater resources or some changes in laws rarely help institutional design defects and public sphere, in which corruption takes place, are not conducible to the operations of the agencies. Set up in a context of systemic corruption that has roots in the political economy of the country, these units fall short of the expectations raised.

Lessons for India

The above discussion provides examples that could be adopted in India. A determined approach against corruption supported by the government and implemented through specialized and empowered investigative agencies can be effective in combating corruption as seen in many nations. The lessons from Singapore and Hong Kong, two Asian nations where corruption was endemic and now almost undetectable, suggest options for India too. The foremost is that anti-corruption agencies and policies cannot be effective unless there is political will to back it up (Quah, 2010). Politicians provide the resources and powers to go after the corrupt, but in order to be effective, at the least the agencies must be independent in their functions. Only when the CBI/EOW and other such anti-corruption units in India demonstrate that they operate in accordance with the law and not base their functions on the political calculations, can people repose faith in them. The citizens must perceive anti-corruption crusade to be professional and impartial before they accept the results as credible. This implies that people who are well connected and are occupying high and powerful posts must be seen to be facing the scrutiny of the agencies without favor or indecisiveness. The commitment of the political leaders, including the Prime Minister, must be unwavering whenever any allegation surfaces against one of their party members or relatives. However, the agencies can only function effectively if competent and professional leaders lead them. The appointment of Director CBI and other senior positions in India remains mired in controversies. The lesson from Singapore and Hong Kong is that the selection of top leaders of anti-corruption units must be carefully and transparently done where only the merit counts and nothing else. Investigators serving in these units must be those with impeccable integrity and professional training.

Nevertheless, even the best-trained and honest officials cannot do much unless they are equipped with strong laws and administrative structures. As the European Commission (2014) discourse suggests, India must ensure that a sophisticated legal and institutional framework must be in place with adequate resources for agencies to show effective performance. Transparency in functioning and regular asset disclosure by the officials is a must for credibility in the agencies to be publicly maintained. This needs further steps like denying lucrative positions after retirement. Today, senior bureaucrats and police officers serving in important posts are regularly given post-retirement benefits. Positions in important bodies like the CVC/CIC/UPSC and even posts of governors and members of numerous commissions are offered to those who seen loyal to the government. This clearly has a pernicious impact upon the functioning of the anti-corruption agencies that stand compromised by mere suspicion of its leaders being aligned with politicians. Related to this is the emerging trend where officers find positions in important private sector industries after completing their public service. This induces a conflict of interest and could create situations where officers use their contacts and insider knowledge to serve the interests of private companies. There must be a system and law in place that creates a time lag before officers serving in anti-corruption agencies could be recruited by the private sector in the country or abroad.

Finally, the US experience with RICO is one that India can emulate with great benefits. As mentioned before, most political parties are violating the law in their election campaigns that has become a major source of corruption in the country (Quraishi, 2014). At present, hundreds of crores of rupees are being spent to finance political campaigns. From offering bribes to voters to spending huge sums over advertisements, the money in electioneering has reached scandalous proportions. The number of candidates who are millionaires is now all-time high (Chauhan, 2013). The only method to deal with this widespread system bribery, influence peddling and corruption is to have a law like the RICO that can bring such pervasive and organized system of patronage under criminal prosecution. RICO also provides for long-term incarceration and seizure of assets that are further deterrence to dishonest political machines and their patrons. Only such comprehensive and determined efforts can begin to curb corruption in the country.

Yet it is pertinent to point to a note of caution in creating such agencies. While independent and empowered agencies are needed to combat corruption, there must be checks and balances in its operations too. Public officials armed with enormous legal and enforcement powers can also misuse it for their personal benefit. Edgar Hoover's unquestioned authority over FBI led to many abuses of power (Omang, 1983). Reportedly, Hoover kept every scrap of information that came his way and used defamatory information to obtain favors from Presidents and other officials. Hoover managed to remain the head of the FBI for almost 48 years and studies suggest that he had little respect for constitutional and libertarian values.

In Finland, traffic fines are based upon the annual income of the delinquent driver. This helps in cautioning rich people from speeding or driving recklessly since their fines will be in proportion to their income. To enforce this provision, the traffic police officers are given a device that can access the income tax returns of the driver under process. However, officers have been charged for using the device to check the incomes of their friends, neighbors and spouses without cause.[1] Any kind of power is likely to be misused and this holds true for officials serving in anti-corruption agencies.

The success of ICAC in Hong Kong has also raised questions about its likely consequences. Its officers have the power to arrest without warrant a person they suspect of indulging in corrupt practices. They also have the power to seize passport, search bank accounts and to examine business and private

---

1   Information shared by a senior officer in Helsinki police to one of the authors.

documents. In the Alex Tsui case, who was sacked from ICAC on charges of corruption and forced a public inquiry, it was revealed that ICAC conducted wiretapping and surveillance and was not accountable to any watchdog bodies (Gidwani, 1994). While ICAC was successful in strengthening public attitudes towards corruption, it also fostered a climate of fear and concerns for trivial matters. 'A faculty member received a box of chocolates from a student, took none and gave it to the entire department to share' (Skidmore, 1996, 129) thus precluding any personal advantage. The ICAC would use tough postures such as knocking on the door of people at 4 am to achieve maximum intimidation. Furthermore, critics have argued that the ICAC propaganda is so extensive that it obscures agency failings. As Skidmore (1996, 130) states, 'after 1997, ... [under the Chinese regime] the ICAC could become the major enforcement authority of a police state'. Who will police the police is an age-old question and one that must be answered before creating a powerful enforcement agency to combat corruption.

8

Alternate Solutions

The common belief in combating corruption is that the independence of investigation agencies must be ensured and guaranteed either by a constitutional or a statutory body. Additionally, the entire Criminal Justice System, including the police, prosecution and the judiciary be reformed and strengthened in terms of personnel, training, technical and financial resources. However, we believe that these measures are inadequate to combat corruption effectively in a country like India, given its size, complexity and historical experience. These agencies are only triggered into motion after the corrupt deed has occurred. The emphasis must equally be upon prevention of corruption. Here we examine some alternate solutions focused on prevention and outside the realm of policing. An innovative 'doctrine of housekeeping', is propounded so that the responsibility and accountability for monitoring and disbursal of funds must essentially devolve on the head of the department/ ministry concerned. We describe how the adoption of this principle will go a long way in the prevention of corruption and economic crimes. Significantly, we argue that corruption can be reduced realistically only by empowering the citizens to hold public officials directly accountable. A vigilant and informed citizenry is needed to safeguard abuse of authority. For this it is necessary that the citizens engage with the functions of administration and have the means to hold officials accountable for performance. We outline some innovations that have evolved by expanding use of ICT platforms, social media, citizen initiatives and rise of informed and concerned citizen groups. We also propose developing a variety of means to bring in the private sector, volunteers, non-governmental bodies and transparency in the functions of public institutions. We argue that open, knowledge-based, publicly-funded institutions best serve the community and help maintain the integrity of public officials.

Introduction

We started this research after witnessing the anger and frustration with the elected officials for their indifference to corruption. The Anna movement is past many years and Lokpal is still to come into action. Yet we believe that we should not be despondent with the politicians and ruling establishment. India is a democracy and the people are supreme who elect their government regularly and astutely. The frequent changes in the government and the undisputed 'incumbency' factor in elections are a testimony to the maturity of Indian voters. The politicians have to listen to the people and take steps to address their concerns and grievances. These may not go far and could be half-hearted but still these add bricks to the edifice of accountability. Accordingly, it is worth describing and analyzing several welcome steps that have been taken by different governments over the past several years to combat corruption.

As discussed previously, the deficiencies and malaise afflicting the anti-corruption agencies are deep-rooted and these agencies cannot by themselves combat corruption effectively. Therefore, there is an urgent need to focus on the preventive aspect rather than only on the enforcement aspect which monopolizes virtually all the limelight. We maintain, therefore, that there is an urgent need to look at alternate solutions to prevent and combat corruption in India. Some such promising and effective ideas and methods are illustrated below:

E-Governance

It is well understood that modern communications and information systems not only help improve efficiency and productivity but also bring about transparency in the organization. E-Governance is the rightful response to the demanding needs and expectations of people of such a vast country like India. By utilizing the online Information and Communication Technology (ICT) based platforms, portals and web sites, the governments are able to discharge their obligatory functions and provide mandatory services in a manageable and efficient manner. Research suggests (Mistry and Jalal, 2012) that the main rationale for E-Governance is that it can reduce costs and delays in processing and delivering services, expand citizen's access to public sector information, increase transparency and public accountability, and weaken authoritarian tendencies. There is some evidence to suggest that E-Government could control corruption (Andersen, 2009). The reason E-Governance can be successful in dealing with corrupt practices is that it can minimize and control the discretionary and monopoly power of public officials often used to extract economic rents. IT-enabled E-Government can improve the transparency of and accountability in the bureaucratic process, thereby minimizing the scope of corruption. The digital foot prints in such a system can be ignored only at one's own peril.

The term E-Governance has become a generic and umbrella word covering a wide range of activities and functions of modern government. E-Governance entails streamlining operational processes, transcribing information held by government agencies into electronic form, linking disparate databases and improving ease of access to services for members of the public. E-Government has also been promoted as a strategy of public sector reform, with a focus on how it can improve the managerial process (Kudo, 2010). However, Bertot, Jaeger and Grimes (2010) point that a culture of openness must be embedded within the government system and this needs to be pooled with technical and social capabilities before E-Governance can take root and become a tool against corruption.

Hooper et al. (2009) argue that E-services such as online submission of applications, requests for services and filing tax returns can help combat corruption by reducing interactions with officials and thus limiting their discretion. Mistry and Jalal (2012, 153) suggest,

> An important strategy for dismantling corruption can be the providing of easy access to information for all citizens through the use of E-Governance initiatives. This can result in greater transparency that reduces the ability of the public-sector official to demand bribes. Thus, E-Government can not only provide greater information to the population but also remove the discretion of the public official and allow citizens to conduct transactions themselves which, in turn, could lead to a reduction in corruption.

Their analysis of several developing countries also demonstrates that as the use of ICT or E-Governance increases, corruption decreases and this benefits the developing nations.

History of E-Governance in India

As far back as 1970, the Government of India established the Department of Electronics recognizing the increasing importance of modern communication systems. The subsequent establishment of the National Informatics Centre (NIC) in 1977 was the first major step towards E-Governance in India as it brought 'information' and its communication in focus. In the early 1980s, use of computers was confined to very few organizations. The advent of personal computers brought the storage, retrieval and processing capacities of computers to government offices. Rajiv Gandhi and Sam Pitroda catalyzed the use of computer in government functions and by the late 1980s, a large number of officials had computers but they were mostly used for 'word processing'. Gradually, with the introduction of better software, computers were put to other uses like managing databases, payroll and accounting and processing information. Advances in communications technology further improved the versatility and reach of computers, and many government departments started using ICT for a number of applications like tracking the movement of papers and files, monitoring development programs, processing of employees' pay rolls, generation of reports, etc.

However, the main thrust for E-Governance was provided by the launching of National Informatics Centre Network (NICNET) in 1987—the national satellite-based computer network. This was followed by the launch of the District Information System of the National Informatics Centre (DISNIC) program to computerize all district offices in the country for which free hardware and software was offered to the state governments. NICNET was extended via the state capitals to all district headquarters by 1990.

In the ensuing years, with ongoing computerization, tele-connectivity and internet connectivity, came a large number of E-Governance initiatives, both at the union and state levels. A national task force on information technology and software development was constituted in May 1998. While recognizing information technology as a frontier area of knowledge per se, it focused on utilizing it as an enabling tool for assimilating and processing all other spheres of knowledge. It recommended the launching of an 'Operation Knowledge' aimed at universalizing computer literacy and spreading the use of computers and IT in education. In 1999, the Union Ministry of Information Technology was created. By 2000, a 12-point minimum agenda for E-Governance was identified by the Government of India for implementation in all the union government ministries/departments (Government of India, 2008).

By 2006, the National E-Governance Plan (NeGP) had been launched and many departments of the Government of India as well as state governments initiated steps to adopt E-Governance. These initiatives are discussed under the following categories for some specific states:

1. Government to Citizen (G2C) initiatives
2. Government to Business (G2B) initiatives
3. Government to Government (G2G) initiatives

Gujarat

The Gujarat Chief Minister's Office (CMO) launched **SWAGAT** (**S**tate-**W**ide **A**ttention on Public **G**rievance by **A**pplication of **T**echnology), a G2C initiative, which is a grievance redressal IT platform on the Gujarat State portal (http://swagat.gujarat.gov.in). The CMO has also been instrumental in implementing IWDMS, an Integrated Workflow and Document Management System, a G2G initiative. It is a multilingual solution developed for automating the functions at all levels of the administrative hierarchy of any governmental department/office. IWDMS provides document management, workflow management, collaborative environment and knowledge management in an integrated fashion and delivers an electronic workplace. This system has resulted in considerable improvements in administrative efficiency. It has also improved transparency and enabled better monitoring of the progress of individual files through the administrative hierarchy.

Andhra Pradesh

The problem of obtaining loans from the bank using fake land records is a major source of corrupt practices across the country. The Revenue Department of AP has taken the initiative to make available all land records online by completing computerization of data relating to private and public land holdings. The government has operationalized two G2C portals—'Webland' and 'Mee Bhumi' that permits citizens to verify and print their land holdings directly. Furthermore, these have been linked to banks to promote faster processing and verification for purposes of taking out loans (*The Hindu*, 2015).

The E-Procurement process was designed to avoid human interface, that is, supplier and buyer interaction during the pre-bidding and post-bidding stages. The system now ensures total anonymity of the participating suppliers, even to the buyers, until the bids are opened on the platform. The E-Procurement application provides automatic bid evaluation, based on the evaluation parameters given to the system. These improved processes help eliminate subjectivity in receipt and evaluation of bids and can reduce corruption to a significant extent.

Saukaryam was the pilot E-Governance project aimed at taking municipal services to the citizens, in a transparent manner. Hitherto, the citizens knew Vishakapatnam Municipal Corporation in the state of Andhra Pradesh for inefficiency, corruption, complicated procedures and poor services. Even simple services like getting a birth certificate or property tax assessment used to take a number of days and citizens had to pay bribes. In the manual system, there was no transparency in approval processes and it used to take unduly long time and where corruption used to thrive. Procurement by the Municipal Corporation was shrouded in secrecy and bids and tenders for public works were fountainheads of corruption. With the introduction of Saukaryam, citizen services were improved and also helped eliminate corruption to a large extent. This could be seen from the increase in municipal tax collections. The Municipal Corporation, which was running in debit of ₹ 35 crores, made a surplus of ₹100 crores after the project was implemented (Pathak and Prasad, 2005, 10).

The Computer-aided Administration of Registration Department (CARD) is also one of the major success stories of E-Governance in Andhra Pradesh. The conventional procedure of registration was cumbersome which included 13 steps like ascertaining the value of the property, calculating the stamp duty, getting the legal document written, verification by sub registrar, copying the document and posting entries into multiple registers. Even a person selling a small piece of land had to go through multiple agencies like stamp vendors, document writers, registration agents (middlemen) and registration offices. Each step and each person in the process caused and contributed to corruption. The most significant achievement of CARD is the elimination of middlemen and organized corruption. In absence of bribes, the savings to the citizens is more than ₹ 100 crores and also increased the revenue to the exchequer (Satyanarayana, 2001 cited in Pathak and Prasad, 2006, 8).

The E-Seva project is designed to provide 'Government to Citizen' and 'E-Business to Citizen' services in Andhra Pradesh. The highlight of the E-Seva project is that all the services are delivered online to consumers/ citizens by connecting them to the respective government departments and providing online information at the point of service delivery. The services include online payment of utility bills, issuing certificates, issuing licenses and permits, e-forms, etc. Payments can be made by cash/check/demand draft/ credit card. The project has become very popular among the citizens especially for payment of utility bills since it has eliminated variety of prevailing corrupt practices. Moreover, from a modest collection of ₹ 43 lakhs in August 2001, the collections went up ₹ 2,500 cores by 2004. For a project which cost ₹ 36 crores, E-Seva centers are now collecting revenues of ₹ 300 crores per month and are serving 35 lakh citizens. E-Seva has succeeded in providing all citizen-related services under one roof and also eliminated corruption while making the entire processes transparent (Pathak and Prasad, 2005).

Uttar Pradesh

The state took the initiative for implementing and adopting E-Governance covering the entire spectrum of interfaces—G2G, G2C and G2B. The government ambitiously sought to introduce E-Governance for the subjects of land record, medical health, secondary education, foods-civil supplies, labor, social welfare, road transport, property registration, agriculture, treasuries, municipalities, gram panchayat, commercial taxes, police and employment exchanges including software technology parks at Agra and Varanasi. The Lokvani (G2C) is a public–private partnership project at Sitapur district in Uttar Pradesh, which was initiated in November 2004. Its objective is to provide a single window, self-sustainable E-Governance solution with regard to handling of grievances, land record maintenance and providing a mixture of essential services. This E-Government project evoked overwhelming response from the citizens. The main attraction was the online grievance redressal system that helped keep track of all the complaints filed by a particular Lokvani Center. All citizen complaints were monitored and sorted at the District Magistrate's Office that could ensure compliance from the concerned officer. Computerization of land records, treasury transactions, vehicle registration and road tax collection and even a tele-medicine project were launched with great fanfare. While these efforts perhaps made an honest attempt to control corrupt practices but a study found that the results have not been satisfactory (Nandan, 2008).

Kerala

The FRIENDS (Fast, Reliable, Instant, Efficient Network for the Disbursement of Services), a G2C initiative, is a state single-window facility providing citizens the means to pay taxes and other financial dues to the state government of Kerala. With the success of the project, efforts have now been initiated to develop FREES (FRIENDS Re-engineered and Enterprises Enabled Software) which would incorporate the 'Any Centre Any Payment Mode'. The state also launched a promising scheme called Akshaya that sought to bridge the digital divide and bring IT services to all the people in their language. One lofty objective was to make at least one member in each family 'e-literate'. However, even in a state with the highest literacy and developmental rates, one study found that 'most of the people in the district of Kottayam [were] not aware about the various services provided by the Akshaya center in their own Panchayath' (Krishnan and Sreehari, 2016, 1557).

Karnataka

The Bhoomi project (G2C) in Karnataka made available a computerized Record of Rights, Tenancy and Crops (RTC) to all landowners at a kiosk in the Taluka office, on a small payment (Bhatnagar and Chawla, 2001). The project sought to eliminate corruption and middlemen, as the farmers had to bribe the village accountants to get their land records in the manual system. Touch-screen kiosks at district offices now help farmers view their records directly. Significantly, it is estimated that the Bhoomi project saved the farmers ₹ 80.6 crores in bribes and ₹ 6.6 crores in wages annually (Pathak and Prasad, 2005, 6).

The Khajane Project (G2G) is a comprehensive online treasury computerization project of the Government of Karnataka. The project has resulted in the computerization of the entire treasury related activities of the state government and the system has the ability to track every activity right from the approval of the state budget to the point of rendering accounts to the government. Not only has this E-Governance project contributed in bringing efficiency in the government and aids the decision-making process, it has eliminated a large number of corrupt practices and frauds in public transactions that could not be detected earlier due manual operations.

Kaveri (G2C) is yet another Karnataka government E-Governance project aimed at speeding up the registration process and delivery of documents to citizens through fully automated registration process. A survey conducted by Skoch International in Bangalore found that the project was user friendly, simple and fast in delivery of service. One of the major findings of the study is that the corruption has come down by 80 per cent and respondents to the survey rated reduction in corruption at 8 on a scale from 0 to 10 (Pathak and Prasad, 2005, 12).

The journey of E-Governance initiatives in India took a broader dimension in mid 1990s for wider sectoral applications with emphasis on citizen-centric services. Later on, as discussed above, many states/UTs launched various E-Governance projects. Though these projects were mainly citizen-centric, their desired impact was less than expected. Unfortunately, the government has not promoted independent research studies to measure their impact, particularly in reducing corruption. Some isolated studies have suggested that E-Governance do not necessarily lead to a reduction in corruption. For instance, the interstate computerized check posts in Gujarat were established with fanfare to eliminate corrupt practices involved in processing vehicles entering the state. These posts were meant to tighten the inspection of incoming trucks for overloading and validity of document. Yet computerization alone was not a sufficient tool to tackle corruption. There was no effort to place this E-Government procedure in a broader context of departmental reform or a drive against corruption within a wider range of governmental functions.

Consequently, officials supervising the check posts continued to extract bribes from truck operators (Bhatnagar, 2003, 6). Still, E-Government projects have continued and 31 Mission Mode Projects covering various domains have been initiated. Irrespective of political affiliations, all governments have realized that digitization would bring greater transparency, better governance and more accountability, thereby reducing the scope of corruption and bribery.

Anti-Corruption Efforts by NDA Government

It will be improper not to discuss the highly publicized efforts of the current NDA government led by Prime Minister Modi to combat corruption. This government won the elections in 2014 promising to combat corruption and usher development of the country. The government at its first cabinet meeting, accepted the direction of the Supreme Court and announced the setting up of a high-level Special Investigation Team (SIT) to help unearth and probe black money stashed away abroad in safe havens (Vinay Kumar and Venkatesan, 2014). The SIT, headed by former Supreme Court Judge, Justice MB Shah and another retired Supreme Court Judge, Justice Arijit Pasayat, as its Vice-Chairman, comprise senior most government officials, including Revenue Secretary, Deputy Governor of RBI, Director of IB, Director of ED, Director, CBI, Director, RAW, Director General of Revenue Intelligence, Chairman of the Central Board of Direct Taxes and Director of Financial Intelligence. The constitution of the SIT followed a directive by the Supreme Court which empowered the SIT with the responsibility of preparing a comprehensive action plan, including the creation of institutional structures that would enable and strengthen the country's battle against generation of unaccounted monies which are usually stashed away either in foreign banks or some other manner domestically.

Regarding the performance of the SIT, the Deputy Chairman, Justice Arijit Pasayat, disclosed that ₹ 70,000 crore of black money has been unearthed so far. He said ₹ 70,000 crore of black money, including more than ₹ 16,000 crore detected after probe launched into global leaks about Indians stashing funds abroad, has been unearthed through different schemes of the government (*The Financial Express*, 2017).

It is educative to know that vast amount of black money is reported to be hidden from tax agencies. Though, there are no official estimates available of black money concealed in various parts of the world, according to an estimate by some economists from the Bank of Italy, of the six to seven trillion dollars of tainted money, Indians' share is estimated at $152–181 billion (Varmal, 2016). All of this wealth is hidden in places with weak regulations and strong secrecy laws. Corrupt use these provisions and shell companies to hide their ill-gotten money. However, there are no official figures available with the Government of India in this regard. Considering the complexity of the task of dealing with sovereign laws of the countries providing safe havens, confidentiality principles of banks and mammoth sums of monies stashed abroad, we feel that the SIT has still a long way to go in unearthing and bringing black money from abroad, as promised by the BJP in its election campaign. It is also pertinent to stress that such enforcement agencies, how-so-ever empowered and supervised even by the Supreme Court simply add to the layers of existing agencies and do not make significant dent in corrupt practices.

Some other anti-corruption measures taken by the current NDA government include *The Benami Transactions (Prohibition) Amended Act , 2016* to curb and detect black money that will make it easier for the income tax authorities to confiscate 'benami' properties. The Act also provides for rigorous imprisonment for a term not less than one year but which may extend to seven years and fine which may extend to 25 per cent of the fair market value of the property. 'Benami' is a Hindi word that means 'without name' or 'no name'. In this Act, the word is used to define a transaction in which the real beneficiary is not the one in whose name the property is purchased. As a result, the person in whose name the property is purchased is just a mask of the real beneficiary.

Another important legislation is *The Black Money (Undisclosed Foreign Income and Assets) Imposition of Tax Act, 2015*. This has been enacted specifically to make deal with the problem of undisclosed foreign income and assets. The Act seeks to speed the procedure for dealing with such income and assets and to provide for imposition of tax on any undisclosed foreign income and asset held outside India and for matters connected therewith or incidental thereto. Similarly, *The Prevention of Money Laundering Act (PMLA), 2002 vide Finance Act, 2015* seeks to enable attachment and confiscation of equivalent asset in India where the asset located abroad cannot be forfeited.

A much-touted initiative is *Digital India,* a program to transform

India into digital empowered society and knowledge economy. Some of the highlights of this rather expansive program are making high speed internet connectivity to all gram panchayats; 'cradle to grave' digital identity; digitization of all government services to improve 'ease of doing business'; moving towards a cashless financial transaction system; making available all government documents and certificates and portability of all entitlements for individuals through the cloud. The digital vision areas have seen the launching of a large number of initiatives totaling altogether 115 digital initiatives! Some significant schemes under this rubric are described below:

Aadhaar

A major technology driven initiative is the so-called Aadhaar that will provide a unique identity to every resident of the country. The largest biometrics based identification system in the world, Aadhaar, is a strategic policy tool for social and financial inclusion, public sector delivery reforms, managing fiscal budgets, increasing convenience and promoting hassle-free people-centric governance. It is designed to eliminate duplicate or fake identities and is meant to be used as a primary identifier for all welfare schemes and for effective service delivery promoting transparency and good governance. The Unique Identification Authority of India (UIDAI) is a statutory authority established under the provisions of the Aadhaar (Targeted Delivery of Financial and Other Subsidies, Benefits and Services) Act, 2016 (Aadhaar Act, 2016) on July 12, 2016 by the current Government of India, under the Ministry of Electronics and Information Technology (MeitY). Prior to its establishment as a statutory authority, UIDAI was functioning as an attached office of the then Planning Commission. It was conceived to check pilferage of transfer of funds to the real beneficiaries in some welfare schemes like MNREGS. The Authority has by end of 2017 issued more than 111 crore Aadhaar to the residents of India.

The UIDAI issues Aadhaar number to residents only after cross-checking their demographic and biometric attributes against its entire database. Aadhaar authentication enables elimination of duplicates under various schemes and is expected to generate substantial savings to the government exchequer. It also provides the government with accurate data on beneficiaries, enables direct-benefit program and allows the government departments/service providers to coordinate and optimize various schemes. Aadhaar will enable implementing agencies to verify beneficiaries and ensure targeted delivery of benefits. Welfare programs, where beneficiaries are required to be confirmed before the service delivery, stand to benefit from UIDAI's authentication services. This will result in curbing leakages and ensuring that services are delivered to the intended beneficiaries only. Examples include subsidized food and kerosene delivery to public distribution system and worksite attendance of MGNREGS beneficiaries. Additionally, Aadhaar can improve disbursement systems and utilize scarce development funds more effectively and efficiently including better human resource utilization involved in the service delivery network.

Aadhaar system provides single source online identity verification across the country for the residents. Once residents enroll, they can use the Aadhaar number to authenticate and establish their identity multiple times using electronic means. It eliminates the hassle of repeatedly providing supporting identity documents each time a resident wishes to access services such as opening a bank account and/or obtaining driving license. By providing a portable proof of identity that can be verified through Aadhaar authentication online anytime, anywhere, the Aadhaar system enables mobility to millions of people who migrate from one part of the country to another. All these provisions are likely to reduce various corrupt practices prevailing in the government departments.

Single Window Interface for Trade (SWIFT)

As part of the 'Ease of Doing Business' initiatives, the Central Board of Excise and Customs, the Government of India, has taken up implementation of the single window project to facilitate the trading across borders in India. The 'India Customs Single Window' would allow importers and exporters, the facility to lodge their clearance documents online at a single point only. Required permissions, if any, from other regulatory agencies would be obtained online without the trader having to approach these agencies. The Single Window Interface for Trade (SWIFT) would reduce interface with governmental agencies, dwell time and the cost of doing business.

Direct Benefit Transfer (DBT)

DBT was initiated with the aim to reform government delivery system by re-engineering the existing process in welfare schemes for simpler and faster flow of information/funds and to ensure accurate targeting of the beneficiaries, de-duplication and reduction of fraud. DBT will bring efficiency, effectiveness, transparency and accountability in the government system and infuse confidence of citizen in the governance.

Government E-Marketplace

This is a single window solution for online procurement of common use goods and services required by various government departments/organizations/PSUs. It is well known that many public-sector undertakings such as Food Corporation of India are mired in corruption. It has been impossible to supervise their operations and procurement of food grains and other commodities have led to immense loss of public funds. Reportedly, 'as much as $14.5 billion in food was looted by corrupt politicians and their criminal syndicates over a decade in Uttar Pradesh' (Misra, 2014). GeM aims to enhance transparency, efficiency and speed in public procurement. It also provides the tools for direct purchase, e-bidding and reverse e-auction, to facilitate the government users to achieve the best value for the money. The portal offers online registration facilities for all stakeholders namely government users, product sellers and service providers.

Passport Seva

Corruption was rampant in the passport offices across the country (Verma, 2010). Now, this scheme called 'Passport Seva' enables simple, efficient and transparent processes for delivery of passport and related services. Apart from creating a countrywide networked environment for government staff, it integrates with the state police for physical verification of applicant's credentials and with India post for delivery of passports. The Passport Seva project is transforming passport and related services in India to provide a best-in-class experience to Indian citizens. PSP is enabling MEA to deliver passport services in a reliable, convenient and transparent manner, within defined service levels.

Goods and Service Tax Network (GST)

One of the most ambitious policy initiative is the GST System that will establish a uniform interface for the tax payer and a common and shared IT infrastructure between the center and the states. This has been described as 'one of the boldest reform in post-independence India' (Krishnan, 2016). It seeks to create a common market throughout India and facilitate free movement of goods and services across the entire country. It is also expected to promote labor intensive manufacturing, including export-oriented manufacturing, in poor regions of India. Arvind Subramanian, the Chief Economic Advisor, has reportedly said that the GST will facilitate 'Make in India' by 'Making One India'.

NREGA-SOFT scheme envisions implementing E-Governance across states, districts and three tiers of Panchayati Raj Institutions. It empowers the common man using the information technology as a facilitator. NREGA-SOFT provides information to citizen in compliance with the Right to Information Act, 2005. It makes transparent and available all the documents like muster rolls; registration and employment register; job card and receipt register which are hidden from public otherwise.

To summarize, all the above described and other initiatives can curb many of the prevailing corrupt practices in public offices. The unique and authentic identity, provided by Aadhaar Card, can be used for 'Know Your Customer' to open bank accounts; including under Jan Dhan Yojna; to acquire passport in 10 days; to avail of Direct Benefit Transfer (DBT) of the LPG subsidy and other funds under various welfare schemes and scholarships; to obtain bank loans; to use it as a proof of address for investing in stock market and for pensioners to obtain Digital Life Certificate, Jeevan Praman helping receive monthly pensions and payment of provident funds. What is going to be a game changer is the digital payment based on this unique 12-digit identification number and biometrics, including thumb impressions. It has also now been made mandatory to link the Aadhaar Card to Pan Card numbers and bank account numbers. Aadhaar and all the other integrated E-Governance schemes will be an effective check to curb corruption by eliminating intermediaries and direct interface with officials as well as other associated economic crimes like impersonation, cheating, criminal misappropriation, forgery and falsification of records. It will also become simpler for the tax authorities to trace the money trail, curb tax evasion and check money laundering.

Perhaps, the most significant step taken by PM Modi was the demonetization of ₹ 500 and ₹ 1,000 notes in November 2016 that represented almost 86 per cent of all the currency in use. This was done with the objective to reduce corruption and 'the country emerged with few obvious scars' (Chakravorti, 2017). At present, it is unknown how much of the currency was returned but seems most of it was deposited. The government backed this initiative with a payment App called BHIM that facilitated E-Banking using Aadhaar identity. While most economists criticized the policy, some reports suggest that it had no impact upon the economy that grew at 7 per cent (*Financial Express*, 2017). However, despite personal hardship, it seems that the people of India felt that the PM is fighting corruption on their behalf and acting boldly.

There is evidence of positive impact of these efforts launched by the NDA government. A Center for Media Studies (2017) survey presents some findings that indicate a reduction in the perception of corruption in the country. The report makes a bold statement, 'Between 2005 and 2017, there is a definite *decline* [our emphasis] in both perception and experience of citizens about corruption in availing public services'. Compared to the survey conducted in 2005 when 73 per cent of the households had perceived increase in corruption level, in the year 2017, this percentage had shrunk to 43 per cent. Furthermore, 'More than half (56 per cent) feel that the level of corruption decreased in public services during demonetization phase (November–December 2016)' (Ibid., 2017, 3). The report is at pains to emphasize that the main data collection was done in October–November 2016 period and then an additional telephonic sub-sample survey was done in January 2017 to understand the effect of demonetization on corruption. Since 'a major part of the reference period was before the "*notebandi*" happened' and the focus was on G2C service delivery phase when money paid in bribes of ₹ 500 and ₹ 1,000 notes were meaningless, 'demonetization phase has no or minimal effect on the findings of CMS-ICS 2017 on petty corruption' (Ibid., 2017, 1).

Limitations of E-Governance in Combating Corruption

E-Governance is effective and holds promise, but by itself cannot remove corruption completely. Interestingly, by way of an example, if we consider the digital payments in Kenya, according to a report (Harford, 2017) just eight months after its launch, a million Kenyans had signed up to M-Pesa. Today, there are about 20 million users. Within two years, M-Pesa transfers amounted to 10 per cent of Kenya's gross domestic product (GDP)—now it accounts for nearly half. Soon, there were 100 times as many M-Pesa kiosks in Kenya as cash machines. However, it is significant to note that despite such a successful digital payment revolution, Kenya remains one of the most corrupt countries in the world. According to the Transparency International's Corruption Perception Index (2016), Kenya is placed lowly at 145 out of 176 countries with a score of 26 out of 100. Clearly just digitized payments do not seem to have contributed much in the reduction of corruption in the country.

Online publication of budgetary allocations and expenditure, electronic systems for tracking status of license applications, processing citizen complaints and grievances and sharing performance data are all known to increase accountability. 'However, increasing availability of information on the Internet does not mean that citizens will automatically use the information to demand greater accountability' (Bhatnagar, 2003, 4). Citizens need to be constantly engaged in the process of governance as well. Efforts to encourage citizens to make conscious efforts to demand better public services are required. Public-spirited groups also need to be involved in checking the performance of public officials and drawing attention to their obstruction in sharing public information.

Bhatnagar (2003) argues that E-Government can be used to combat corruption in two ways. First, it can become one of the key components of a broader anti-corruption strategy as is demonstrated by the Online Procedures Enhancement Civil Applications (OPEN) system installed in the Seoul municipality in Korea. This system provides information on application procedures and supervisors to contact, which assists citizens to follow the handling of their applications. Second, service delivery improvement initiatives can be implemented in corrupt departments, specifically targeting transparency and reduced corruption as objectives. Moreover, E-Government can also reduce the tolerance for corruption amongst citizens who would no longer be required to compromise their honesty by paying a bribe to public officials. Above all, there must be the free access to information guaranteed by the Right to Information. Bhatnagar (2003) further recommends an approach of learning by trial and consolidating small gains. A few pilot projects in departments known to be corrupt, which have some exposure to computerization and a large interface with public, could be the beginning for experimentation and evaluation. Efforts must be made to inform about the benefits of implementing the new processes. Impact on transparency and corruption must be the underlying concern of these new forms of delivering public services.

Nandan (2008) also pointed that the analysis of various E-Governance schemes launched by Uttar Pradesh government shows that planning alone cannot ensure success. To be successful, all these schemes must engage the citizens, educate them about the potential benefits and seek their involvement before rolling them out. Furthermore, the officials must also be motivated to become change agents. Detailed planning and determined leadership is required to transform old practices and bring bureaucratic practices in the twenty-first century. The computerization of police station records and criminal tracking systems were conceived in the early 1980s and have yet to be implemented in most of the states. Bureaucratic culture, indifference to public service and resistance to change are major obstacles that even an active Prime Minister cannot tame easily. Many of the measures taken by PM Modi are laudable and can contribute effectively to combat corruption and black money effectively. However, it is the issue of enforcement that remains a major challenge. The bureaucratic machinery remains the same and the enforcement agencies, including Income Tax Department, as also the entire criminal justice system, remain afflicted by the problems of acute shortage of personnel and technical resources vis-à-vis the mammoth number of complaints/cases to be handled. This matter has been amply amplified and discussed in great detail with empirical data in Chapter 5.

Promising Global Efforts

There are now a large number of global cooperative efforts to engage, assist and promote governmental and non-governmental efforts in combating corruption. Amongst various methods of combating corruption, most suggest economic reforms that open the markets for competition and ensure proper taxation. Other suggestions include strengthening the institutions; reforming the public sector; financial management and civil service reform to develop accountable and effective governance. Furthermore, reform of tax and revenue departments; transparency in public procurement; a decentralized system of governance and citizen accountability along with legal and judicial reforms are also recommended. What seems important is that the civil society must be engaged and special anti-corruption bodies be created to bring probity and integrity in public functions.

The United Nations Office on Drugs and Crime (UNDOC, 2017) moved a resolution in the General Assembly to adopt the United Nations Convention against Corruption (UNCAC) on October 31, 2003. UNCAC has become a major legally binding universal anti-corruption instrument. The Convention's far-reaching approach and the mandatory character of many of its provisions make it a unique tool for developing a comprehensive response to a global problem. The Convention covers five main areas: preventive measures, criminalization and law enforcement, international cooperation, asset recovery and technical assistance and information exchange. The Convention covers many different forms of corruption, such as bribery, trading in influence, abuse of functions and various acts of corruption in the private sector.

UNCAC provides for codes of conduct for public officials; transparency in public procurement and public finances, forfeiture of the proceeds of corruption crimes in terms of both moveable and immoveable assets, steps to prevent private sector corruption and money laundering. It also seeks participation of civil society and non-governmental organizations to fight against corruption and demands measures ensuring public access to information and participation in educational programs. The Convention provides for the protection of whistleblowers, witnesses, victims and experts. Ever since the adoption of the UNCAC, December 9 has been designated as the 'International Anti-Corruption Day'.

A Conference of States Parties (CoSP) has also been established to improve the capacity of and cooperation between the nations and to promote and review implementation of various measures. This body has evolved an interesting peer review process that supports and supervises the implementation of the guidelines into domestic laws and regulations. This system promotes international cooperation, sharing of good practices and even challenges of the respective member states in their efforts to combat corruption. A significant number of anti-corruption tools and resources are now being shared to assist all the states in dealing with corruption (UNDOC, 2017, see Documents, Publications and Tools).

As a signatory to the resolution in 2005, India asserted its commitment to take all necessary steps to fight corruption and indeed many legislations, including the Lokpal and Lokayuktas Act, Protection of Whistleblowers Act and Right to Information, are examples of this commitment. After amending domestic laws to bring about greater transparency in funding election campaigns and political parties, among other crucial legislative steps, to bring it at par with the international instrument, India ratified this Convention in May 2011. Significantly, India was reviewed for its anti-corruption efforts and implementation of the UNCAC resolutions in 2015 by two foreign country experts (UNDOC, 2017). India has also provided full information about the laws and competent authorities that deal with corruption-related subjects. Furthermore, a 'national anti-corruption' strategy has also been formulated and placed on record with the United Nations. This strategy not only describes a large number of steps that are being taken but also which body—the government, civil society organizations, CVC, judiciary, the media and even the political parties are responsible for undertaking these steps. For instance, the document states, 'political parties should demonstrate political will to fight corruption by adopting and enforcing a code of ethics among members' (UNDOC, 2017, India- National Anti-Corruption Strategy Summary Section 2.1). At least, in principle, the Indian state remains committed to combat the scourge of corruption! While a corruption-free world remains a utopian dream, these conventions, resolutions and promises of cooperation do provide a blueprint, guidelines and framework for the prevention and combating of corruption effectively.

GRECO

An interesting feature that is worth considering for India is the Group of States against Corruption (GRECO) organization established in 1999 by the Council of Europe to monitor states' compliance with the organization's anti-corruption standards. GRECO's objective is to improve the capacity of its members to fight corruption by monitoring their compliance with Council of Europe anti-corruption standards through a dynamic process of mutual evaluation and peer pressure. It helps to identify deficiencies in national anti-corruption policies, prompting the necessary legislative, institutional and practical reforms. GRECO also provides a platform for the sharing of best practice in the prevention and detection of corruption. Furthermore, membership in GRECO is not limited to Council of Europe member states. Any state may join by notifying the Secretary General of the Council of Europe. Moreover, any state, which becomes party to the Criminal or Civil Law Conventions on Corruption automatically, accedes to GRECO and its evaluation procedures. Currently, GRECO comprises 49 member states (48 European states and the United States of America).

GRECO monitors all its members on an equal basis, through a dynamic process of mutual evaluation and peer pressure. The GRECO mechanism ensures the scrupulous observance of the principle of equality of rights and obligations among its members. All members submit themselves without restriction to the mutual evaluation and compliance procedures. GRECO monitoring comprises a 'horizontal' evaluation procedure (all members are evaluated within an Evaluation Round) leading to recommendations aimed at furthering the necessary legislative, institutional and practical reforms. The second compliance procedure is designed to assess the measures taken by its members to implement the recommendations.

GRECO works in cycles that are organized as evaluation rounds, each covering specific themes. For instance, GRECO's first evaluation round (2000–02) dealt with the independence, specialization and means of national bodies engaged in the prevention and fight against corruption. It also dealt with the extent and scope of immunities of public officials from arrest, prosecution, etc. The second evaluation round (2003–06) focused on the identification, seizure and confiscation of corruption proceeds; the prevention and detection of corruption in public administration and the prevention of legal persons (corporations, etc.) from being used as shields for corruption. The third evaluation round (launched in January 2007–10) addressed the transparency of party funding. The fourth evaluation round was launched on January 1, 2012 to examine the themes of 'prevention of corruption in respect of members of parliament, judges and prosecutors' regarding ethical principles and rules of conduct; conflict of interest in public responsibilities and personal matters; prohibition of certain activities; declaration of assets, income and liabilities of interests and enforcement of the rules regarding conflict of interest and general awareness of public interest.

The evaluation process follows a well-defined procedure, where GRECO appoints a team of experts for the evaluation of a particular member. The analysis of the situation in each country is carried out on the basis of written replies to a questionnaire and information gathered in meetings with public officials and representatives of civil society during an on-site visit to the country. Following the on-site visit, the team of experts drafts a report, which is communicated to the country under scrutiny for comments before it is finally submitted to GRECO for examination and adoption. The conclusions of evaluation reports may state that legislation and practice comply—or do not comply—with the provisions under scrutiny. The conclusions may lead to recommendations which might require action within 18 months or to it may lead to observations that members are supposed to take into account but are not formally required to report on in the subsequent compliance procedure.

One of the strengths of GRECO's monitoring is that the implementation of recommendations is examined thoroughly. The assessment of whether a recommendation has been implemented satisfactorily, partly or has not been implemented, is based on a situation report, accompanied by supporting documents submitted by the member under scrutiny. In cases where not all recommendations have been complied with, GRECO will re-examine outstanding recommendations within another 18 months. GRECO pursues compliance of its recommendations from member states. As an international organization its reports carry weight and pressure the states to make strong efforts in combating corruption.

This is clearly a mechanism that may be worth following in India. Although, questions about independence and external interference in national institutions may arise but the admissibility of an external evaluation is something that is likely to spur much needed reforms and compliance with well-recognized international standards of probity in public institutions and processes. Combating corruption is a continuous battle and joining hands with others will always be beneficial.

Learning from Other Countries' Experience

Corruption affects every society and many countries have evolved promising methods to combat corruption that can be customized and adopted in India. For example, Hong Kong and Singapore conceptualized and implemented successful anti-corruption agencies as discussed in Chapter 7. The leadership displayed commitment in launching large-sale investigations and going after high-profile individuals to establish the effectiveness of the agencies. The key to their success is that, rather than restricting the activities to law enforcement, they also worked on changing the attitudes of the people who consider personal loyalties more important than formal rules and public duties.

Situational crime prevention (Clarke, 1992) that we have discussed in Chapter 2 suggests that many ways to combat specific crimes is to understand how the offenders perceive and execute their deeds. One specific way is to control the facilitators that enable offenders to commit the crime. Free coffee and gifts from merchants has been seen to be a common form of corrupt practice amongst American police forces that continues to this day. The administrators have simply not been able to control this visible form of corruption. However, the German police made a rule that strictly prohibits its officers from visiting any food outlet in uniform to avoid public perception of misuse of authority. Once it was made known that violation of this rule will mean disciplinary action, drinking coffee without paying for it stopped in the organization. In India, where constables openly extort from street vendors, a similar rule prohibiting any constable from acting against the vendor in absence of senior officer may help prevent public extortion.

Similarly, strict and symbolic leadership also plays an important role in establishing probity in public offices. President Sirleaf of Liberia displayed her commitment to tackling corruption and even suspended her own son along with 46 other senior government officials for failing to disclose assets to Liberia's anti-corruption officials. This example provided an incredibly effective way to demonstrate to the citizens and business people of Liberia that she and her government are taking the fight against corruption seriously.

President Jahjaga of Kosovo recognized corruption to be the major problem affecting the country and planned on tackling it head on. She established a presidential anti-corruption council to coordinate the work and activities of major agencies fighting corruption. This was done on the understanding that combating corruption requires setting up an effective information exchange mechanism between law enforcement agencies and other involved actors. Her efforts have gained the trust of citizens and investors and also show how a genuinely committed leader can make a difference to a country's graft culture (Newtactics, 2014).

'Ask Your Government' Initiative

Another significant international initiative is the 'Ask Your Government' movement that is designed to reflect the fundamental guiding principle that citizens have the right to know how their government is spending public money. The movement began in 2010, when 100 civil society organizations launched an ambitious effort to document public access to budget information in 80 countries. The aim was to highlight the problems civil society faces in accessing public budget information in a wide range of countries. The government responses were assessed on two levels. First, whether or not the government responded at all to the queries. Activists gave government agencies up to three opportunities to respond to their inquiries. If no formal response was provided in a reasonable time frame, or officials refused to provide an answer to the question posed, the result was categorized as a failure to respond to the citizen information request. Second, when governments did respond to citizen requests, the information provided was analyzed based on whether or not it substantively addressed all aspects of the inquiry.

Surprisingly, only one country, New Zealand, provided all the answers substantively including the budget information. An additional 22 countries (28 per cent of the total) offered an official answer to all six information requests, though with varying degrees of comprehensiveness that included India. However, the officials in these nations struggled to provide some of the required budget information. Key pieces of the requested budget information were not provided on excuses such as, not available, not held centrally, or not organized in a way that allowed the responsible agencies to respond to the question as it was posed. This initiative is a test of government responsiveness to public enquiries for budget information. If officials declined to provide the information, or the government agency was not able to produce a timely or complete response, the end result is that citizens are not informed about how public funds are spent. This gap is particularly troubling when the information sought relates to government's investments in development. The lessons are clear, active citizen participation is needed to understand how the officials spend public funds on development. This needs to be made transparent to enable citizens to hold governments accountable for the use of public funds (International Budget Partnership, 2014).

Competitive Bureaucracy

A creative solution is the concept of competitive bureaucracy as a response to the problem of corruption (Rose-Ackerman, 1978; Shleifer and Vushny, 1993). Drugov (2007) examined the impact of competition amongst bureaucrats on their power to misuse discretionary judgments. For example, corruption prevails in India in procuring the driving license since a single office in the district handles the process. In Russia, such a license can be obtained from any police office situated in the district. The choice of going to more than one office to obtain a license induces competition amongst various officials and this reduces the extortion that prevails when operating through a single office. The Indian case is described as a monopoly regime where the license must be obtained from a pre-specified office and bureaucrat. Hence this bureaucrat has a monopoly power over the applicants in his district. The Russian case is akin to a competition regime. Any applicant can request the license from any bureaucrat; therefore, bureaucrats must compete for the applicants. Drugov's (2007) analysis provides an empirical argument to suggest that the competitive bureaucracy creates more incentives for the citizens to seek out less corrupt officers and thereby reduce corrupt practices of the specific department.

Unfortunately, competitive bureaucracy is an arrangement rarely seen in the real world. But it is an idea that is worth experimenting in India where the citizen may be given the option of filing a criminal case at any police station and not restricting the jurisdiction of the investigator to a particular region. Thus, any police officer will have the power to investigate any crime in the district. Drugov's analysis suggests that competition amongst the police investigators and the choice given to the citizen will reduce bribery and obstacles in registration of cases. This will also give incentive to the officers to act professionally in order to attract citizen complainants in larger numbers.

The above is based on the experiences of one of the authors. In a particular police station, the author, then serving as the superintendent of the district police, did not specify who would serve as the Station House Officer (SHO) of the police station. All sub-inspectors serving in that police station were to be evaluated after a month to determine who should be appointed as the SHO. This became an incentive for the officers to do well and serve the citizens in order to attain the coveted position. For a month, the citizens were surprised to receive helpful and professional attention. The officers courted the citizens and would do their best to quickly address their grievances and complaints. For that month, the numbers of crimes solved increased significantly and most importantly the citizens happily informed the SP about the safety, security and service they experienced.

While not really formulated as a method to induce competition but the establishment of kiosk in Bangalore to provide online registration of complaints attracted media attention and popular citizen support. To ensure better access to the citizens and to combat corruption in the registration of complaints, Bangalore police established a remote FIR registration system. The IT company, Cisco, helped design and install a kiosk at a popular shopping mall where people could go and file a complaint about crime. This involved a remote FIR filing system using Cisco's tele-presence technology and Remote Expert Government Service system. The kiosk was equipped with high-definition video and high-quality audio, a touch screen and a virtual keyboard to connect the complainant to a designated police officer based at the traffic management center. The complainant was virtually transported to a police control room where the FIR was registered after incorporating digital signatures as required by the law. The citizen was also able to review the complaint with an experienced officer to ensure that the FIR was error free. Once the document was prepared, the citizen received a free copy as an instant acknowledgement. The system also permitted the citizen to submit his own complaint by digitally signing, scanning, printing and submitting it online. The kiosk was also equipped to provide other services such as police verification certificates and taking report of lost items. This system initially attained popularity amongst the residents but gradually lost its attraction. Perhaps, the system was taking too much time to register the FIR or may be the officers were not very helpful. Unfortunately, no study about its effectiveness in reducing corrupt practices has been done and the police have discontinued this kiosk.

However, it is clear that if citizens have a choice, then they will avail the easiest one to navigate the complex and indifferent bureaucracy. Citizens would prefer to connect with the police officers from a remote system rather than face the challenges of going to the police station where harassment is common. The 911 call system is now ubiquitous across the United States and almost all developed nations have a similar system that helps citizen call for police or emergency help. Indeed, Bayley (2001) argues that modern professional policing involves a system where the citizen need not go to the police but the officer comes to the citizen in the shortest possible time. This system enhances the legitimacy of the government by ushering a responsive service-oriented style of policing. In India, such a mechanism has emerged with the 100-call system, but unfortunately, it is not designed to register the complaint as an FIR for which the citizen has to go to the nearest police station. Research suggests that a sense of distance and indirect communication emboldens the people who interact with the police to engage on an equal basis. This adds to their sense of entitlement and empowerment. Clearly, E-FIR has the potential to reduce corruption in registration of cases by the police. Most significantly, the complainant does not have to face the foul mood of the officer nor experience subordination!

Empowering Citizens

Though not widely known, over the past 10 years, there has been a grass-roots, bottom-up 'eruption against corruption' to borrow a popular slogan from the Fifth Pillar movement in India (http://www.5thpillar.org). Citizens can and are fighting to curb corruption in their communities and countries. They are organizing and strategically using non-violent actions such as civil disobedience; petitions; vigils; marches; sit-ins; Right to Information laws, demanding information; monitoring and auditing of authorities, budgets, spending and services; social networking and blogging; coordinated low-risk mass actions; creation of parallel or independent institutions; social and economic empowerment initiatives; street theatre; songs; humor and public pledges (*NewTactics.org*, 2014).

These grass root movements are important since they present a more promising bottoms-up approach involving citizens who are generally the ones facing corruption and hardship. Grass root movements also help mobilize the people and help highlight the practices that generally go unnoticed by anti-corruption agencies. In contrast, the top-down approach fails since many of the functionaries responsible for combating corruption are themselves involved or indifferent to these practices. Furthermore, top-down approach involves working within the complex administrative rules largely designed to protect the officials rather than making them accountable to the people.

However, bottoms-up protests can only come from better education and information. Protestors must know the laws and administrative rules as well as the rights enshrined in the constitution. The democratic polity of India, particularly the freedom struggle launched by Gandhiji, has outlined the methods to stand against injustice and abuse of public office. The non-violent and peaceful struggles adopted against the British authorities have been replicated in independent India when the elected representatives and the bureaucracy have misused their powers. The Narmada Bachao Andolan against illegal methods to take away land from the people, the Chipko movement to prevent deforestation and the recent Anna Hazare movement to demand Lokpal, provide numerous examples of citizen-led initiatives to force accountability from public officials.

Such examples can be found from other parts of the world too. The 2009 CICAK (acronym for 'Love Indonesia, Love Anti-Corruption') campaign mobilized citizens in Indonesia through creative non-violent tactics, including a 1.7-million-member Facebook group, humor and anti-corruption ringtones, to defend the Corruption Eradication Commission and secure the release of senior commissioners, who were jailed under false charges. The Muslims for Human Rights NGO is empowering communities to fight poverty by curbing misuse of community development funds. It conducts local education and training in social audits, while using non-violent tactics such as street theatre, marches and site visits, to organize people against corrupt practices in Kenya.

In South Korea, a coalition of 1053 civil organizations called the 'Civil Action for the General Election 2000' was formed to clean up politics by identifying corrupt and ineligible candidates in the general election. They set up transparent guidelines to define corrupt and anti-human rights activities, held street rallies, petitions, phone and email campaigns, and launched youth websites that included TV, movie and music-celebrity endorsements.

Similarly, the Dejemos de Hacernos Pendejos is a citizen's movement in Mexico that seeks to alter the apathy of people, foster a sense of civic responsibility and demand accountability from public officials. The group use street actions, stunts, social networking and humor as innovative tactics to involve citizens and gain access to information. Their efforts have forced members of parliament to return bonuses they gave to themselves.

Another interesting initiative is by Controlarios Ciudadanas that has grown into a network of 70-citizen watchdog groups covering every province in Paraguay. They share expertise on filing criminal reports of corruption and getting information to the media about corrupt officials. They also support politicians and judges displaying integrity. When a district attorney's life was threatened, they organized marches and placed newspaper ads highlighting his bravery and honesty (*Newtactics.org*, 2014).

The growth of social media has also spurred innovative efforts to combat corruption. Social media allows citizens to speak up about their concerns and access information on corruption. They can also draw attention using blogs, petitions, video, etc., and at the same time maintaining anonymity. Moreover, this electronic communication can quickly spread all over the country and even around the world in no time. This provides means to organize, support and draw attention towards the corrupt practices. For example, *Avaaz.org* created an online petition to draw attention to the Ficha Limpa campaign, which targets corrupt officials in Brazil and holds them accountable. These efforts helped to get a bill through Congress that was the reason for the potential disqualification of over 330 candidates for political office in the elections. Undoubtedly, advantages of using social media are that it disrupts systems of corruption, strengthens citizen participation, strengthens campaign organization and capacity, wins people over and weakens sources of support and control for unaccountable and corrupt power holders (*Newtactics.org*, 2014).

Mobilizing People through Humor to Combat Corruption

A creative method to involve people in combating corruption comes from using humor. Philip Duhame, a strategist and a civil resistance organizer, based in Quebec, has rightly stated, 'because after all, isn't laughing the best way to show teeth that bite?' Humor is a powerful tool to captivate a wide range of audiences, attract media attention, provoke contemplation and disarm the opponent without giving offense. Moreover, humor can reduce tension and sense of confrontation. Humor is a tactic which entertains, surprises and engages the otherwise uninterested audience into the issue. By making activism fun, the apathetic can find motivation in a meaningful way. As George Orwell said, 'every joke is a tiny revolution'.

The Venezuelan group El Chiquire Bipolar used a humorous video in response to President Hugo Chávez threat to the movement as 'Twitter birdie'. In response to this harmless humor, thousands of people created 'remixes' of the President's response video, furthering the humrous campaign. Political satire is a very social thing. To seem funny and pitiful in the eyes of most of the public is near death for a politician. Ridicule is absolutely deadly, politically speaking.

The Egyptian revolution was not only marked by protests but also humor that ridiculed the regime and ultimately brought it down. 'The steady stream of comedy flowing throughout the Tahrir Square functioned to build community, strengthen solidarity and provide a safe, thug-free outlet for Egyptians to defy the regime' (Sussman, 2011). The Turkish uprising started as a peaceful sit-in against the demolition of Taksim Gezi Park. However, what gave the Turkish protests their viral effect was the constant use of political humor and the protesters' willingness and ability to turn every heavy-handed move into an occasion for social media satire.

Citizen Initiatives in India

Indian democracy may have its limitations and wide-spread corruption may even lead one to question if democracy suits the country but there is little doubt that democracy has empowered the citizens to hold their rulers accountable. As Amartya Sen (1999) says, 'a country becomes fit through democracy' and this is reflected in the large number of NGOs and citizen coordinated determined efforts that combat prevailing asymmetry of power between officials and citizens. The key is to address the core problems through civil society led projects that mobilize citizen engagement and persist with sophisticated strategies that aim to yield sustainable results. This is well demonstrated by a case study from Khariar block in the state of Odisha. The women of this block were eligible to receive free maternal and child health care services under the National Rural Health Mission program of the Government of India. However, official corruption and apathy was denying them this benefit. An NGO Ayauskam got involved in helping citizens' access and collect information and used it to raise community awareness and motivate them to demand accountability. It helped citizens form collective action groups, trained them and established performance monitoring tools such as customer feedback surveys. The groups were trained to pursue effective advocacy and public communications. As may be expected the persons benefiting from the corruption tried to retaliate but retreated only when they saw that the groups had strength in numbers and were succeeding in getting the support of public authorities and local media. The NGO was able to use the existing laws, particularly the Right to Information Act to force the officials to be responsive to the demands of the citizens. The strength and persistence of collective action groups resulted in the officials' acting to resolve grievances and improve citizen satisfaction (Partnership for Transparency, 2012).

Citizen group's willingness to participate and constructively engage with service providers made a crucial difference. Bhargava (2012) notes that substantial results can be secured when citizens are aware of their rights, organized and mobilized for collective action, for example, to promote activities comprising access to information about service entitlements and standards prescribed by the law, granting voice to beneficiaries regarding design and implementation of service programs, providing grievance redress mechanisms and citizens with tools and access to demand accountability from service providers like third party monitoring, public hearings, social audits, etc.

A most unusual citizen initiative, Bribe Busters, was launched by entrepreneur Shaffi Mather. Based on his understanding that 'Bribes and corruption have both a demand and a supply side, with the supply side being mostly of greedy corporate unethical businesses and hapless common man. And the demand side being mostly politicians, bureaucrats and those who have discretionary power vested with them' (Mather, 2009). This is a promising and innovative approach that is emerging in the country. A group of concerned citizens are developing a service that will fight the demand for a bribe and or corrupt practice.

Bribe Busters in Kerala was set up as a BPO-like social venture with a team of legal experts to help citizens and institutions fight bribery. For a fee, an individual or an institution, when confronted with a request for a bribe, can hire Bribe Busters to prevent it from taking place. Bribe Busters uses only legally established means to stop the action. One such is the Right to Information Act that allows any citizen to request public information from a government body, which must revert within 30 days.

Being market driven and based upon a token fee this service uses other tools like, hidden cameras and surveillance, peer pressure to ensue fulfillment of citizen grievances without paying a bribe. This group has set up standard processes that are available through a call center based franchise system to serve anyone confronted with a bribe. So far, Bribe Busters has handled about 100 cases successfully, mainly in its home state of Kerala. Interestingly, in many cases the perpetrator simply backed off after Bribe Busters made the first contact. At this stage, the cases are smaller ones, ranging from getting a passport renewed to registering a new company. Over the next several years, Shaffi plans to take Bribe Busters national, and with his keen eye for injustice, will certainly make anyone in a position of power think twice before asking for a bribe. A fee-based BPO kind of service to stop payment of bribes and prevent corruption appears to be the ultimate weapon to combat corruption in the country.

Kaushik Basu (2011), former consultant with the Finance Ministry in UPA II government proposed a 'novel' idea for cutting down incidents of bribery. Basu states that there are different kinds of bribes and amongst these those that people have to give for services that are legally entitled to can be addressed. He has called these as 'harassment bribes' for these occur when citizens are denied basic public services by dilatory tactics of officials or by deliberate misuse of their discretion. As Basu mentions, 'harassment bribery is widespread in India and it plays a large role in breeding inefficiency and has a corrosive effect on civil society' (ibid., 3). His idea is to declare such bribe giving as a legitimate action on part of the citizen and ensure full immunity from any punitive action by the anti-corruption agencies or state authorities. Basu believes that this immunity will enable the citizen to be willing to cooperate with police in trapping the bribe taker or getting caught for the act. Furthermore, if the bribe taker is caught then the bribe giver will go free and will also be able to collect his or her money back. This will encourage the bribe giver to cooperate with the anti-corruption agents and get his work done as well as get his money back. Basu is cautious in emphasizing that public officials may become vulnerable to blackmail and false charges of taking a bribe. For this he recommends that the punishment for levying false charges be increased to act as a deterrent. While the proposition is interesting the government has not shown interest in pursuing this preventive measure. We believe this could be a good attempt and one that can be effective in controlling such harassment forms of bribery cases.

Alternate Solutions Proposed by Authors

We believe that good governance in India is inversely proportional to corruption! It is apparent that corruption is primarily responsible for poor governance, lack of desirable inclusive growth, development and implementation of welfare schemes. The most important challenge for the development of the country is to eradicate or at least minimize corruption by a two-pronged strategy of short-term measures and preventive mechanisms. We describe these two approaches in some detail below.

The restructuring, reinforcement and strengthening of existing anti-corruption mechanisms in terms of personnel and training, technical and financial resources is an urgent first step. These agencies need to transform by adopting strategic rather than reactive approach to detect and curb corruption in key susceptible departments/ministries and plans/schemes. Instead of awaiting random complaints and responding to them, a more proactive thrust is required by the anti-corruption agencies in key vulnerable departments/ schemes to prevent, detect and neutralize corruption in the first place.

This could be possible with the generation of greater actionable and strategic intelligence. Special intelligence units within the anti-corruption bodies, as in the Economic Offenses Wing of Madhya Pradesh, are needed to supplement pro-active anti-corruption efforts. A plethora of agencies have been created to deal with corruption and other illegal activities. Anti-corruption agencies exist in the Finance Ministry and the Home Ministry while statutory bodies like the CVC, CIC, ED and CAG have their own mechanisms to handle citizen complaints about corrupt or questionable practices of public officials. Unfortunately, each unit tends to function in isolation and rarely designs a multipronged effort to deal with corrupt practices in public organizations in a systematic and long-term manner. At present, close coordination among enforcement agencies at various levels to deal comprehensively with this menace is an urgent need. In particular, intelligence needs to be shared at all levels, both formally and informally, particularly at the cutting-edge levels involving illegal financial transactions. For too long turf wars and acrimonious center–state relations have plagued the efforts to combat corruption.

Furthermore, urgent need to evolve a National Data Base of offenders of corruption and other economic crimes is a much-needed requirement. Each Anti-Corruption Bureaus should have access to this Data Base. It should also be linked to the Data Base of the Banking Sector, Income Tax and Enforcement Departments as well as other financial and regulatory bodies. Any limitation of jurisdiction or functionality is going to be exploited by the unscrupulous elements and all such loop holes need to be plugged. Such proactive efforts cannot succeed unless there are more dialogue and cooperation amongst the various stakeholders both at the level of central government as also the state governments. There is thus an urgent need to set up an effective state level anti-corruption intelligence coordination committee that comprises the state CBI, Lokayukta, EOW, ACB, CID, Vigilance, Special Branches and others for both formal and informal sharing of intelligence. As pointed out in previous chapters, in MP the Lokayukta has been given its own investigative agency instead of working with a powerful and resourceful agency like the EOW. Rulers have established independent fiefdom for their vested interests which have divided and weakened the anti-corruption efforts of these agencies.

It goes without saying that investigators need to be continuously trained and exposed to the latest technology, hardware and software applications that are prevalent in the market. Everyday new technology strengthens the hands of the offenders to exploit the system and cover up their tracks. The police investigators need extensive and quality training within the state, at the national level as well as international level, to develop their professional skills. At present, the training programs and schedules are poorly organized and do not seek to adequately prepare the investigators for probing complex financial transactions that hide the inherent corrupt practices. A beginning has been made with annual conference hosted by the CBI of all the anti-corruption enforcement agencies but zonal conferences with specific agenda can help share good practices and train officers at the subordinate levels.

Doctrine of Housekeeping

We have already argued citing EOW MP's data that in view of plethora of complaints and limited resources, a couple of enforcement agencies at the

Government of India level and at the states' level cannot curb corruption effectively in the country. Hence, alternate solutions have to be looked into, primarily those that seek to prevent corruption. One of the authors has proposed this 'doctrine of housekeeping' to Leaders of the CBI as well as the Chiefs of the ACBx that has been well received though no action has been taken so far. This doctrine emulates the practice of a family where the head is responsible and accountable for keeping track of the household budget and overseeing that the money is spent in the most effective manner for family needs. In the same manner, the Ministry/Department Head must be made responsible and accountable for the proper utilization of the funds allotted to it by the Parliament/Legislative Assemblies in the budget. After all, an organization is nothing more than an extension of family on a larger scale.

Besides the earthy commonsense approach behind this doctrine of housekeeping, the concept is actually enshrined in the financial codes of this country. The MP Financial Code Volume II begins by quoting in its opening paragraph: 'The cardinal principle governing the assessment of responsibility is that every public officer should exert the same vigilance in respect of public expenditure and public funds generally as a person of ordinary prudence would exercise in respect of the expenditure and the custody of his own money'. The Code goes on to state: 'While, therefore, Government are prepared to condone an officer's honest errors of judgment involving financial loss, provided the officer can show that he has done his best up to the limits of his ability and experience, they are determined to strictly enforce personal liability against all officers who are dishonest, careless or negligent in the duties entrusted to them'. The same principle has been reiterated in the financial codes of other states as also that of the Government of India. But there is still no effective mechanism to implement the letter and spirit of these postulations of the financial codes. There is even scarce attempt to understand the institutional instruments needed by which senior officers and organizational heads could exercise vigil and monitor the budget made available to them.

In view of the fact that enforcement agencies step in only after the damage has been done, such a system of houskeeping would have the added advantage of preventing the funds from being misused in the first place. This governance model would also cut down on the number of complaints being received by the ACBx and thus take a big load off the shoulders of the enforcement agencies.

It would also reinforce the concept of accountability right at the doorsteps. Furthermore, it would do away with the current practice of haphazard receipt of complaints by the anti-corruption agencies, if and when it is made or ever made by a vigilant citizen or an interested party or an aggrieved individual. It is no secret that often misuse of funds goes unnoticed if no complaints are lodged.

In continuance with the doctrine of housekeeping, we also propose that in keeping with the proverbial principle of 'charity begins at home', all major flag ship welfare schemes and plans, like Mahatma Gandhi National Rural Employment Guarantee Scheme (MNREGS), involving huge sums of money running into thousands of crores of rupees, must provide for a suitable percentage of funds from within to ensure that the public money is not misused in the first place and proper anti-corruption mechanisms are put in place. This can be done by providing for and setting up of in-built internal vigilance, security and third-party audit systems to ensure proper utilization of the funds, instead of waiting for misappropriations to take place and then asking anti-corruption machinery to step in. Clearly, the social audit system envisaged in these schemes has failed to prevent large-scale misuse and misappropriation of funds. This 'housekeeping' system will help in ensuring that corruption is nipped in the bud and that the funds are genuinely utilized for the deprived sections of the people for whom they are meant. The above innovative concept was adopted as a resolution and sent to the government for consideration, by one of the authors but appears to have been lost in transit!

Conclusion

Despite all the promises and expectations from the NDA government and PM Modi in particular, it is rather disconcerting that the battle against corruption seems to be at a standstill. The large number of schemes and stress on E-Governance have not changed the perception of a large proportion of people that corruption is going down (Center for Media Studies, 2017). While corruption at the top seems under control the common experience of bribing the police and other officials remains unchecked. Significantly, Lokpal has yet to be appointed by current NDA government, on the ground that the Leader of Opposition (LoP) is not in existence in the selection committee. It is noteworthy that the requirement of the presence of the LoP in the selection of the CVC, Director CBI and Chief Information Commissioner (CIC) has been circumvented by amending relevant laws and substituting the Leader of the Largest Opposition Party in place of the LoP. It is, therefore, significant that similar amendment has, so far, not been made in the Lokpal and Lokayuktas Act, 2013. We wonder if the provision that the Lokpal, under certain circumstances, can also investigate the Prime Minister and other ministers is inhibiting the process.

It is worth mentioning the anguish of the Supreme Court that reflects the disappointment with the current government in being serious about curbing corruption. Peeved with the delay in the appointment of Lokpal, the Supreme Court (April 2017) found the Lokpal and Lokayukta Act of 2013 an 'eminently workable piece of legislation' which provides for the appointment of Lokpal chairperson and members even in the absence of a recognized Leader of Opposition (LoP). The Supreme Court reiterated that Section 4 (2) of the said Act males it amply clear that 'No appointment of a Chairperson or a Member shall be invalid merely by reason of any vacancy in the Selection Committee'. However, this advice is yet to be accepted by the government.

We feel that a viable corruption combating policy requires a multipronged approach. The deterrence effect of punishment through well investigated cases by independent and professional anti-corruption agencies with requisite manpower, financial and technical resources and speedy delivery of justice by the criminal justice system is first and foremost requirement for battling corruption effectively. In any case, it is the sovereign function of the state to enforce its laws rigidly. While such a deterrence would lead to prevention and thereby reduction of corruption due to the fear of and respect for law, we simultaneously need a system that prevents corrupt practices in the first place and controls the facilitators of corruption. A number of such institutions and systems have been discussed in the book and we have examined their strengths and weaknesses. We have also suggested that through the 'doctrine of housekeeping', checking and preventing corruption at the functional levels within the ministry/department itself is a far better proposition than conducting elaborate investigations at a later stage after corruption has taken place.

The Government of India's thrust on providing statutory and obligatory services and empowerment of the people vide its flagship program, *Digital*

India, will certainly have a substantial impact on actually preventing corruption. However, these initiatives have to be consistently monitored and sustained over several years to attain their objectives. Simultaneously, the states need to get their acts together and follow the positive initiatives of the central government as much of the anti-corruption programs need to be closely monitored at the local levels which come under purview of the state governments. Digital delivery of mandatory services by various governments would reduce the human interface and thus curb petty corruption afflicting the masses. All this also needs to be supplemented by the efforts of vigilant and concerned citizens. People also would need to be sensitized to spread awareness and thereby usage of ICT-based projects launched by the government. An empowered people's movement that acts as a watchdog over the functioning of public officials is an effective mechanism to combat corruption.

We stated that corruption must be regarded as 'evil' and one that damages the fabric of any society. The culture and history of India reminds us that evil is fought through morality and goodness. In the land of Buddha and Gandhi, where corruption is ubiquitous we must realize that at present moral values are in decline. Corruption is invariably linked with lust, greed and an exploitative lifestyle that is indifferent to the future. The strongest weapon in the arsenal to combat corruption is thus a revival of moral principles that shame the corrupt. Ethical behavior, truthfulness and humanism are values that could revive the society where tolerance and simplicity were practiced. These cannot be imposed from the top nor realized by institutional mechanisms. Rather than harking upon the cliché of 'political will' and waiting for the day when there will be honest politicians in India who will work for public good, each citizen has to ponder and question his or her actions and contribution in building the society. Citizens must believe that in a democracy, it is the 'public will' that is paramount. Ultimately, the people of India are the critical factor in ensuring that corruption is shackled and righteousness prevails in the nation.

Bibliography

Abedin, Najmul. 2010. 'The Ombudsman in Developing Democracies: The Commonwealth Caribbean Experience.' *International Journal of Public Sector Management* 23(3): 221–53.

Abraham, Ann. 2012. 'Ombudsman, Tribunals and Administrative Justice Section: Making Sense of the Muddle: The Ombudsman and Administrative Justice, 2002–2011.' *Journal of Social Welfare and Family Law* 34(1): 91–103.

Aji, Sowmya. 2012. 'Toothless Watchdogs.' *India Today*, 11 February. Accessed on 26 March 2017. Available at http://indiatoday.intoday.in/story/lokpal-lokayukta-offices-lack-basic-infrastructure/1/173027.html.

Andersen, Thomas Barnebeck. 2009. 'E-Government as an Anti-corruption Strategy.' *Information Economics and Policy* 21(3): 201–10.

Andvig, Jens Chr and Karl Ove Moene. 1990. 'How Corruption May Corrupt.' *Journal of Economic Behavior and Organization* 13: 63–76.

Association for Democratic Reforms. 2014. *Election Watch*. Accessed on 31 May 2017. Available at http://adrindia.org/.

Bainbridge, John. 1965. 'A Civilized Thing.' *The New Yorker*, 13 February, 136–40.

Bandiera, Oriana, Andrea Prat and Tommaso Valletti. 2009. 'Active and Passive Waste in Government Spending: Evidence from a Policy Experiment.' *American Economic Review* 99(4): 1278–308.

Barbados. 2006. *Annual Report*. Bridgetown: Ombudsman Office.

Barr, A and D. Serra. 2006. *Culture and Corruption*. Global Poverty Research Group. Accessed on 31 May 2017. Available at http://www.gprg.org/pubs/workingpapers/pdfs/gprgwps-040.pdf.

Basu, Kaushik. 2011. 'Why, for a Class of Bribes, the Act of Giving a Bribe should be Treated as Legal.' Working Paper, Economic Division, Department of Economic Affairs, Ministry of Finance. New Delhi: Government of India.

Bayley, David H. 2001. 'Democratizing the Police Abroad: What to Do and How to Do It.' *Issues in International Crime, National Institute of Justice.* Washington DC: US Department of Justice. Accessed on 28 August 2018. Available at www.ncjrs. gov/pdffiles1/nij/188742.pdf.

BBC News. 2012. 'India's Corruption Scandal'. 18 April. Accessed on 31 May 2017. Available at http://www.bbc.com/news/world-south-asia-12769214.

Bent, Christensen. 1961. 'The Danish Ombudsman.' *Univ. Pennsylvania Law Review* 109(8): 1100–26.

Bertot, John C., Paul T. Jaeger and Justin M. Grimes. 2010. 'Using ICT to Create a Culture of Transparency: E-Government and Social Media as Openness and Anti-corruption Tools for Societies.' *Government Information Quarterly* 27(3): 264–71.

Bertrand, Marianne, Simeon Djankov, Rema Hanna and Sendhil Mullainathan. 2007. 'Obtaining a Driving Licence in India: An Experimental Approach to Studying Corruption.' *Quarterly Journal of Economics* 122(4): 1639–76.

Bhargava, Vinay. 2012. 'Strategies for Empowering Communities to Demand Good Governance and Seek Increased Effectiveness of Public Service Delivery.' *Partnership for Transparency Fund,* Working Paper 4. Accessed on 31 May 2017. Available at http://ptfund.org/2012/04/demand-good-governance-public-service-delivery/.

Bhatnagar, Subhsh and Rajeev Chawla. 2001. 'Bhoomi: Online Delivery of Land Titles in Karnataka.' Accessed on 25 June 2017. Available at http://www1.worldbank. org/publicsector/egov/bhoomi_cs.htm.

Bhatnagar, Subash. 2003. 'Transparency and Corruption: Does E-Government Help?' Draft Paper prepared for the compilation of CHRI 2003 Report 'Open Sesame: looking for the Right to Information in the Commonwealth.' Delhi: Commonwealth Human Rights Initiative.

Brantingham, P. J. and P. L. Brantingham. 1993. 'Nodes, Paths and Edges: Considerations on the Complexity of Crime and the Physical Environment.' *Journal of Environmental Psychology* 13: 3–28.

——————— (eds). 1981. *Environmental Criminology.* Prospect Height, Ill.: Waveland Press.

Brasz, H. A. 1978. 'The Sociology of Corruption.' In *Political Corruption: Readings in Comparative Analysis,* edited by Arnold J. Heidenheimer and Michael Johnston. New Brunswick: Transaction Books.

Brooks, Graham. 2016. *Criminology of Corruption: Theoretical Approaches.* London: Palgrave Macmillan.

Bureau of Police Research and Development. 2017. *Data on Police Organization: As on 1.1.2016.* New Delhi: BPRD.

Byrne, Elaine. 2007. 'The Moral and Legal Development of Corruption: Nineteenth and Twentieth Century Corruption in Ireland.' PhD Thesis, University of Limerick.

Cadeddu, Simone. 2004. 'The Proceedings of the European Ombudsman.' *Law and Contemporary Problems* 68(1): 161–80.

Caiden, G. 1984. 'Ombudsman in developing democracies: Comment.' *International Review of Administrative Sciences* 50(3): 221–26.

Center for Media Studies. 2010. *India Corruption Study 2010: Is the Scenario Changing?* New Delhi: CMS Research House.

———. 2017. *India Corruption Study 2017: Perception and Experience with Public Services and Snapshot View for 2005–17*. New Delhi: CMS Research House.

Central Bureau of Investigation. 2013. *Annual Report 2013*. New Delhi: Government of India Press.

Central Information Commission. 2017. *Annual Report 2015–2016*. New Delhi: CIC

Central Vigilance Commission. 2017. *Annual Report 2016*. New Delhi: Government of India Press. Accessed on 31 May 2017. Available at http://www.cvc.nic.in/ar2016.pdf.

Chakravorti, Bhaskar. 2017. 'Early lessons from India's Demonetization Experiment.' *Harvard Business Review*, 14 March. Accessed on 8 July 2017. Available at https://hbr.org/2017/03/early-lessons-from-indias-demonetization-experiment.

Chambliss, William J. and Robert B. Seidman. 1971. *Law, Order and Power*. Reading, MA: Addison-Wesley.

Chandrashekaran, Sumathi. 2014. 'Our Poorly Written Lokpal,' *The Indian Express*, 15 Juanary. Accessed on 31 May 2017. Available at http://indianexpress.com/article/opinion/columns/our-poorly-written-lokpal/2/.

Chauhan, Chetan. 2013. 'No Business Like Politics in India; Re-elected Leaders Triple Wealth,' *Hindustan Times,* 16 June. Accessed on 31 July 2017. Available at http://www.hindustantimes.com/India-news/NewDelhi/No-business-like-politics-in-India-re-elected-leaders-triple-wealth/Article1-1077016.aspx.

Cheng, Hongming and Ling Ma. 2009. 'White Collar Crime and the Criminal Justice System: Government Response to Bank Fraud and Corruption in China.' *Journal of Financial Crime* 16(2): 166–79.

Chowdhary, Anil. 2013. 'Independence of CBI: Myth and reality.' *Rediff.com,* 15 May. Accessed on 5 July 2017. Available at http://www.rediff.com/news/column/independence-of-cbi-myth-and-reality/20130515.htm.

Clarke, J. R. and Dwight R. Lee. 2011. 'Markets and Morality.' *Cato Journal* 31(1): 1–25.

Clarke, Ronald V. 1992. *Situational Crime Prevention: Successful Case Studies*. New York: Harrow and Heston Publishers.

Cornish, Derek B. and Ronald V. Clarke (eds). 1986. *The Reasoning Criminal: Rational Choice Perspectives on Offending*. New York: Springer-Verlag.

Corrupt Practices Investigation Bureau. 2013. *Annual Report.* Singapore.

Danish Parliamentary Ombudsman. 2011. *Annual Report.* Copenhagen: Directorate of Enforcement.

Dhawan, Himanshi and Pradeep Thakur. 2015. 'Here's Proof That Poor Get Gallows, Rich Mostly Escape.' *Times of India,* 21 July. Accessed on 5 July 2017. Available at http://timesofindia.indiatimes.com/india/Heres-proof-that-poor-get-gallows-rich-mostly-escape/articleshow/48151696.cms.

Doig, Alan and David Norris. 2012. 'Improving Anti-Corruption Agencies as Organizations.' *Journal of Financial Crime* 19(3): 255–73.

Dong, Ben, U. Dulleck and Benno Torgler. 2012. 'Conditional Corruption.' *Journal of Economic Psychology* 33: 609–27.

Dong, Ben and Benno Torgler. 2012. 'Corruption and Social Interaction: Evidence from China.' *Journal of Policy Modeling* 34(6): 932–47.

Drugov, Mikhail. October 2007. *Competition in Bureaucracy and Corruption.* Department of Economics, Oxford University Discussion paper series # 369. Accessed on 31 May 2017. Available at http://www.economics.ox.ac.uk/materials/working_papers/paper369.pdf.

Durkheim, Emile. 1965. *The Division of Labor in Society.* Translated by George Simpson. New York: The Free Press.

Economist. 2011. 'A Rotten State,' 10 March. Accessed on 31 May 2017. Available at http://www.economist.com/node/18332796.

Ed., ———. 2014. 'Campaign Finance in India: Black Money Power,' 4 May. Accessed on 31 May 2017. Available at http://www.economist.com/blogs/banyan/2014/05/campaign-finance-india.

Enforcement Directorate. 2017. *Performance from 2012-2015.* Accessed on 31 May 2017. Available at http://www.enforcementdirectorate.gov.in/Performance_of_ED_2012_to_2015.pdf.

European Commission. 2014. *Report from the Commission to the Council and the European Parliament: EU Anti-Corruption Report.* Brussels: European Commission.

Faccio, Mara. 2006. 'Politically connected Firms.' *American Economic Review* 96(1): 369–86.

Fisman, Raymond and Edward Miguel. 2007. 'Corruption, Norms, and Legal Enforcement: Evidence from Diplomatic Parking Tickets.' *Journal of Political Economy* 115(6): 1020–48.

Frank, B. 1975. 'The Ombudsman Revisited.' *The Journal of International Bar Association* May: 48–60.

Ganguly, Sumit. 2012. 'Corruption in India: An Enduring Threat.' *Journal of Democracy* 23(1): 138–48.

Gardiner, John A. 1993. 'Defining Corruption.' In *Coping with Corruption in a Borderless World,* edited by Maurice Punch et al. Boston: Kruwer.

Gargan, Edward A. 1992. 'Corruption's Many Tentacles are Choking India's Growth', *NY Times*, 10 November.

Gellhorn, Walter. 1965. 'The Ombudsman in New Zealand.' *California Law Journal* 53: 1155–211.

Ghosh, S. K. 1978. *Economic Offences*. Kolkata: Satchidananda Prakashani.

Gidwani, Anoop Gulab. 1994. 'The Impact and Accountability Implications of the Bill of Rights in Relation to the Independent Commission against Corruption.' MPA Thesis, University of Hong Kong.

Godbole, Madhav. 2001. *Report of the One-man Committee on Good Governance*. Nasik: Government of Maharashtra Press.

Goel, Rajeev K. and Michael A. Nelson. 2010. 'Causes of Corruption: History, Geography and Government.' *Journal of Policy Modelling* 32(4): 433–47.

Goldstein, Herman. 1979. 'Improving Policing: A Problem-Oriented Approach.' *Crime and Delinquency* 25(2): 236–58.

Gottehrer, Dean M. 1974. *Ombudsman Committee, International Bar Association Resolution*. Vancouver: International Bar Association.

———. 2009. 'Fundamental Elements of an Effective Ombudsman Institution.' Paper presented at the 'Annual US Ombudsman Association Conference'. Estes Park, CO: 29 September to 3 October.

Gottfredson, Michael and Travis Hirschi. 1990. *A General Theory of Crime*. Stanford: Stanford University Press.

Government of India. 2008. *Promoting e-Governance- the Smart Way Forward*. Second Administrative Reforms Commission, 11ᵗʰ Report. Accessed on 31 May 2017. Available at http://arc.gov.in/11threp/ARC_11thReport_preface_contents.pdf.

Gregory, Roy and Philip J. Giddings. 2000. 'The Ombudsman Institution: Growth and Development.' In *Righting Wrongs: Ombudsman in Six Continents*, edited by Roy Gregory and Philip J. Giddings, 1–20. Amsterdam: IOS Press.

Gupta, Anandswarup. 1979. *The Police in British India: 1861–1947* New Delhi: Concept Publishing Company.

Harford, Tim. 2017. 'Money Via Mobile: The M-Pesa Revolution,' *BBC News*, 13 February. Accessed on 31 May 2017. Available at http://www.bbc.com/news/business-38667475.

Heineman Jr. Ben W. 2012. 'Can America Lead the World's Fight against Corruption?' *The Atlantic*, 3 February. Accessed on 7 December 2017. Available at https://www.theatlantic.com/international/archive/2012/02/can-america-lead-the-worlds-fight-against-corruption/252448/.

Hill, L. B. 1974. 'Institutionalization of the Ombudsman and Bureaucracy.' *The American Political Science Review* LXVIII(3): 1075–85.

Hirschi, Travis. 1969. *Causes of Delinquency*. Berkeley, CA: University of California Press.

Holmgren, K. 1968. 'The Need for an Ombudsman Too.' In *The Ombudsman: Citizen's Defender*, edited by D. C. Rowat, 225–30. London: George Allen and Unwin.

Hood, Christopher. 1995. 'The "New Public Management" in the 1980s: Variations on a Theme.' *Accounting, Organizations and Society* 20(2–3): 93–109.

Hough, Dan. 2015. *Corruption, Anti-Corruption and Governance*. Basingstoke: Palgrave MacMillan.

Huisman, Wim. and Judith van Erp. 2013. 'Opportunities for Environmental Crime: A Test of Situational Crime Prevention Theory.' *British Journal of Criminology* 53(6): 1178–200.

Inamdar, Nikhil. 2013. 'Fraud at Public Sector Banks - A Rampant Occurrence?' *Business Standard*, 27 November. Accessed on 31 May 2017. Available at http://www.business-standard.com/article/finance/fraud-at-public-sector-banks-a-rampant-occurrence-113112700132_1.html.

Independent Commission against Corruption. 2017. *Conditions Which May Allow Corruption to Occur*. ICAC- New South Wales. Accessed on 31 May 2017. Available at http://www.icac.nsw.gov.au/about-corruption/conditions-allowing-corruption.

Inge, Amudsen. 1999. 'Political Corruption: An Introduction to the Issues.' Working Paper 7. Bergen, Norway: Michelson Institute

International Anti-Corruption. 2017. *About the IAC*. Accessed on 31 May 2017. Available at http://internationalanticorruption.com/about-the-iac/.

International Budget Partnership 2014. *Ask your Government*. Accessed on 31 May 2017. Available at http://internationalbudget.org/what-we-do/major-ibp-initiatives/international-advocacy/ask-your-government/.

Jayaprakash Narayan. 2002. 'Corruption in Civil Services,' *Times of India*, 10 August. Accessed on 31 May 2017. Available at http://timesofindia.indiatimes.com/city/hyderabad/Corruption-in-civil-services/articleshow/18605547.cms.

Jha, Giridhar. 2016. 'Suitcases, Cell Phones, Microwave Ovens; It's Raining Gifts for Bihar MLAs,' *Indiatoday.in*, 19 March. Accessed on 25 June 2017. Available at http://indiatoday.intoday.in/story/suitcases-cell-phones-microwave-ovens-its-raining-gifts-for-bihar-mlas/1/624119.html.

Jharkhand Lokayukta. 2011. *Annual Report*. Ranchi: Government Press.

Jones, Stephens. 2006. *Criminology*. Third edition. Oxford: Oxford University Press.

Justia. 2014. *Criminal Law: Racketeer Influenced and Corrupt Organizations [RICO] Law*. Accessed on 31 May 2017. Available at https://www.justia.com/criminal/docs/rico.html.

Kapur, Vikram. 2013. 'Lest we forget,' *The Hindu*, 26 November. Accessed on 26 March 2017. Available at http://www.thehindu.com/opinion/op-ed/lest-we-forget/article5390637.ece.

Karnataka Lokayukta. 2012. *Annual Report*. Bangalore: Government Press.

Kaufmann, Daniel. 2006, 'Corruption, Governance and Security.' *World Economic Forum*- Global Competitiveness Report 2004/2005, September.

Kelkar, Vijay and Ajay Shah. 2011. 'Indian Social Democracy: The Resource Perspective.' Working Paper 2011–82. New Delhi: National Institute of Public finance and Policy.

Kirkpatrick, David D. 2010. 'Does Corporate Money Lead to Political Corruption?' *New York Times*, 23 January. Accessed on 31 May 2017. Available at http://www.nytimes.com/2010/01/24/weekinreview/24kirkpatrick.html.

Krishnan, Aswani and K. G. Sreehari. 2016. 'A Study on E- governance and User Satisfaction through Akshaya Centers in Kerala; with Special Reference to Marangattupilli Panchayath in Kottayam District.' *Imperial Journal of Interdisciplinary Research* 2(10): 1547–58.

Krishnan, Chandrasekhar. 2010. 'Tackling Corruption in Political Party Financing: Lessons from Global Regulatory Practices.' Edmond J Safra Research Lab, Working paper 43. Boston: Harvard University.

Kudo, Hiroko. 2010. 'E-Governance as Strategy of Public Sector Reform: Peculiarity of Japanese IT Policy and its Institutional Origin.' *Financial Accountability and Management* 26(1): 65–84.

Kulkarni, Dhuval. 2013. 'Toothless Maharashtra Lokayukta Deals Mostly with Service Issues.' *DNA*, 11 December. Accessed on 31 May 2017. Available at http://www.dnaindia.com/mumbai/report-dna-exclusive-toothless-maharashtra-lokayukta-deals-mostly-with-service-issues-1933024.

Kumar, Tarun. October 2012. *Corruption in Administration: Evaluating the Kautilyan Antecedents, Issues in Brief.* New Delhi: Institute for Defense Studies and Analysis. Accessed on 31 May 2017. Available at http://idsa.in/issuebrief/CorruptioninAdministrationEvaluatingtheKautilyanAntecedents_TarunKumar_121012.

Kumar, Vinay and J. Venkatesan. 2014. 'SIT to go after Black Money,' *The Hindu*, 27 May.

Lambsdorff, Johann G. 2002. 'Corruption and Rent-Seeking.' *Public Choice* 113(1): 97–125.

Law Commission of Trinidad and Tobago. 1998. *The Ombudsman: Improving His Effectiveness.* Trinidad: Government Printer.

Lazarski, Christopher. 2012. *Power Tends to Corrupt: Lord Acton's Study of Liberty.* Dekalb: Northern University Press.

Lee, Julak. 2015. 'Formal Approaches in Controlling White Collar Crime: The Criminal Justice System and the Regulatory System.' *Journal of Public Administration and Governance* 5(4): 76–83.

Lemieux, Andrew M. (ed). 2014. *Situational Prevention of Poaching.* London: Routledge.

Liu, Christine. 2014. 'India's Whistleblower Protection Act – An Important Step, But Not Enough.' *Blog*. Massachusetts: Center for Ethics, Harvard University. Accessed on 7 May 2017. Available at http://ethics.harvard.edu/blog/indias-whistleblower-protection-act-important-step-not-enough.

Madhya Pradesh Lokayukta. 2017. *Statistical Reports*. Accessed on 1 July 2017. Available at http://mplokayukt.nic.in.

Maharashtra Lokayukta. 2013. *Annual Report*. Nasik: Government Press.

Maiorano, Deigo. 2014. 'The Empress's Long-term Legacies,' *The Hindu*, 31 October. Accessed on 31 May 2017. Available at http://www.thehindu.com/opinion/op-ed/comment-the-empresss-longterm-legacies/article6549343.ece?homepage=true.

Mather, Shaffi. 2009. 'A New Way to Fight Corruption.' *Ted Talk*. Accessed on 23 January 2017. Available at www.ted.com/talks/shaffi_mather_a_new_way.

Mazumdar, Prasanta. 2013. 'Guwahati High Court Questions Validity of the Formation of CBI.' *DNA*, 8 Friday. Accessed on 31 May 2017. Available at http://www.dnaindia.com/india/report-guwahati-high-court-questions-validity-of-the-formation-of-cbi-1915322.

Merton, Robert K. 1968. *Social Theory and Social Structure*. Glencoe, Ill.: The Free Press.

Meško,Gorazd, Klemen Bančič, Katja Eman. 2011. 'Situational Crime-Prevention Measures to Environmental Threats.' In *Understanding and Managing Threats to the Environment in South Eastern Europe*, edited by Gorazd Mesko, Dejana Dimitrijević, Charles B. Fields. NATO Science for Peace and Security Series C: Environmental Security, Volume 2. Dordrecht: Springer.

Misra, Pankaj. 2011. 'A Curzon without an Empire,' *Outlook India*, 31 January.

Misra, Prabhudatta. 2014. 'Food Corporation of India in Need of Restructuring as Corruption Mars Operations.' *LiveMint*, 5 November. Accessed on 24 June 2017. Available at http://www.livemint.com/Politics/vesoR5XxwEK0mrfSaeOVZI/Food-Corporation-of-India-pays-labourers-7250-a-month.html.

Mistry, Jamshed J. and Abu Jalal. 2012. 'An Empirical Analysis of Relationship between e-Government and Corruption.' *The International Journal of Digital Accounting Research* 12: 145–76.

Mukherji, Anahita. 2013. 'Maharashtra Tops Country in Attacks, Murder of RTI Activists.' *Times of India*, 22 December. Accessed on 31 May 2017. Available at http://timesofindia.indiatimes.com/india/Maharashtra-tops-country-in-attacks-murder-of-RTI-activists/articleshow/27743408.cms.

Munroe, T. 2004. 'The Ombudsman and Parliament.' Paper presented at the 'Third Regional Conference of the Caribbean Ombudsman Association (CAROA)', Runaway Bay.

Myint, U. 2000. 'Corruption: Causes, consequences and cures.' *Asia Pacific Development Journal* 7(2). Accessed on 26 April 2017. Available at www.unescap.org/drpad/publication/journal_7_2/myint.pd.

Nandan, Shjefali. 2008. 'Lesson from E-Governance Initiatives in Uttar Pradesh.' Working Paper. Allahabad: Motilal Nehru National institute of Technology. Accessed on 23 June 2017. Available at http://www.iceg.net/2008/books/3/4_26-32.pdf.

National Crime Records Bureau. 2016a. *Crime in India 2015*. Faridabad: Government of India Press.

———. 2016b. *Prison Statistics in India 2015: Table 5.2*. Faridabad: Government of India Press.

National Democratic Institute for International Affairs. 2005. *The Role and Effectiveness of the Ombudsman Institution*.Rule of Law Series Paper. Washington DC: NDI.

NDTV. 2011. 'What is 2G Scam?' 5 May. Accessed on 31 May 2017. Available at http://www.ndtv.com/india-news/what-is-2g-spectrum-scam-439271.

Newman, Oscar. 1972. *Defensible Space*.New York: Macmillan.

Newtactics.org. 2014. *Empowering Citizens to Fight Corruption*. Accessed on 31 May 2017. Available at https://www.newtactics.org/conversation/empowering-citizens-fight-corruption.

Norway Ombudsman. 2012. *Annual Report*. Oslo.

Nova Scotia Ombudsman. 2013. *Annual Report*. Halifax.

OECD (The Organisation for Economic Co-operation and Development). 2011. *OECD Integrity Review of Brazil: Managing Risks for a Cleaner Public Service*. Accessed on 31 May 2017. Available at http://www.oecd.org/governance/ethics/48947397.pdf.

Olken, Benjamin A. and Rohini Pande. 2012 'Corruption in Developing Countries.' *Annual Review of Economics* 4(1): 479–509.

Omang, Joanne. 1983. 'Secret Hoover Files Show Misuse of FBI.' *The Washington Post*, 12 December. Accessed on 8 July 2017. Available at https://www.washingtonpost.com/archive/politics/1983/12/12/secret-hoover-files-show-misuse-of-fbi/6ba74dc7-a6b7-447b-95a1-ea2ff28ecacc/?utm_term=.cf8e92544338.

Ombudsman of Jamaica. 1981. *Annual Report*. Kingston: Ombudsman Office.

———. 1993. *Annual Report*. Kingston: Ombudsman Office.

Ombudsman of Trinidad and Tobago. 1981. *Annual Report*. San Fernando: Ombudsman Office.

Orfield, Lester B. 1966. 'The Scandinavian Ombudsman.' *Administrative Law Review* 19(1): 7–74.

Pai, Sandeep and Mahua Venkatesh. 2014. 'Frauds Ripped Public Sector Banks of Rs. 23,000 Crore.' *Hindustan Times*, 30 January. Accessed on 31 May 2017. Available at http://www.hindustantimes.com/business-news/frauds-ripped-public-sector-banks-of-rs-23-000cr/article1-1178173.aspx.

Parker, Wilmer. 1984. 'Every Person Has a Price?' In *Corruption: The Enemy Within*, edited by Barry Rider. The Hague: Kluwer Law International.

Parliamentary Ombudsman of Finland. 2013. *Summary of the Annual Report 2012*. Translation by Greg Coogan. Sastamala: Vammalan Kirjapaino Oy.

Partnership for Transparency. 2012. 'Controlling Corruption to Improve Health Services for the Poor in Odisha State, India.' 13 April. Accessed on 25 June 2017. Available at https://ptfund.org/controlling-healthservices-corruption-odisha-india/.

Pathak, R. D. and R. S. Prasad. 2005. 'Role of E-Governance in Tackling Corruption and Achieving Societal Harmony: Indian Experience.' Paper presented at the 'Workshop on Innovations in Governance and Public Service to Achieve a Harmonious Society', Beijing, 5–7 December. Accessed on 31 May 2017. Available at http://www.napsipag.org/pdf/tackling_corruption.pdf.

Pearsall, Beth. 2010. 'Predictive Policing: The Future of Law Enforcement?' *National Institute of Justice*, 266. Accessed on 31 May 2017. Available at https://www.nij.gov/journals/266/Pages/predictive.aspx.

Phelps, Edmund S. 1975. *Altruism, Morality and Economic Theory*. New York: Russell Sage Foundation.

Philp, Marks. 2001. 'Contextualizing Political Corruption.' In *Political Corruption: Concepts and Contexts*, edited by Arnold J. Heidenheimer and Michael Johnston. Third edition. New Jersey: Transaction Publishers.

Pocha, Jehangir S. 2014. 'How Money Subverts Indian Elections,' *The Huffington Post*, 9 July. Accessed on 31 May 2017. Available at http://www.huffingtonpost.com/jehangir-s-pocha/india-elections-money_b_5293211.html.

Quah, Jon ST. 1995. 'Controlling Corruption in City States.' *Crime, Law and Social Change* 22: 39–414.

Quinney, Richard. 1970. *The Social Reality of Crime*. Boston: Little Brown.

Quraishi, S. Y. 2014. 'Money in Elections Root Cause of Corruption: Ex-CEC Quraishi,' *Zee News*, 21 December. Accessed on 31 May 2017. Available at http://zeenews.india.com/news/india/money-in-elections-root-cause-of-corruption-ex-cec-quraishi_1518039.html.

Raghavan, Muralee D. 2010. 'Corruption Grips India,' *The Verdict Weekly*, 17 August. Accessed on 26 April 2017. Available at http://www.countercurrents.org/rmuralee170810.htm.

Rashid, Omar. 2013. 'Mafia's Role in Sand Mining in UP,' *The Hindu*, 5 August. Accessed on 31 May 2017. Available at http://www.thehindu.com/news/national/other-states/mafias-role-in-sand-mining-in-up/article4992599.ece.

Reif, Linda C. 2008. 'Foreword.' In *The International Ombudsman Yearbook*, edited by Linda C. Reif, Volume 9, 1–2. Leiden and Boston, MA: Martinus Nijhoff Publishers.

Roosbroek, Steven V. and Steven Van de Walle. 2008. 'The Relationship between Ombudsman, Government, and Citizens: A Survey Analysis.' *Negotiation Journal* July: 287–302.

Rose-Ackerman, S. 1978. *Corruption: A Study in Political Economy*. New York: Academic Press.

———. 1997. 'The Political Economy of Corruption.' In *Corruption and the Global Economy*, edited by Kimberly Ann Elliott, 31–60. Washington DC: Institute for International Economics.

Rowat, D. C. (ed). 1968. *The Ombudsman: Citizen's Defender*, Second Edition. London: George Allen & Unwin.

———. 1984. 'The Suitability of the Ombudsman Plan for Developing Countries.' *International Review of Administrative Sciences* L(3): 207–11.

Rowe, Mary. 2001. 'Effectiveness of organizational ombudsman, with Mary Simon.' In *The Ombudsman Association Handbook*, Chapter IV, 1–22. Hillsborough, NJ: The Ombudsman Association. Accessed on 7 December 2017. Available at https://www.ombudsassociation.org/IOA_Main/media/SiteFiles/effectiveness_final-6_TOA.pdf.

Sawer, G. 1968. 'The Ombudsman and Related Institutions in Australia and New Zealand.' *The Annals of The American Academy of Political and Social Science* 377(1): 62–72.

Scott, James C. 1972. *Comparative Political Corruption*. Englewood Cliffs, NJ: Prentice Hall.

Sen, Amartya. 1999. 'Democracy as a Universal Value.' *Journal of Democracy* 10(3): 3–17.

Shah, Anup 2011. 'Corruption,' *Global Issues*, 4 September. Accessed on 26 April 2017. Available at http://www.globalissues.org/article/590/corruption.

Shaxson, Nicholas. 2007. 'Oil, Corruption and the Resource Curse.' *International Affairs* 83(6): 1123–40.

Sherman, Lawrence. 1978. *Scandal and Reform: Controlling Police Corruption*. Berkeley: University of California Press.

Shihata, Ibrahim F. I. 1997. 'Corruption: A General Review with an Emphasis on the Role of the World Bank.' In *Corruption: The Enemy Within*, edited by Barry Rider, 255–58. The Hague: Kluwer.

Shleifer, Andrei and Robert W. Vishny. 1993. 'Corruption.' *Quarterly Journal of Economics* 108(3): 599–617.

Singh, Gyanant. 2013. 'Hauled over the Coals: Supreme Court Slams CBI and Government for "Changing the Heart" of Coalgate Report.' *Mail-online India*, 8 May. Accessed on 26 March 2017. Available at http://www.dailymail.co.uk/indiahome/indianews/article-2321552/Hauled-coals-Supreme-Court-slams-CBI-Government-changing-heart-Coalgate-report.html.

Singh, Nirvikar. 2014. *Essays on India's Political Economy*. Santa Cruz: Center for Global, International and Regional Studies, UCSC. Accessed on 23 January 2017. Available at <https://escholarship.org/uc/item/2669k2ww>.

Skidmore, Max J. 1996. 'Promise and Peril in Combating Corruption: Hong Kong's ICAC.' *The Annals of the American Academy of Political and Social Science* 547: 118–30.

Smith, Brian. 2008. 'Edmund Burke, the Warren Hastings Trial, and the Moral Dimension of Corruption.' *Polity* 40(1): 70–94.

Sousa, Luis de. 2010. 'Anti-Corruption Agencies: Between Empowerment and Irrelevance.' *Crime, Law Social Change* 53(1): 5–22.

Stacey, F. 1978. *Ombudsman Compared*. Oxford: Clarendon Press.

Stark, R. 1987. 'Deviant Places: A Theory of the Ecology of Crime.' *Criminology* 25(4): 893–909.

Sunday Express. 1984. 'Retrieving the Ombudsman from the Shadows,' 23 September.

Sunshine, Jason and Tom Tyler. 2003. 'Moral Solidarity, Identification with the Community, and the Importance of Procedural Justice: The Police as Prototypical Representatives of a Group's Moral Values.' *Social, Psychology Quarterly* 66(2): 153–65.

Sussman, Anna L. 2011. 'Laugh, O Revolution: Humor in the Egyptian Uprising.' *The Atlantic*, 23 February. Accessed on 31 May 2017. Available at http://www.theatlantic.com/international/archive/2011/02/laugh-o-revolution-humor-in-the-egyptian-uprising/71530/.

Sutherland, Edwin H., Donald R. Cressey and David F.Luckenbill. 1992. *Principles of Criminology*. Eleventh edition. Dix Hills, NY: General Hall.

Sykes, Gresham M. and David Matza. 1957. 'Techniques of Neutralization: A Theory of Delinquency.' *American Sociological Review* 22(6): 664–70.

Szech, Nora and Armin Falk. 2013. 'Morals and Markets, Research Article.' *Science* 340 (6133): 707–11.

Tavares, Samia C. 2005. 'Do Rapid Political and Trade Liberalizations Increase Corruption?' *European Journal of Political Economy* 23(4): 1053–76.

Taylor, Alan. 2014. 'Bhopal: The World's Worst Industrial Disaster, 30 Years Later,' *The Atlantic*, 2 December. Accessed on 31 May 2017. Available at https://www.theatlantic.com/photo/2014/12/bhopal-the-worlds-worst-industrial-disaster-30-years-later/100864/.

Taylor, Ian, Paul Walton and Jock Young. 1973. *The New Criminology*. New York: Harper and Row.

The Hindu. 2013. 'UP Information Commission Issues Notice to Lokayukta on RTI,' 21 June. Accessed on 31 May 2017. Available at http://www.thehindu.com/news/national/other-states/up-information-commission-issues-notice-to-lokayukta-on-rti/article4836778.ece.

Time. 1966. 'People's Watchdog,' 22 December.

Times of India. 2012. 'Beni Prasad Verma Says Rs 71 Lakh Too Little for a Central Minister,' 16 October. Accessed on 26 March 2017. Available at http://timesofindia. indiatimes.com/india/Beni-Prasad-Verma-says-Rs-71-lakh-too-little-for-a-central-minister/articleshow/16829095.cms.

———. 2013. 'CBI a "Caged Parrot", "Heart" of Coalgate Report Changed: Supreme Court,' 8 May. Accessed on 5 July 2017. Available at http://timesofindia.indiatimes. com/india/CBI-a-caged-parrot-heart-of-Coalgate-report-changed-Supreme-Court/articleshow/19952260.cms.

———. 2016. 'CIC Not Competent to Bring Political Parties under RTI: Cong,' 20 June. Accessed on 8 July 2017. Available at http://timesofindia.indiatimes.com/city/delhi/CIC-not-competent-to-bring-political-parties-under-RTI-Cong/articleshow/52836288.cms.

———. 2017. 'Bank Officials Held for Rs 25 Crore "Exchange",' 5 January. Available at http://timesofindia.indiatimes.com/city/ahmedabad/bank-officials-held-for-rs-25-crore-exchange/articleshow/56345457.cms.

Tiwari, Deeptiman. 2015. 'UP Worst Offender in Transfer of SPs before 2-year Tenure Ends.' *Indian Express*, 29 November. Accessed on 8 July 2017. Available at http://indianexpress.com/article/india/india-news-india/up-worst-offender-in-transfer-of-sps-before-2-yr-tenure-ends/.

Transparency International. 2011. *Bribe Payers Index*. Accessed on 8 July 2017. Available at https://www.transparency.org/research/bpi/overview.

———. 2017. *Corruption Perceptions Index 2016*. Accessed on 8 July 2017. Available at www.transparency.org/cpi.

———. 2017. *People and Corruption: Asia Pacific Global Corruption Barometer*. Accessed on 8 July 2017. Available at https://www.transparency.org/whatwedo/publication/people_and_corruption_asia_pacific_global_corruption_barometer.

Treisman, Daniel, 2000. 'The Causes of Corruption: A Cross National Study.' *Journal of Public Economics* 76(3): 399–457.

Tummala, Krishna K. 2009. 'Combating Corruption: Lessons out of India.' *International Public Management Review* 10(1): 34–58.

Turk, Austin. 1969. *Criminality and Legal Order*. Chicago: Rand McNally

Underkuffler, Laura S. 2005. *Captured by Evil: The Idea of Corruption in Law*. Duke Law School: Working Papers in Law.

UNODC (United Nations Office on Drugs and Crime). 2017. *UNODC and Corruption*. Accessed on 5 July 2017. Available at unodc.org.

Van Rijckeghem, C. and B. Weder. 2001. 'Bureaucratic Corruption and the Rate of Temptation: Do Wages in the Civil Service Affect Corruption, and by How Much?' *Journal of Development Economics* 65(2): 307–31.

Varmal, Subodh. 2016. '$181 Billion Indian black Money in Tax Havens?' *Times of India*, 21 March. Accessed on 23 June 2017. Available at http://timesofindia.

indiatimes.com/india/181-billion-Indian-black-money-in-tax-havens/articleshow/51487042.cms.

Verma, Arvind and Madhukar Shetty. 2013. 'Constructions of White Collar Crimes and Corruption.' Paper presented at 'American Society of Criminology' Atlanta 22 November.

Verma, Arvind. 1999. 'Cultural Roots of Police Corruption in India.' *Policing: An International Journal of Police Strategies and Management* 22(3): 264–79.

———. 2001. 'Taking Justice Outside the Courts: Judicial Activism in India.' *The Howard Journal of Criminal Justice* 40(2): 148–65.

———. 2005. *Indian Police: A Critical Evaluation.* Delhi: Regency Publications.

———. 2007. 'Anatomy of Riots: A Situational Prevention Approach.' *Crime Prevention and Community Safety: An International Journal* 9(3): 201–21.

———. 2010. *The New Khaki: The Evolving Nature of Policing in India.* Boca Raton, FL: CRC Press.

Vittal, N. 2004. *Musings on Governance, Governing and Corruption.* Hyderabad: ICFAI University Press, 8–16.

Vold, George, Thomas J. Bernard and Jeffrey B. Snipes. 1998. *Theoretical Criminology.* Fourth edition. New York: Oxford University Press.

Wagner, Marsha L. 2000. 'The Organizational Ombudsman as Change Agent.' *Negotiation Journal* 16(1): 99–114.

Walecki, Marcin. 2003. 'Political Money and Political Corruption: Considerations for Nigeria.' Paper presented at the INEC Civil Society Forum Seminar on Agenda for Electoral Reform, 27–28 November, Abuja.

Walzer, Michael. 2008. 'Does the Free Market Corrode Moral Character? Of Course it Does'. In *Thirteen views on the Question. John Templeton Foundation*, Autumn. Accessed on 4 July 2017. Available at http://www.templeton.org/market.

Ward, Robert. 1982. 'The System of Administrative and Political Corruption: Canal Irrigation in South India.' *Journal of Developmental Studies* 18(3): 287–328.

Wilson, Ronald, Timothy Brown and Beth Schuster. 2009. 'Preventing Neighborhood Crime: Geography Matters.' *National Institute of Justice, Journal No. 263.* Accessed on 2 July 2017. Available at https://www.nij.gov/journals/263/pages/neighborhood-crime.aspx.

World Bank. 2017. *Worldwide Governance Indicators.* Accessed on 21 June 2017. Available at http://info.worldbank.org/governance/wgi/#home.

Xu, Beina. 2014. 'Governance in India: Corruption.' *Council on Foreign Relations*, October. Available at http://www.cfr.org/corruption-and-bribery/governance-india-corruption/p31823

Zee News. 2011. 'Lokayukta Appointment To Be Again Taken Up,' 31 December. Accessed on 1 July 2017. Available at http://zeenews.india.com/news/karnataka/lokayukta-appointment-to-be-again-taken-up_749765.html.

Index